To Marilee —

Thanks for your marvelous
courage — so professional,
breezy and professional

Congratulations

Margaret Brady

# FINAL CURTAIN

To Marilee —
That's not all folks!

Gary

# FINAL CURTAIN

*Eternal Resting Places of*
*Hundreds of Stars, Celebrities,*
*Moguls, Misers & Misfits.*

by

**MARGARET BURK**      **GARY HUDSON**

**SEVEN LOCKS PRESS**
Santa Ana, California
Minneapolis, Minnesota
Washington, D.C.

Library of Congress Cataloging-in-Publication Data

Burk, Margaret Tante.
    Final Curtain: Eternal Resting Places of Hundreds of Stars, Celebrities, Moguls, Misers & Misfits / by Margaret Burk. Gary Hudson.
        p. 384    cm.
    Includes index.
    ISBN  0-929765-53-2
    1. Motion pictures actors and actresses--California, Southern--Tombs. 2. Celebrities--California, Southern--Tombs.   I. Hudson, Gary.   II. Title.

    PN1998.2.B87      1996
    920.073--dc21                                                      96-45257
                                                                      CIP


Picture acknowledgments:
From the collections of Roger Karnbad, Marvin Paige, Paul Froehlich, Jimmy Bangley, Richard Biegert and Margaret Burk.
Page 273   Photo of Police Motorcade (back), °Jeff Dye, courtesy of the photographer


Manufactured in the United States of America

SEVEN LOCKS PRESS
P.O. Box 25689
Santa Ana, CA 92799
(800) 354-5348

*Final Curtain* is dedicated to

all of you who have gone before,

to prepare a place for the rest of us.

# Table of Contents

Foreword . . . . . . . . . . . . . . . . . . . . . . . . . . . . . . . . . . . . . . . . .ix
Acknowledgments . . . . . . . . . . . . . . . . . . . . . . . . . . . . . . . . . . .xi
Introduction . . . . . . . . . . . . . . . . . . . . . . . . . . . . . . . . . . . .xiii

Part I — "The End"
Chapter 1     Famous Last Lines . . . . . . . . . . . . . . . . . . . . . . . .1
Chapter 2     Deathstyles of the Rich and Famous . . . . . . . . . . . .9
Chapter 3     Death by Mysterious Circumstance . . . . . . . . . .21
Chapter 4     Body Parts . . . . . . . . . . . . . . . . . . . . . . . . . . . .45
Chapter 5     The Out-of-Towners . . . . . . . . . . . . . . . . . . . . . .55
Chapter 6     Where Are They Now? . . . . . . . . . . . . . . . . . . . .73
Chapter 7     Pet Cemeteries . . . . . . . . . . . . . . . . . . . . . . . . . .81
Chapter 8     Welcome to the Afterworld, Online . . . . . . . . . .83
Chapter 9     Opening Pandora's Coffin . . . . . . . . . . . . . . . . .85
Chapter 10    The Monster Mortician . . . . . . . . . . . . . . . . . .89
Chapter 11    Gaucheries . . . . . . . . . . . . . . . . . . . . . . . . . . .93
Chapter 12    Taps . . . . . . . . . . . . . . . . . . . . . . . . . . . . . . . . .97

Part II — Who's Who and Where?
Chapter 13    Angelus-Rosedale . . . . . . . . . . . . . . . . . . . . . .103
Chapter 14    Chapel of the Pines . . . . . . . . . . . . . . . . . . . . .111
Chapter 15    Calvary Cemetery . . . . . . . . . . . . . . . . . . . . . .115
Chapter 16    Crystal Cathedral Memorial Gardens . . . . . . . .121
Chapter 17    Eden Memorial Park . . . . . . . . . . . . . . . . . . . .123
Chapter 18    Heaven Bound . . . . . . . . . . . . . . . . . . . . . . . .127
Chapter 19    Forest Lawn, Glendale . . . . . . . . . . . . . . . . . .131
Chapter 20    From the Cradle to the Grave . . . . . . . . . . . . . .195
Chapter 21    Forest Lawn, Hollywood Hills . . . . . . . . . . . . .197
Chapter 22    Forest Lawn, Covina . . . . . . . . . . . . . . . . . . . .219
Chapter 23    Forest Lawn, Cypress . . . . . . . . . . . . . . . . . . . .221

Chapter 24 Forest Lawn, Long Beach . . . . . . . . . . . . . . . . . .223

Chapter 25 Hillside Memorial Park . . . . . . . . . . . . . . . . . . . .225

Chapter 26 Hollywood Memorial Park . . . . . . . . . . . . . . . .231

Chapter 27 Holy Cross Cemetery . . . . . . . . . . . . . . . . . . . . .271

Chapter 28 Home of Peace Memorial Park . . . . . . . . . . . . .297

Chapter 29 Inglewood Park Cemetery . . . . . . . . . . . . . . . .301

Chapter 30 Mission Hills Cemetery . . . . . . . . . . . . . . . . . .307

Chapter 31 Mt. Sinai Memorial Park . . . . . . . . . . . . . . . . . .311

Chapter 32 The Richard Nixon Presidential
        Library and Birthplace . . . . . . . . . . . . . . . . . . . .315

Chapter 33 Oakwood Memorial Cemetery . . . . . . . . . . . . .317

Chapter 34 Pacific View Memorial Park . . . . . . . . . . . . . . .319

Chapter 35 Rose Hills Memorial Park . . . . . . . . . . . . . . . . .323

Chapter 36 Valhalla Memorial Park . . . . . . . . . . . . . . . . . . .325

Chapter 37 Westwood Memorial Park . . . . . . . . . . . . . . . .329

Chapter 38 Woodlawn Cemetery . . . . . . . . . . . . . . . . . . . . .343


Epilogue . . . . . . . . . . . . . . . . . . . . . . . . . . . . . . . . . . . . . . . . . .347

Appendix  (Cemetery Locations) . . . . . . . . . . . . . . . . . . . . . . .349

Glossary . . . . . . . . . . . . . . . . . . . . . . . . . . . . . . . . . . . . . . . . . .351

Index . . . . . . . . . . . . . . . . . . . . . . . . . . . . . . . . . . . . . . . . . . . .353

About the Authors . . . . . . . . . . . . . . . . . . . . . . . . . . . . . . . . . .367

*"That's All, Folks!"*

# Foreword

I never thought that anyone could ever put a new slant on a Hollywood book, but Margaret Burk and Gary Hudson have done it with a revealing look at celebrity death in *Final Curtain*.

I have known Margaret for many years. During most of our friendship she was the publicist for the Ambassador Hotel and its fabulous Cocoanut Grove, Hollywood, the nation's most glamorous nightclub. I knew she was privy to many secrets of the stars, and this book proves it.

For instance, Margaret discloses why no pictures of a wasted and terribly thin Sammy Davis Jr., in his open coffin were ever printed. Sammy's daughter, Tracey, told Shirley MacLaine how the photographer had appeared out of nowhere and shot a picture of the open casket. Shirley took the problem to David Steinberg, Sammy's longtime press agent. Steinberg told the photographer that Frank Sinatra was so furious, he was going to have the photographer killed. The shaken photographer couldn't hand over the pictures fast enough.

The book is full of juicy items like that, and it is not confined to show business celebrities. William Randolph Hearst, J. Paul Getty and even Abe Lincoln are included among those taking the *Final Curtain*.

Margaret sent the galley proofs to me with instructions to skim through the pages and write a foreword. I read the whole book. I couldn't put it down. It was too fascinating and revealing.

Margaret and Gary, you made a winner out of death. And that's quite a feat.

James Bacon
Hollywood Columnist
*October 1996*

# Acknowledgments

The authors are grateful to those who aided with this book especially our friends at Seven Locks Press; Heather Slade for design and production of the book; Marylin Hudson for research and inspiration; Tray Burk for computer expertise; Kimberly Kasimoff for research; Paula Becker for editing; Sharon Goldinger for assistance; Laura Ordonez for data entry; and the cemeteries, some more than others.

# Introduction

There is something very touching about where people are buried. Perhaps it is because while you are near their final resting place, you feel traces of their spirits, the lives they lived or their thoughts brought out by an epitaph.

Good Night, Sweet Prince
Flights of Angels Sing Thee to Thy Rest.
— Douglas Fairbanks

"Over My Dead Body," George Bernard Shaw

"This Is Too Deep for Me," Hedy Lamarr

"Nite, Nite, Jiminy Cricket," on an infant's headstone

"She Was a Woman of True Grit," a simple expression

"That's all, folks," of course, Mel Blanc

The last resting places of people who have passed this way in Southern California are as varied as their occupants. Some cemeteries are small and not very well cared for, mostly last resting places of people who have lived simple lives. Others are lavish, filled with miles of flowers, opulent shrines and soaring mausoleums. Some are so like a theme park you begin to wonder, as writer Peter Theroux did at Holy Cross, if the Ascension is a Disneyland ride. The only things missing are the tour trams.

Many of the parks are equal opportunity resting places, with Christian, Jewish and other ethnic sections. Forest Lawn, the most glamorous and glitzy of them all, offers you a pictorial map and guide that urges "Please allow yourself at least two hours to visit all the attractions." Actually, that's not long enough.

Perhaps the most perplexing thing about Southern California's last resting places is finding a common attitude. When you tour New England, you get somber moss-and-tree-filled grassy church yards, touched with a Pilgrim flavor. In Paris the great Pere-Lachaise

Cemetery, last resting place of Jim Morrison of The Doors, reflects a sexy city of rooftops, a "Come play with me" flavor. London's cathedrals, and specifically Westminster Abbey, tell you this is the home of poets such as Chaucer, kings, queens and statesmen, the guardians and guides of the mighty British Empire, and don't you dare think or do anything foolish.

But what of Southern California's last resting places? Do they have a common theme that can be shared? Could it be the one-liner that Dr. Hubert Eaton, who calls himself "The Builder," wrote for Forest Lawn? "I believe in a happy Eternal Life."

In this land of surf, sunshine, Hollywood, riots, fires, boats, earthquakes, immigration, unemployment, rock and roll, theme parks, carjackings, Rolls Royces, race problems, eternal youth, power lunches, rest homes, the homeless, Beverly Hills, Watts, glitter and grunge, what do we have in common? A Shiny Optimism, that's what. There may be kings, queens, Quakers, popes, emperors and poets in other cemeteries, but we've got Jack Benny, Gracie Allen, Armand Hammer, the Chandlers, Bugsy Siegel, Marilyn Monroe, and Aimee Semple McPherson in ours.

We take a backseat to no one. We like our cemeteries sunny-side up, filled with that shiny optimism about what our next life is going to be.

# Part I

◆

## "The End"

Douglas Fairbanks Jr. — Good night, Sweet Prince.

# 1

## Famous Last Lines

### Celebrity Self Epitaphs

Some exit lines reveal that the famous are not without their wit and wisdom when it comes to thinking about that final curtain.

"He was an average guy who could carry a tune." **Bing Crosby**

"On the whole, I'd rather be in Philadelphia." **W.C. Fields**

"He was lucky—and he knew it." **Cary Grant**

"A nice part—only 'four sides,' but good company and in for a long run." **Edward Everett Horton**

"Well, I've played everything but a harp." **Lionel Barrymore**

"This is too deep for me." **Hedy Lamarr**

"Did you hear about my operation?" **Warner Baxter**

"Here's something I want to get off my chest." **William Haines**

"A gentleman farmer goes back to the soil." **Lewis Stone**

"Do not disturb." **Constance Bennett**

"At last I get top-billing." **Wallace Ford**

"Excuse my dust. This is on me." **Dorothy Parker**

"Over my dead body." **George Bernard Shaw**

"Go away. I'm asleep." **Joan Hackett**

This charming little verse commemorates the resting place of **Preston Sturges:**

> Now I lay me down to die
> I pray my neighbors not to pry
> Too deeply into sins that I
> Not only cannot here deny
> But much enjoyed as time flew by.

◆

Not all the creative passages are found on the tombstones of the stars. Some unknowns also have had their final say.

"The reptilian form stepped from the shadows, often stalked and bit me. Finally it did not let go, so now I am here," a 1994 message at Fairhaven.

"Caught the wave to heaven," seen on a surfer's grave.

"I'd rather be in Vegas," adorns one marker.

At Forest Lawn you can find "Having a Wonderful Time. Glad You're Not Here," along with "Off to The Greener Fairways." "I Told You I Was Sick" is another common line.

In Tombstone, Arizona, we find "Here lies Lester Moore, Four slugs from a .44. No Les. No Moore."

◆

Some cemeteries have been known to reject a few of the more questionable parting shots. This one was turned down by a cemetery in Los Angeles: "He was quite a salesman. This was his last deal." Catholic cemeteries are reported to be the toughest literary critics. They turned down "Boop Boop E Doop" (no reason given) and "666," a no-brainer. But they allowed rock singer **Ritchie Valens** to include on his marker the musical notes and lyrics to his hit "La Bamba."

◆

**Rudyard Kipling** declares:
> And the end of the fight is a tombstone white
> With the name of the late deceased.

Tombstones are big business and another means of creative self-expression for the departed. *MB News,* the Illinois-based trade magazine for the Monument Builders of North America, reports on a few of the more notable headstones. One spells out the life, death and hobbies of the occupant on a giant Scrabble board. Others feature a full-sized granite Mercedes, diesel trucks, juke boxes, soccer balls, a giant Coke bottle, and an intact car engine. A life-size sculptured baby elephant is found on the grave of a circus owner.

Tombstones at the Valley Monument Company in San Gabriel, California, come in white as well as mahogany, gray and black. Gravestones weigh anywhere from 2 to 1,700 pounds.

Owners Blain Sutton Montgomery, 82, and Blain Julian Montgomery, 62, have almost 90 years combined experience operating their business. According to the younger Montgomery, the standard joke around the company begins with the question, "How's business?"

The reply: "Oh, it's on the rocks."

Montgomery says, "Anything in bad taste, such as profanity, isn't permitted." About 15 years ago, the family of a deceased beautician asked them to put "At last, I'm out of the Goddamn beauty shop" on her marker. The cemetery insisted they drop the "God." Some of the images the Montgomerys have created for their customers include the UCLA Bruins' logo, a trapeze, a slot machine, a Ferrari Testarossa, and the entrance to Disneyland for a child's tombstone. Some other images found on Southland markers include dolphins, space shuttles, tennis rackets, airplanes, pigs, sewing machines, Ninja turtles, Mormon temples and city skylines.

Craftsmen have learned to "paint" with their etchings, including one artisan who created a scene from the movie *Backdraft* for a dead fireman; a ghostly farmer alongside a grain elevator; and Jesus in the clouds, reaching toward a little girl who spent her life in a wheelchair. Another created the Idaho "Spud King," who is shown as a potato ascending to heaven where angels await him.

◆

## In Their Own Words

"You understand that last night was only a comedy." **Paul Bern,** in his suicide note to his wife, Jean Harlow.

"Why should I talk to you? I've just been talking to your boss." **Wilson Mizner,** on his deathbed, to a priest.

"Did I say not, old fellow? No Barrymore would allow such a conventional thing to happen to him." **John Barrymore,** during his final illness.

"I was very ill last summer. For a while, I thought I was a goner. I woke up one night in my hospital bed, and I saw standing there a tall man, wearing a white robe, with a long white beard. I said, 'Who are you?' He said, 'I am the Holy Ghost.' I said, 'Where are the Father and the Son?' He said, 'They're out of town.' I'm not a religious man, but it's things like this that make you stop and think." **Harry Ruby**

"I don't want to achieve immortality through my work; I want to achieve it through not dying." **Woody Allen**

"One day I shall probably talk myself to death. Those who live by the word shall perish by the word." **Alexander Woollcott**

"When I die, just skin me out and put me up on old Trigger and I'll be happy." **Roy Rogers**

"I'm not afraid to die, honey. In fact, I'm kind of looking forward to it. I know that the Lord has his arms wrapped around this big, fat sparrow." **Ethel Waters**

"I never killed a man, but I have read many obituaries with a lot of pleasure." **Clarence Darrow**

"She thinks she doesn't get old. She told me once it was her cameraman who was getting older. She wanted to fire him." **Joe Pasternak,** about Doris Day.

"He's the kind of guy that when he dies, he's going up to heaven and give God a bad time for making him bald." **Marlon Brando,** about Frank Sinatra.

"When I die, be sure the services are in the morning, so my friends can get to the track." **Arthur Caesar**

Guns aren't lawful;
Nooses give;
Gas smells awful;
You may as well live.
— **Dorothy Parker**

"Being an old maid is like death by drowning; a real delightful sensation after you cease to struggle." **Edna Ferber**

"I look wonderful for a woman my age, but not for a man. I was downtown last week and saw a building as old as I am. It looked terrible." **Ed Wynn**

"No, get me a people doctor." **Max Baer,** when asked if he wanted a house doctor.

> Do not go gentle into that good night.
> Old age should burn and rave at close of day;
> Rage rage against the dying of the light.
> — **Dylan Thomas**

"Goodbye, everybody!" **Hart Crane,** as he jumped overboard to his death.

"There will soon be only five kings left; the King of England, Diamonds, Hearts, Spades and Clubs." **King Farouk of Egypt**

"Southerly gales, squalls, lee rail under water, wet bunks, hard tack, bully beef. Wish you were here instead of me." **Richard Haliburton,** his last message while lost at sea.

"Turn up the lights. I don't want to go home in the dark." **O. Henry**

"Don't worry, it's not loaded." **Terry Kath,** rock musician killed while playing Russian roulette.

"You will do my postmortem? And look at the intestines carefully, for I think there is something there now." **Elie Metchnikoff,** Russian bacteriologist.

"Yes. Hurry it up you Hoosier bastard! I could hang a dozen men while you're fooling around." **Carl Panzram,** mass murderer, on the day of his hanging.

"Sister, you're trying to keep me alive as an old curiosity, but I'm done. I'm finished. I'm going to die." **George Bernard Shaw,** to his nurse.

"Curtain! Fast music! Lights! Ready for the last finale! Great! The show looks good." **Florenz Ziegfeld,** in his last delirium.

◆

## "Oh the Pain, the Bliss of Dying!" — Death in the Movies

"They aren't forgotten because they haven't died. They're living, right out there, Collingwood and the rest, and they'll keep on living as long as the regiment lives. The pay is $13 a month. The diet, beans and eggs—maybe horse meat before this campaign is over. They fight over cards or rot-gut whiskey, but share the last drop in their canteens. The faces may change. Names. But they're there. That's the regiment—the regular army—now and 50 years from now." **John Wayne,** *Fort Apache*

"I aim to kill you in one minute, Ned, or see you hang in Fort Smith at Judge Parker's convenience. Which will it be?" **John Wayne,** *True Grit*

"They tell me he was so crooked that when he died, they had to screw him in the ground." **Bob Hope,** *The Cat and the Canary*

"Death's at the bottom of everything, Martins. Leave death to the professionals." **Trevor Howard** to Joseph Cotten, *The Third Man*

"I can't sleep anymore—too much like death." **Cher,** *Moonstruck*

"Mother of Mercy, is this the end of Rico?" **Edward G. Robinson's** last gasp in *Little Caesar*

"It is a far, far better thing I do than I have ever done. It is a far, far better rest I go to than I have ever known." **Ronald Colman,** *A Tale of Two Cities*

"Made it Ma. Top of the world!" **James Cagney,** on the top of the oil tank, *White Heat*

"Heathcliff, can you see the gray over there where our castle is? I'll wait for you until you come." **Merle Oberon** dying in Laurence Olivier's arms, *Wuthering Heights*

"Prew, Prew, listen. Fatso done it, Prew. He liked to whack me in the gut. He asks me if it hurts, and I spit at him like always—only yesterday it was bad. He hit me. He hit me. He hit me. I—I hadda get out, Prew." **Frank Sinatra's** dying words to Montgomery Clift, *From Here to Eternity*

◆

## "He Is Dead and Gone, Lady. . ."—Movie Eulogies

"Oh no! It wasn't the airplanes. It was beauty killed the beast." **Robert Armstrong,** *King Kong*

"You are now in heaven and on earth. Your life begins, oh Bernadette." **Charles Bickford** eulogizing Jennifer Jones, *The Song of Bernadette*

"Rosebud." **Orson Welles'** dying word, *Citizen Kane*

"Mr. Kane was a man who got everything he wanted, and then lost it. Maybe Rosebud was something he couldn't get or something he lost. Anyway, it wouldn't have explained anything. I don't think any word can explain a man's life. No, I guess Rosebud is just a piece in a jigsaw puzzle—a missing piece." **William Alland,** *Citizen Kane*

"I don't suppose anybody would think that she was a good person. Strangely enough, she was. On the surface, she was all sex and devil-may-care, yet everything in her was struggling toward respectability. She never gave up trying." **Laurence Harvey,** on the death of his mistress, **Elizabeth Taylor,** *Butterfield 8*

"What can I say about a 25-year-old girl who died? That she was beautiful. And brilliant. That she loved Mozart and Bach. And the Beatles. And me." **Ryan O'Neal** about Ali McGraw, *Love Story*

"He used to be a big shot." **Gladys George's** goodbye to James Cagney, gunned down in *The Roaring Twenties*

"Yes, it was my privilege to know him and to make him known to the world. He was a poet, a scholar and a mighty warrior . . . He was also the most shameless exhibitionist since Barnum and Bailey." **Arthur Kennedy,** *Lawrence of Arabia*

"He was some kind of man. What does it matter what you say about someone?" **Marlene Dietrich's** short and sweet goodbye to Orson Welles, *Touch of Evil*

"One Rocco more or less isn't worth dying for." **Bogie** in *Key Largo*

"Here's looking at you, kid." from *Casablanca*

Writers on writers: **Thomas Babington Macaulay,** commenting on the death of Socrates, said, "The more I read him, the less I wonder that they poisoned him."

**Fran Lebowitz** adds: "I prefer dead writers because you don't run into them at parties."

William Randolph Hearst, Louella Parsons and Marion Davies hosting a costume party at San Simeon.

# 2

◆

## Deathstyles of the Rich and Famous —
## Fascinating Funerals and Wakes

### William Randolph Hearst, 1863–1951

With the passing of William Randolph Hearst on August 14, 1951, America lost one of its most powerful, articulate, eccentric and flamboyant power players. For some 88 years, Hearst had it all his way. From the day he talked his father into giving him the anemic *San Francisco Examiner* in 1887, Hearst was off and running. He championed the common man while building a newspaper empire with which he created as much news as he reported. Along the way, he took a gorgeous, fun-loving mistress, Marion Davies from the Ziegfeld Follies, who was to be his lover and companion for the next 32 years.

During these years, Hearst financed Marion's movie career as an actress and dabbled in politics by getting elected to Congress as a representative for the state of New York. He then lost runs for mayor of New York City and governor of New York on what he thought then was the path to the presidency of the United States. He would also, during this time, be the first to declare war on Spain while spending $30 million on what he called his "ranch," San Simeon. All this would end when he died of a brain hemorrhage in Marion's mansion in Los Angeles.

The flamboyant era of William Randolph Hearst was over. Now his wife of 47 years, Millicent Wilson Hearst, and her five sons would take charge. There would be no Hollywood high jinks at this funeral. This would be a powerful, conservative family saying a final goodbye to a father and husband, carried off as though he had never had a romantic dalliance with Marion. Hearst would lie in state for a day and a half, wearing a dark blue suit, blue tie, monogrammed shirt and cuff links, as friends, statesmen and business associates filed by to pay their respects. "He's mine now. He's finally mine," Millicent Hearst told her sons. More than 300 floral arrangements overflowed the Chapel of Grace in the Grace Episcopal Cathedral on Nob Hill in San Francisco, where Hearst lay in state.

Honorary pallbearers included Earl Warren, governor of California, San Francisco Mayor Elmer E. Robinson, President Herbert Hoover, General Douglas MacArthur, Arthur Hayes Sulzberger, Bernard Baruch, Roy Howard, Colonel Robert McCormick, John N. Garner, and Mrs. Ogden Reid. On the day of the funeral, some 1,500 invited guests filled the cathedral, while hundreds more stood outside. Guests included Hearst's newspaper people, such as Louella Parsons, Gene Fowler and Adela Rogers St. Johns, along with friends, including Louis B. Mayer, Hugh Baillie, president of United Press, A.P. Giannini, president of the Bank of America and University of California president, Robert G. Sproul. The half-hour service was delivered by the Right Reverend Karl M. Block, Episcopal bishop of California. The bishop read from the Book of Common Prayer, including "Oh, death where is thy sting? Oh, grave where is thy victory?" There was no eulogy or homily. The organist played Bach and Caesar Franck. The men's chorus sang Mallotte's *Lord's Prayer* followed by a full chorus that sang Dvořák's arrangement of the 23rd Psalm.

Following the short ceremony, two dozen limousines drove slowly down the peninsula to Cypress Lawn Cemetery, where Hearst was interred in the Grecian Mausoleum with his parents. At the service, Bishop Black read a poem written by the deceased, *Song of the River.*

> For life was born on lofty heights
> And flows in a laughing stream
> To the river below
> Whose onward flow
> Ends in a perfect dream.

William Randolph Hearst was gone, and Marion Davies was not allowed to say goodbye. She had been administered sleeping pills so that she would not appear. (More on Marion Davies in the "Hollywood Memorial Park" section.)

### John Barrymore—One Last Drink

John Barrymore, who died May 29, 1942, was a legendary stage and movie star known as "The Great Profile," who rose to the heights of his profession as a young man. The youngest of the "Fabulous Barrymores," which included Ethel and Lionel, his interpretations of Shakespeare's Hamlet and Richard III showed him to be the most talented actor to ever work on the American stage. In motion pictures he played both romantic leads as well as comedy roles in hit after hit, including *Grand Hotel.* However, Barrymore's drinking and wild lifestyle soon began to take its toll, and by 1941, he was behaving like a buffoon, reading from cue cards, mugging rather than acting before the camera and not displaying the dignity his talents had earned.

Hollywood columnist James Bacon tells the story of Barrymore's wake. A bunch of his pals, Gene Fowler, Errol Flynn, Raoul Walsh, David Chasen and Tony Quinn, were celebrating at the Irish-style wake being held at the funeral home. Errol Flynn recalled:

"We all got very drunk. I left first ... I felt to get drunk (and laid) after Jack's wake was the best way I could pay my respects to this greatest of actors. But that son of a bitch Walsh bribed a young funeral attendant with $500 to lend him Barrymore's body for a few hours. He and some of his nefarious pals transported Jack's corpse from its coffin to my house. There they propped him into a chair in front of the fireplace and put a drink in his hands.

"Can you imagine the shock I felt after being at Jack's wake to come home and find that son of a bitch sitting there in my favorite chair? I aged 30 years on the spot, drunk as I was. It scared the living bejesus out of me, but you know what I did? I just sat down in the chair next to him and cried. The funeral attendant then showed up and took Jack back to his coffin. And then Raoul came in and had a big laugh. So did I. It was the crazy sort of thing that Jack would have appreciated. I told Raoul that he must have loved Barrymore as much as I did, else he wouldn't have gone to all that trouble. And then, of course, we had another drink."

## A Power Wake at a Power Place—Don Simpson

When your personal physician is found dead in your pool house from an overdose of drugs, can you be far behind? Don Simpson wasn't. A few months after his doctor died, on January 19, 1996, Don followed at age 52. His autopsy showed that he died of heart failure caused by a massive overdose of cocaine, a stimulant, and a variety of drugs used in the treatment of depression, anxiety and sleeplessness, including Unisom, Atarax, Vistaril, Librium, Valium, Compazine, Xanax, Desyrel and Tigan.

Ten days later, Simpson's power wake was held at Mortons, the "You are where you sit" entertainment industry's favorite restaurant. Simpson would have loved it as 500 supermoguls, celebrities, agents and fringe feeders gathered before a poster-sized photo of Don to watch highlights of his colorful life played out on nine television screens to the driving beat of rock music that had become the Simpson-Bruckheimer trademark.

A native of Anchorage, Alaska, Simpson was a driven, intense, even reckless man to whom nothing mattered except the making of movies. And make movies he did. With his partner Jerry Bruckheimer, he produced hot, big box office pictures, such as *Flashdance, Beverly Hills Cop, Top Gun* and *Officer and a Gentleman.* On the set of *Officer*, Simpson said to one of the gofers sent to meet him, "I'm hung over and exhausted. Now tell me, whose got the best whorehouse and the best drugs?"

"Don lived the way he wanted to and never made excuses. There are a lot of frauds out there, but he walked it like he talked it. Don was an original—the real thing," said Simpson's long-time partner, Bruckheimer, who tossed the wake along with ICM president Jim Wiatt, DreamWorks' Jeffery Katzenberg and producer Steve Tisch.

"Around Don every aspect of every day was magnified in its intensity," Katzenberg added. Simpson, as head of worldwide production for Paramount, also made such hits as *American Gigolo, 48 Hours, Bad Boys, Dangerous Minds,* and *Crimson Tide.*

Former Columbia studio chief Dawn Steele, whom Simpson elevated out of *Star Trek* merchandising at Paramount, said, "The business is all about money now, and Don was about passion. Like John Kennedy and Elvis, he had to go early. I could never picture him growing old."

Simpson's wake had to be the power cocktail party of the year. Others attending were Disney CEO Michael Eisner and studio chief Joe Roth, Bob Daly of Warner Brothers, Paramount's Jonathan Dolgen, Mark Canton of Columbia, MCA's Ron Meyer and DreamWork's

David Geffen. Celebrities included Richard Dreyfuss, Michelle Pfeiffer, Will Smith and Martin Lawrence.

*Days of Thunder,* a poor box office performer produced by Simpson in 1990, probably cost him his producing deal at Paramount. This was followed by some unhappy months at Disney, which, because of the heavy-handed way they handled producers, Simpson dubbed the place "Mouschwitz" and "Duckau."

"I want to be a legend," he said, and he was.

## Last Cruise to Eternity—Victor Ajax Browning Sr.

For his last cruise in his dearly beloved baby-blue Cadillac, Victor wore his red corduroy cap at a jaunty angle, his favorite jogging clothes, a big smile and his seat belt snugly fastened. He was driven from Texas to California in style. The interesting part? Victor Ajax Browning Sr. was dead.

Browning's son, Victor Browning Jr., and his grandson were about to honor Browning Sr.'s final request—to be driven in his precious 1990 Cadillac Seville the final 1,000 miles to his cremation in California. He made the trip in style, propped up in the back seat all the way to Hesperia. "That's the best he's looked in years," said his grandson, Victor "Shane" Browning.

Browning, an insurance executive and bond underwriter, died following bouts with diabetes, leukemia, heart surgery and several strokes. And it was his lifelong love of Cadillacs that inspired his final wish. For the last two years of his life he insisted that his dream be fulfilled—his last ride to eternity. So, after strapping Victor in, and armed with appropriate documents, the trio headed off down Interstate 10, bound for Victor's final destination.

"This wasn't a time of mourning for us," Shane said. "It was a time to do what Grandad wanted us to do. We'd be having a conversation between ourselves and we'd turn around and say 'Hey, Grandad, what'd you think of that?' And Dad and I would laugh, because we'd almost expect him to lift that cap off his eyes and say 'Give me a beer!'"

Their only brush with the authorities came at a border patrol checkpoint outside of Blythe, California. According to Shane, "When the patrol agent stuck his head in, looked at Grandad and said, 'How you doin', sir?' I said, 'Oh, he's asleep.'

"'Damn, he's sleepin' pretty hard,' the agent said.

"'Oh, he's been asleep ever since Texas,' I told him."

And so Victor, a passenger with a grin on his face, riding in his beloved baby-blue Cadillac, took his last cruise to eternity.

## Bela Lugosi—Dracula's Last Goodbye

Internationally syndicated columnist James Bacon tells this story about Lugosi's funeral in 1956. Lugosi, a Hungarian, first played Dracula on Broadway in 1927. He insisted on being buried wearing his famous black Dracula cape. He starred in a long string of chillers, including *Murders in the Rue Morgue, Chandu the Magician*, and Ed Wood's fever dream, *Plan 9 From Outer Space*, during which Lugosi died. Yet the actor was still best known and recognized as *Dracula* from the 1931 film.

"At the conclusion of the funeral services," Bacon recalls, "Boris Karloff and Peter Lorre (both actors of the same macabre genre) and I were invited to view the body. As I watched Boris and Peter looking down on Bela's remains—and what a picture that would have made—I heard Peter say to the oft-filmed actor, who on film had died and risen countless times, 'Come now Bela, quit putting us on!'"

## David Janssen's Big Goodbye

A handsome man from a handsome family, Janssen was the son of a beauty queen and Ziegfield Girl; his sister was a Miss California.

With his mother, his ex-wives, and his current wife all not speaking to each other and the Hillside Chapel jammed with real friends, girlfriends and newly found friends, David Janssen's last honors were given in a nonsectarian service consisting of four eulogies.

Janssen was one of the most popular of the male action/adventure TV stars working in Hollywood. His death brought out the "A" list of Hollywood movers and shakers, along with some less pedigreed close friends, for an expensive, well-planned, glamorous funeral. There were 500 invited guests inside the Hillside Chapel and another 1,000 plus fans standing outside. Seated near Janssen's dark coffin, which was covered with white gardenias, were Johnny Carson, Milton Berle, Buddy Hackett, Gregory Peck, James Garner, Angie Dickinson, George Peppard, Jack Klugman, Richard Harris, Gene Kelly, George Hamilton, Nancy Sinatra, Robert Stack and other celebrities. Linda Evans was there with her best friend, David's wife, Dani.

Eulogies were given by Paul Ziffren, Olympic Committee chairman, director Richard Lang, and producer Quinn Martin, who would sell a syndication package of *The Fugitive* for $17 million the day after Janssen's death. Suzanne Pleshette, David's close friend, read a tender eulogy that included these thoughts: "He was Peter Pan and at his best when he didn't have to act as a grownup. Being with him was like playing hookey and not getting caught."

Also at the service were Nicky Blair, the restaurateur; Tommy Gallagher, Chasen's dining room captain; and Benny Massi, David's favorite waiter at the Brown Derby.

Joey Tata, Janssen's closest pal, described the service: "All the old friends, the ones crying their eyes out, were in the back, ignored, while the famous strangers were up front. There was an entire legion of mourning ladies."

Columnist Rona Barrett described David this way: "He was a romantic puzzle. He could keep deep friendships with women without ever having sex with them, and have sex with others, and have absolutely no commitment with the ladies."

And Janssen's valet and confidant summed the day up this way: "It isn't so surprising that all his girlfriends were at the funeral—all of them were firmly convinced that he was about to divorce Dani (Janssen's wife), and marry them. But, David is not around to tell us if any of them were even close." (For a description of where Janssen is buried, see "Hillside Memorial Park.")

### Sammy Davis Jr.—Goodnight, Mr. Bojangles

When Sammy Davis Jr. died on May 16, 1990, the lights on the Vegas strip went dark for an unheard-of ten minutes in tribute to their beloved "Mr. Bojangles." The only other times the lights had been dimmed were for Martin Luther King Jr., President John F. Kennedy

Sammy Davis Jr. — Entertainer
*extraordinaire*.

and later, briefly, for Dean Martin.

According to his daughter, Tracey Davis, the first hours after Sammy's death went badly. Ignoring Sammy's last request that his headstone should simply read, "The Entertainer," his wife, Altovise, changed it to read "The Entertainer. He Did It All; Your Loving Wife Altovise. Father of Tracey, Mark, Jeff and Manny." Manny was a young man who was never adopted by Davis. Further, against Tracey's wishes, the casket was left open, revealing Sammy's thin body that had been ravaged by cancer. And worse, a photographer had appeared from nowhere and had taken pictures of Sammy in the casket.

Tracey, almost hysterical, had called their dear friend Shirley MacLaine and told her about the incident. Shirley told their mutual friend David Steinberg about the pictures. He then immediately went to the photographer and told a big lie: Frank Sinatra was so angry about the pictures he was going to have the photographer killed. The shaken photographer immediately surrendered the pictures. Only later did Tracey find out that Altovise asked him to take the pictures.

Sammy's death was the lead story in newspapers, on radio and television. When the motorcade left Sammy's house, it looked like a presidential procession—thousands of people lined the streets, taking off hats, crying, many shouting, "Sammy, we love you."

Legions of celebrities showed up for the services, and so many thousands of fans showed up at the park they had to be led through in groups. Jesse Jackson spoke, referring to Sammy as "Mr. Bojangles." The Rabbi Allen Freehling spoke of Sammy going "gently into the good night." Stars who were present included Shirley MacLaine, Frank Sinatra, Berry Gordy, Tony Danza and

Billy Crystal. Recordings of Sammy singing "Mr. Bojangles" and "I've Gotta Be Me" were played.

Sammy Davis Jr. was laid to rest in the family plot next to his father, his grandmother PeeWee, and "Uncle" Will Mastin of the Will Mastin Trio. (Sam Cooke is nearby on the other side of the garden in the Garden of Honors, high on a hill at Forest Lawn.)

After the funeral, Sammy's closest friends went to his house to be with his family and to share the food, drink and good times that Sammy had so dearly loved. The celebration had been arranged by Shirley MacLaine. Bill Cosby called to send his love, and Tracey's baby, young Sam, was there with Billy Crystal doing the honors as babysitter. It was a great day for Sammy's family, friends and fans to say goodnight to "Mr. Bojangles." (In 1996, Tracey Davis wrote a beautiful biographical tribute to her father, entitled *Sammy Davis Jr., My Father.*)

## Death of an Oilman, J. Paul Getty

When J. Paul Getty died early one Sunday morning in June of 1976, the *New York Times* described him as "A symbol of wealth and power" and estimated his personal fortune at $2 billion. His body was placed in view in the Great Hall of Sutton Place, his mansion in England, guarded by a dozen German shepherds during the day and armed guards at night. The 72-room mansion was further protected by bars on its 500 windows. Only two visitors came to view him at Sutton Place: Rosabella Burch, a Nicaraguan beauty whom he had supported for years; and his lover Anna Hladka, an art researcher from Czechoslovakia. However, his memorial service on June 21, 1976, at the American church of St. Mark on North Audley Street in London, was packed with those who came to say their last goodbyes, including Lord and Lady Southbrough of Surrey; C.Y. Tung, the Chinese shipping tycoon; Joseph Floyd, distinguished chairman of Christie's; and assorted earls, countesses, lords, ladies and members of his family. J. Paul Getty Jr. was there with Bianca Jagger, as was his ex-wife Gail. She never forgave the old man for dragging his feet before coming up with the ransom for their kidnaped son, J. Paul Getty Jr., which caused the kidnappers to cut off his ear in order to speed up the process. Paul Jr.'s son,

Mark, was there with his two sisters, Aileen and Ariadne. The only speaker at the service was the Duke of Bedford, a friend who gave the funeral oration.

The real fun began when the terms of J. Paul Getty's will, which had been changed some 21 times over the years, was made public. As Penelope Kitson, a close friend of Getty's put it, upon hearing the will's details, "He was frightfully wrong in the will. He hurt a great many people." However, Penelope didn't hurt too badly. She was left with 5,000 shares of Getty stock, worth $825,000, and a monthly allowance of $1,167.

His lover, Anna Hladka, was given only $17,500 for her children's education; and Robina Lund, his public relations consultant, who expected a million, was left $209 a month. Rosabella Burch got $82,000 in shares, which was later increased to $150,000 to stop her outrageous screams. One of the big winners was Getty's museum, patterned after a first-century Roman villa, a building Getty never saw during his lifetime. The art museum, located in Malibu, received $661,943,577.50. Bingo!

The bulk of Getty's estate, $1.3 billion, went to the Sarah Getty Trust, which was created for Getty's grandchildren. His son Ronald, who got a trite $3,000 a month and stock worth $320,000, started to sue the estate and was given $10 million by the museum to calm him down. That move cost the museum $30 million in taxes, but they felt it was worth it in case the whole thing caved in like a house of cards. Ronald's half brothers, Paul Jr. and Gordon, were the fat cats. Their daughters split $28 million a year, with Gordon and lawyer Haye splitting an additional $1.65 million a year as trustees of the estate. Other old flames of Getty got monthly money or money and stock, including Marianne von Alvensleben, Mary Teissier, Gloria Bigelow, Mary Maginnes, Belene Clifford, Karen Mannhardt, Ursula d'Abo, Hildegard Kuhn, and Robina Lund. Three of his ex-wives had their monthly income cut off completely. The fourth, Teddy Getty Gaston, had hers lowered to $4,583 a month.

Getty made his first million off Oklahoma oil leases in 1916. After the sale of Getty Oil, the trust appreciated to $4 billion and the museum endowment to $2.2 billion. He had $16.41 on him when he died.

Getty's remains were shipped to the United States in a coffin that was so badly made, someone remarked that "It looked like a coffin for a Western outlaw." Getty's remains had to be moved to a new coffin before authorities would release the body to his attorneys. For over two years Getty occupied several temporary locations at Forest Lawn in Glendale while his attorneys argued with the Malibu City Planning Commission, zoning office and the California Coastal Commission. Finally he was allowed to be interred near his Getty museum under a granite slab on a slim promontory jutting out into the Pacific, guarded by closed-circuit TV.

**A Fond Goodbye for a Shoeshine Man**

You not only left Sam Eason's three-seat shoeshine stand with gleaming footwear, you left with a happy spring in your stride because with a few caring and humorous words, Sam could rejuvenate the weariest of people, both sole and soul.

Then one day Sam's stand, which was located in a parking garage in the Los Angeles business district, was empty. Sam's friends and customers, corporate executives and other businessmen traveled to South Los Angeles to bid their farewells to this man whose wit and wisdom were as bright as his "spit" shines. Sam had died of diabetes and was being buried on his 59th birthday.

"If you were down, Sam brought you up," said commercial realty executive Bill Dougherty, a 28-year, three-times-a-week customer of Sam's. "If you were feeling good when you sat down, you were feeling even better when you got up."

"It didn't matter the color of your skin or the color of your shoes, only the color of your mood. Sam was a good friend to everyone," said office systems manager Timothy Matthews. Added copier company executive Phil Cannon, "There was nothing phony about Sam." And lawyer Forbes said he often tested his trial arguments on Eason before heading for court. "He'd tell me if it worked or didn't. He understood Everyman."

Eason followed his customers west when the financial district moved from Spring Street, and his customers stayed loyal to him, returning after being transferred to places such as Century City and the San Fernando Valley. Ray Cano drove back twice a week from Alhambra to see Sam, even after he had retired from his downtown job.

On the day of Sam's funeral, flowers covered his stand back at 8th and Flower. Shock filled the face of real estate broker John Eichler when he saw the hand-printed sign announcing Sam's death. And parking attendant Astor Gebre remembered how Sam's dancing and joking would always cheer her up.

Sam was eulogized at his funeral by Highway Patrol Officer John Bavetta, who was wearing the motorcycle boots Sam had kept gleaming for so many years. In tears he reminded Sam's 100 friends of Sam's penchant for playing the horses. Saluting Sam's plain gray coffin he said, "It would have been the final tribute if Sam had hit it big and could let somebody else shine his shoes. Right now Sam is probably kicking back and having his halo shined."

Goodbye, good friend, we know our Shoeshine Man has gone to join God's other angels.

# 3

◆

## "A Riddle, Wrapped in a Mystery, Inside an Enigma" Death by Mysterious Circumstance

**William Desmond Taylor** (William Deane-Tanner), 1877–1922. His crypt is at Hollywood Memorial to the right as you enter the Cathedral Mausoleum.

William Desmond Taylor was known as one of Hollywood's finest directors and a perfect gentleman. He was thought to be a man without an enemy, except for the one who shot him dead with one bullet through his heart on the night of February 1, 1922.

Taylor's body was discovered in his elegant Alvarado Street apartment the next morning by Henry Peavey, an employee who had just arrived to cook Taylor's breakfast. Peavey's yelling quickly attracted a next-door neighbor, Edna Perviance, an actress and favorite leading lady of Charlie Chaplin. She immediately made two phone calls—the first one to Mary Miles Minter, a 17-year-old actress who had been a Hollywood star and Mary Pickford imitator for 13 years. Edna told Mary, "If you've left anything in that house you don't want anyone else to see, you better get it out now." The second call was to Mabel Normand, a popular silent film star and another paramour of Taylor's.

Peavey, meanwhile, had called Taylor's doctor, who in turn called the coroner. Word quickly got to Taylor's studio, the Famous Players-Lasky Studio, and soon the movie executives were on their way, hoping to remove anything "disagreeable" from Taylor's house.

The police arrived to find the studio executives, who had already removed Taylor's stock of bootleg whiskey, busily burning papers. Also present were Mabel Normand and Edna Perviance, searching for love letters. The last to arrive were Mary Miles Minter with her overbearing stage mother, Charlotte Shelby. They were refused admittance at the door by police officers.

As the investigation progressed, a neighbor, Faith MacLean, came forward to say she had heard what could have been a shot fired at 7:50 P.M. Moments later she saw someone leaving Taylor's apartment, a person she described as 5 feet 10 inches tall, about 185 pounds and wearing a large, dark coat, a cap pulled over the eyes, with a muffler hiding the lower part of the face. She recalled the person was dressed like a man but walked like a woman.

From Peavey the police also learned that Mabel Normand had visited Taylor the previous night but stayed only a few minutes to pick up two books. Later, the police would find Mabel Normand's love letters to Taylor, along with the startling information that Normand had a $2,000-a-month cocaine habit. When this fact was made public, it ended her movie career. In a further search of Taylor's house, the police found a lacy nightgown with the monogram "MMM" and a note that said "Dearest, I love you-I love you-I love you! XXXXXXXXX! Yours always, Mary." The news of this find quickly spread through town and brought Mary Miles Minter's career to a halt.

Then came the strangest revelation of all: William Desmond Taylor's real name was William Deane-Tanner. He had been a well-known New York art connoisseur before disappearing without a word, leaving behind a wife and child. His brother, Dennis, pulled the same disappearing trick four years later.

Suspicion now fell on a man named Edward Sands as the murderer. Sands, a former servant of Taylor's, had forged thousands of dollars in checks before disappearing with Taylor's car, clothes and jewelry. Pawn tickets for the jewelry were later mailed back with the name "William Deane-Tanner" on them. Faith MacLean, when she was shown photos of Edward Sands, said he was definitely not the person she had seen the night of the murder. Further information led the police to speculate that Edward Sands was really Taylor's brother, Dennis.

"We know, of course, who committed the murder," said E.C. King, an investigator from the district attorney's office. He suggested the murderer was a woman, but there was no evidence to take her to court.

But which woman? A good guess would be Minter's stage mother, Charlotte Shelby. Why Shelby? First, she was known to have had an affair with Taylor, who obviously had been sleeping with her 17-year-old daughter, Mary, at the time he was murdered. But we will never know for sure who had Taylor first raise his hands high in the air and then calmly put a bullet in his heart.

Famous film writer and national news reporter Adela Rogers St. Johns was not only involved in reporting the event, she was also close to all the key people. Her theory? Powerful studio executives had the murder, the story and the investigation killed. The case was never prosecuted or solved.

**Dr. Haing S. Ngor** died in 1996 and is buried at Rose Hills.

Ngor escaped the Cambodian killing fields of the Khmer Rouge, where he had spent four years as a slave laborer. An obstetrician and gynecologist, he escaped to Thailand and eventually made his way to the United States, where he continued his medical career. A casting director spotted him at a Cambodian wedding, and although he had no acting experience, he was cast to play a major part in the 1984 film *The Killing Fields.* Ngor won the best supporting actor Oscar for his portrayal of Dith Pran, a real-life Cambodian who had worked for *New York Times* reporter Sydney Schanberg covering the war in Cambodia and Vietnam.

A hero to the Thai community, Ngor was gunned down in the carport of his apartment building in a high-crime area of Los Angeles' Chinatown. On April 26, 1996, three members of a local Chinese gang were arrested in connection with the homicide. The police believe their motive was robbery, but some members of the Cambodian community believe the killing was a political assassination to stop Ngor's efforts to bring Khmer Rouge perpetrators of the Cambodian holocaust to justice.

**Freddie Prinze,** 1954-1977. His crypt is in the Court of Remembrance at Forest Lawn, Hollywood Hills.

"We love you. Psalm 23" reads his epitaph. Freddie was only 19 years old when he first appeared on *The Tonight Show* on December 6, 1973. By April he was the star of his own TV series, *Chico and the Man.* Shy and very vulnerable, his friends say fame came too fast for young Freddie to handle. Born to a Puerto Rican mother and a Hungarian-Jewish father, Freddie loved to tell audiences, "You know, a Puerto Rican mother and a gypsy father? They met on the bus trying to pick each other's pockets."

Once on the celebrity fast track, Freddie took drugs—cocaine, Quaaludes, Valium and Ritalin—to hide his insecurity and started carrying a .357 magnum pistol after receiving death threats from Chicanos who were angry that a Puerto Rican was playing the Mexican character, Chico.

On October 13, 1975, Freddie married Kathy Cochrane, a travel agent, former cocktail waitress and co-owner of a beauty supply store. Twice divorced, Kathy was vulnerable and unsophisticated, and she fought continually with Freddie over his out-of-control drug problem. Kathy and Freddie had one son.

Freddie's psychiatrist wrote, "This person feels unable to deal with the environmental pressures facing him." Performing for President Carter's Inaugural Ball was the high point of Freddie's life. This joy was quickly shattered when he returned home to find that Kathy had obtained a restraining order to keep him away from their son.

Freddie had always had a fixation with the idea of dying young. Despondent, on January 29, 1977, he proved it. Freddie Prinze killed himself with one gunshot to the head.

"He was so incredibly different from the rest of us. At 19, to do what he did with *Chico*, at 22 to host *The Tonight Show*, he was a grown-up, charming, troubled, brilliant little boy," said Jimmy Komack, producer of *Chico and the Man*.

**George Reeves,** 1914–1959. Mountain View Cemetery, Altadena, California.

From 1951 to 1957, Reeves played Superman, "The Man of Steel," in 104 TV episodes, broadcast worldwide to homes in 30 countries, reaching an audience of 34 million viewers. As Superman, he could outrun the fastest train, but he couldn't stop a speeding bullet that took his life in the early hours of June 16, 1957.

Officially, Reeves' death is listed as "indicated suicide" by Beverly Hills officials. Others however, including crime experts, friends and private detective Milo Speriglio, who now owns the famous Nick Harris Detectives School and Agency, call it murder. Motive? Reeves' torrid and very visible love affair with a married woman, Toni Mannix. The affair had been going on for years when Reeves announced he intended to marry another woman. Toni was outraged and began calling him with death threats, mostly late at night, for the next two months, until finally Reeves filed reports about her with the Beverly Hills Police and the Los Angeles County District Attorney. After investigating, the authorities discovered both Toni and Reeves had been receiving threatening calls. The suspect behind the calls was Toni's husband, Eddie Mannix, tough guy and right hand to Louis B. Mayer at MGM.

Eddie was crude, common, uncouth, dangerous and hated by most of his associates. Known as "The Ape" because of his looks, he was made out to be an even bigger fool when Reeves dumped his wife from their open affair for another woman. Mannix had the power, the temper and the means to have Reeves taken out.

George Reeves, on the last night of his life, had dinner with Lenore Lemmon, the woman he planned to marry, and a house-guest, writer Robert Condon. After dinner, the three went into the living room to watch some television. A short time later, they went to bed, having consumed a lot of alcohol. Around midnight, two of Reeves' friends showed up, Carol Von Ronkel and William Bliss. Their late arrival made Reeves angry, and after one drink and words on the subject, he retired again to his bedroom. "Well, he's sulking; he'll probably go up to his room and shoot himself," Lenore said. She was referring to Reeves' favorite and well-known trick of pretending to kill himself by firing a blank from his pistol at his head, which he always managed to hold well away from his face to avoid powder burns.

This night, however, there was a real bullet in the gun. The Beverly Hills Police's official position would be "that without explanation, Reeves just suddenly decided to commit suicide." But why? His career was on an upswing; he had a boxing exhibition coming up with Archie Moore, a feature film in the works that he would both star in and direct, and more Superman episodes coming up for syndication. Reeves had everything to live for.

According to the police report, there were no powder burns on Reeves' face, suggesting he had held the pistol at least a foot and a half away, as he always did when firing a blank. Experts say that when committing suicide, one holds the gun as close to the head as possible to avoid a miss or possible maiming.

One theory is that someone, without Reeves' knowledge, had entered his bedroom, removed the blank bullet and substituted a real one. Another is that someone had been hiding in Reeves' bedroom and, taking advantage of the large amount of alcohol Reeves had consumed, killed him. And of course there is the official version, "indicated suicide."

**Benjamin "Bugsy" Siegel,** 1906–1947. Located in the mausoleum at Beth Olam in Hollywood Memorial, his marker is inscribed "In Loving Memory from the Family."

"My friends call me Ben; strangers call me Mr. Siegel; and guys I don't like call me Bugsy, but not to my face." Siegel first appeared on the west coast in the 1940s and soon became very popular with the Hollywood crowd, especially George Raft, who had been a boyhood pal. Jailed in Los Angeles in 1940 for the murder of "Big Greeny" Greenburg, Bugsy lived it up in style in his cell, with his own chef, wine and women delivered to the door, until he was released after the only two witnesses against him conveniently died. Called "the most dangerous man in America" by "Joey A." Adonis, Bugsy was Meyer Lasky's protégé and pals with mob bosses Lucky Luciano, Frank Costello, Tony Accardo and Joey A.

"Bugsy" Siegel — The "hit" scene.

Bugsy soon had a girlfriend, Virginia Hill. Even before Bugsy, Hill threw lavish parties, tipped and spent big on everything from food, jewelry, clothes and caterers to homes. Hill claimed her money came from her dead husband, George Rogers. But there was no Rogers. The money came from the mob, and Hill had actually grown up in rural Alabama, one of ten children born to an alcoholic handyman. Her big break came while she was slinging hash in Chicago. Joseph Epstein, who was in charge of Al Capone's bookmaking racket, fell in love with her. Hill moved on to become Joey A.'s mistress. Since Joey A. was involved with heroin, cocaine and mob money loans and laundering, Hill quickly became the mob's most trusted bag lady.

Bugsy, who was sent to head the west coast operations for the mob, also fell in love with Hill. And with World War II over, Bugsy decided the mob needed a legitimate front, so he talked the capos into building Las Vegas' first big casino and 280-room hotel. He named the hotel after his nickname for Virginia, "The Flamingo."

From its opening day, the Flamingo was a nightmare for Bugsy. His casino employees were thieves. The hotel lost so much money the dons worried not only about their investment, but also about their reputations as they appeared to be "patsies." They asked Bugsy for their money back. Bugsy told them to go to hell. He would pay them back when he was damned good and ready. Then he made the biggest mistake. He threatened to kill Lucky Luciano. Virginia, fearing the worst, begged him to apologize to Luciano. When Bugsy refused, Hill left for Paris, at Luciano's insistence, on a quick "business trip."

Shortly after Virginia left, on July 7, 1947, someone pumped nine rifle shots through the picture window at Bugsy's Beverly Hills mansion, hitting him three times in the head. The murder of Bugsy was never solved, but in those days no one threatened Lucky Luciano unless they were crazy. Benjamin seemingly earned his nickname, "Bugsy."

**Marilyn Monroe,** 1926–1962. The crypt is located in the northeast corner of the Corridor of Memories in Westwood Memorial.

There would seem to be two Marilyn Monroes: one was Norma Jean Mortenson, a frightened, immature girl who had grown up in an insecure world that included a mad mother and two years in an orphanage. The other was the Marilyn Monroe who became a Hollywood Legend. The Norma Jean part, unfortunately, left her incapable of building a lasting affair or marriage. Her three marriages included her first husband Jim Dougherty, whom she married as a convenience just out of high school. He joined the Merchant Marines. She waited for him on Catalina Island, but his destination was Shanghai and their marriage was soon dissolved. He later became a Los Angeles police officer.

Her second husband was baseball slugger Joe DiMaggio, and her third and last was playwright Arthur Miller.

DiMaggio so loved her that, even though their marriage lasted only nine months, he arranged to have red roses placed on her crypt every Tuesday, Thursday and Saturday following her death. Susan Hail of Parisian Florists says, "It was 20 years that we delivered those roses—more than 180,000 in all—and we never raised the price for Mr. DiMaggio."

As Marilyn Monroe, her love affairs were spectacular and showed her to be a very bright and funny woman. When the news broke that she had posed naked for a calendar, a reporter asked Marilyn what she had on when the photos were taken. She replied, "The radio." Some of her rumored affairs included Marlon Brando, Frank Sinatra and Yves Montand. And even though they had divorced, DiMaggio considered himself her protector. Reporter James Bacon tells the story of DiMaggio becoming incensed at the rumor that Marilyn was shacked up in an apartment with some makeup guy. DiMaggio went there with Frank Sinatra, who supposedly guided him to the wrong apartment, scaring the hell out of a spinster who was in bed asleep. Marilyn, when she heard the story later, said "Joe is such a gentleman. Who else but a gentleman would kick in the wrong door?"

Another of Marilyn's lovers, powerful William Morris agent Johnny Hyde, gave her career a boost in the 1950s with parts in *Asphalt Jungle* and *All About Eve.* Then came *Gentlemen Prefer Blondes, How to Marry a Millionaire,* and *The Seven Year Itch,* which firmly planted her in the minds of America as the sexy, sensual "girl toy" with the pouty lips and little girl voice. These

Marilyn Monroe — "Only the public can make a star."

films were followed with more challenging parts in *Bus Stop* and *The Prince and the Showgirl.* But it was Billy Wilder's *Some Like It Hot* in 1959 that showcased Marilyn's magnetic allure at its hottest and made her a Hollywood goddess.

Her two miscarriages with Miller, three wrecked marriages, memories of her unhappy childhood and a failed picture, *The Misfits,* caused the star to seek help in a psychiatric clinic, a bad mistake from which she called on Joe DiMaggio to rescue her.

Her movements during the following months were somewhat of a mystery. Back in California, rumors flew about Marilyn's alleged affair with President John F. Kennedy and frequent visits to Peter Lawford's beach house. Finally rumors of another affair surfaced, this time with Attorney General Robert F. Kennedy.

Her frustrations, ailments and perpetual tardiness caused Fox to drop her as the female lead in *Something's Got to Give.* On the last night of her life, August 4, 1962, Marilyn closed the door of her bedroom after speaking to her housekeeper, Eunice Murray. Eunice claimed to be the last person to see her alive and the first person to find her dead. Murray said it was 10:00 P.M. when she awakened, fearing something was wrong with Marilyn. She summoned the doctor at midnight. She would later change her story to waking up at midnight and summoning the doctor at 3:00 A.M.

With the Kennedys and most of the other players now dead, the details of what happened that night, and what went on before, will never be known. One rumor said that Marilyn was furious at being passed around by John and Bobby "like a piece of meat" and intended to make their affairs known at a press conference on August 6.

Los Angeles Police Department watch commander Jack Clemmons was the first police officer on the scene. "In my opinion Marilyn Monroe was murdered that night," he said. "In fact, it was the most obvious case of murder I ever saw. Everything was staged."

Dr. Lionel Grandison, deputy coroner, said he was forced to sign a false death certificate listing the cause of death as "acute barbiturate poisoning." Grandison went on to tell about Marilyn's infamous, supposedly tell-all "Little Red Diary," which was placed in the coroner's hand as evidence. "The next day, the diary not only had disappeared, but its very existence was struck from the inventory."

Famous Hollywood private investigator Fred Otash had a telephone interview with the *Los Angeles Times* in 1985. He stated that at 2:00 A.M. on the night of Marilyn's death, he met with Peter Lawford in his office at Lawford's request. "He had just left Monroe's house. He said that she was dead and that Bobby Kennedy had been there earlier. Lawford said they had gotten Bobby out of the city via helicopter."

So ends the life of Marilyn Monroe.

"Only the public can make a star," she once said. "It's the studios who try to make a system."

**Natalie Wood** (Natasha Gurdin), 1938–1981. Her grave is located southeast of the entrance and just south of the Hammer Mausoleum in Westwood Memorial.

Born to Russian immigrant parents, Natalie landed her first bit part in a motion picture when she was four. By the age of seven she was earning $1,000 a week in pictures, and at nine, she became a full-fledged star in *Miracle on 34th Street*. At seventeen, she became a bona fide teenager and got her first on-screen kiss from James Dean in *Rebel Without a Cause,* along with her first Academy Award nomination as Best Supporting Actress. At nineteen, she married a star's boy-next-door equivalent, Robert Wagner.

The first year of the Wagners' marriage was sheer bliss. Natalie was under suspension from Warner's on a salary dispute, and she and Robert became inseparable. Then as they both returned to work, their marriage problems began. Natalie wasn't used to being alone, and by the time she made *Splendor in the Grass* in 1961, for which she got a Best Actress Academy Award nomination, she was close to having a nervous breakdown. Without Wagner around, she slipped into an affair with Warren Beatty. A divorce soon followed.

Natalie confessed, "I didn't know who or what I was." She entered therapy that was to continue five days a week for eight years. During this time

31

Natalie Wood — "The only thing I don't like is being in the water."

her professional life flourished with such hits as *Westside Story* and *Gypsy.* Then in 1969 she married a British screenwriter, Richard Gregson, and gave birth to their daughter, Natasha. This marriage soon ended, and in 1972 she remarried Robert Wagner. They became what appeared to be Hollywood's most perfect couple. Three years later Natalie gave birth to their daughter, Courtney, and by 1981, at age 42, Natalie was at the peak of her career. She was wonderfully happy, sound and stable, a beautiful, mature woman.

Thanksgiving of that year, the Wagners decided to spend the weekend on their 55-foot yacht, the *Splendor,* at Catalina Island. They invited Christopher Walken, Natalie's then co-star in *Brainstorm,* to join them. On Saturday, November 28, while anchored at the Isthmus, the Wagners and Walken returned to the yacht after a stormy dinner ashore. They had spent the evening at Doug's Harbor Reef and Saloon. Years later, their yacht's Captain Davern claimed that Wagner had smashed a bottle of wine in anger and had accused Walken of "trying to seduce my wife in front of me." Davern went on to say, "Natalie was intrigued with Walken. He was a young, good-looking guy and she played it up with him."

That same night, while making his final check of the boat, Davern discovered the yacht's dinghy, *Valiant,* was not tied to the *Splendor.* At the time no one worried about this because Natalie was an excellent sailor who often took the dinghy out alone on clear nights. At 1:00 A.M., Wagner became worried and called ashore to Don Whiting, the night manager of the restaurant where they had eaten dinner. Whiting immediately dispatched three patrol boats, one to pick up Wagner and two to look for Natalie. At 3:25 A.M., the Coast Guard was alerted and at dawn, lifeguards on the island and an L.A. County sheriff's helicopter joined the search.

Natalie was found floating face down near Blue Cavern's Point. Nearby was the dinghy *Valiant.* The key to her ignition was turned off and the gear shift was in neutral. Her four life jackets were untouched. Scratches on Natalie's wrists and hands suggested to the authorities that she has been trying to cling to the nearby rocks before she gave in to hypothermia and drowned. (The waters in the winter at Catalina are very cold, averaging 49° to 63°F.)

Police and locals came up with one theory: she never boarded the boat but slipped while untying it, hit her cheek, and ended up falling into the harbor. Another similar theory was that she may have been attempting to move the dinghy to keep it from banging into the *Splendor* when she lost her balance and fell into the sea.

However, Marilyn Wayne, a Los Angeles commodities broker anchored nearby, heard a woman calling for help about midnight. "I didn't help because I heard someone answer, 'Take it easy,' in a laid-back voice, 'We'll be over to get you.'" Who was that person who cried for help? And who was the person who promised to help?

Natalie once declared, "I always feel very serene when I'm near the water or on the water. The only thing I don't like is being *in* the water."

**Sharon Tate,** 1943–1969. Located just west of the gate at Holy Cross Cemetery, in the garden behind the Grotto. The headstone, level with the ground, reads "Beloved wife of Roman, Sharon Tate Polanski" and "Paul Richard Polanski, their baby."

Sharon was 26 and 8 1/2 months pregnant that hot summer night in 1969. She was at the home she and her husband had rented on Cielo Drive, in a secluded canyon off Benedict Canyon Road. Also in the house were Jay Sebring, 35, a famous hair stylist with clients such as movie stars Paul Newman and Steve McQueen; Wojtek Frykowski, a countryman of Roman's and a charismatic motion picture producer; and Wojtek's lover, Abigail "Gibby" Folger, 26, the coffee heiress. Outside was Steve Parent, 18, a departing guest of the groundskeeper, William Garretson, 19, who lived in the remote guest house on the estate. Garretson was the only survivor of the massacre. He spent the night listening to music through headphones, unaware of the murders taking place at the mansion.

Sharon Tate Polanski was an actress and the wife of famous Polish film director Roman Polanski, the genius behind such movies as *Rosemary's Baby*. The daughter of an army intelligence officer, Sharon had grown up leading a nomadic life in dozens of military towns in the United States. As a teenager, against the wishes of her father, she decided to become a film actress. Stunningly beautiful, Sharon quickly found some bit work in TV. When producer Martin Ransohoff thought she was ready, he cast her in

*Eye of the Devil*, a low-key thriller with an excellent cast, including David Niven and Deborah Kerr. Then in 1966, Tate met Polanski in London, where she was cast in his film *The Fearless Vampire Killers*. They quickly fell in love and married two years later in 1968. "She was sweet and lovely. . .an angel who I'll never meet again in my life," Roman said.

However, on that hot August night in 1969, four people were looking for Sharon's rented house—Tex Watson, Patricia Krenwinkle, Susan Atkins and Linda Kasabian. They were the disciples of Charles Manson, a man whom they described as "Jesus Christ," and the four of them were part of his "family." On this night, they had been sent from the abandoned Spahn Movie Ranch, a place of group sex, LSD, and Manson's daily sermons, on a mission of death. They had been ordered to kill anyone they found in Sharon's house. Why? Because in that house some songs Manson had written were turned down by a music producer, who by now had moved away. They were going there to begin playing out the plot of *Helter Skelter,* Manson's plan to start a race war between blacks and whites. "Make it as gruesome as possible," he ordered his followers. "Use knives. Mutilate them. Write something on the wall that will shock the world."

Parent, the 18-year-old visitor, was the first to die. As he was trying to open the driveway gate, Tex Watson slashed his arm with a knife held in one hand. Then he shot Parent dead with a pistol held in his other hand. Krenwinkle and Atkins quickly joined Tex, and they silently made their way to the main house. Inside, Tex and the others quickly rounded up Sharon and her guests. Sebring, protesting, would be the next to die, shot by Watson. Frykowski was the next victim, shot twice, his head beaten by Tex's pistol, his body stabbed numerous times with a knife. Following this, Folger tried to escape by running away. Krenwinkle tackled her; she was then stabbed 28 times by Atkins and Watson.

Sharon, the last to die, pled "Please, let me have my baby" before Watson stabbed her 16 times. Susan Atkins then dipped her finger in Sharon's blood, tasted it, soaked a towel in the blood and wrote on the door "Pig."

Years later, in 1984, Polanski wrote, "Even after so many years I

Jean Harlow — There was a directness, a simplicity, a hearty good humor and a joy of life about her.

find myself unable to watch a spectacular sunset, or visit a lovely old house, or experience visual pleasure of any kind without telling myself how she would have loved it all. In these ways I shall remain faithful to her until the day I die."

**Jean Harlow** (Harlean Carpentier), 1911–1937. Located in the Great Mausoleum at Forest Lawn, Glendale, in an alcove in the Sanctuary of Benediction. Outside the room is her name, and behind the gate is a $25,000 room made of beautiful, colored European marble, paid for by William Powell, a famous actor whom she had loved.

It is a good thing Jean Harlow had guts, beauty, intelligence and a great sense of humor. She would not only have to battle a tough life, she would have to battle the people she loved to survive the few years she was allowed to live. Called the "Platinum Venus," Harlow was unbelievably gorgeous. She came to Hollywood when she was barely 16, with a worthless husband and a money-grubbing mother and stepfather, Mama Jean and Marino Bello.

Harlow managed to land a few "going nowhere" parts in the movies the first few months. Then she was discovered by Howard Hughes in 1927. He gave her a starring role in *Hell's Angels,* his film about World War I flyers. Harlow was an instant hit. Even staid England called her "Sexquisite," and America had a new star, one with a super sexy, sassy appeal. Writer Adela Rogers St. Johns remembers the first time she met Harlow at a party:

"She walked in and a cry went up from every woman in the room, 'There's Harlow—where's my husband?' I found myself liking the girl! There was a directness, a simplicity, a hearty good humor and a joy of life about her that were irresistible."

Harlow went on to star with Clark Gable in *The Secret Six.* He immediately took a liking to Jean and they made five more films together. These were followed by *Public Enemy* with James Cagney and *Goldie* with Spencer Tracy, both of which won the critics' approval. Tracy genuinely liked Harlow. He told her to stop being phony about her acting and taught her to just be herself. Harlow took Tracy's advice, and the two made two more films together that brought out Harlow's natural gift for wisecracking comedy.

Having sent her first husband to the showers years ago, Harlow found herself fighting off passes from half of Hollywood, including Louis B. Mayer. But it was Paul Bern, an MGM studio executive, that she became attracted to. She saw in him the comfort and stability her life had never had, and as she described it, "his friendship, his sane wisdom and his understanding were the great influences in my life." Paul Bern was so sensitive to the feelings of people around him that he was known as "Father Confessor" and "St. Francis of Hollywood." Jean and Paul were married on July 2, 1932.

In the early morning hours following the ceremony, Jean called her friend Arthur Landau in hysterics. "Come and get me!" Back at Landau's house, Harlow told Arthur and his wife, Jean, about Paul's terrible secret. His sex organ was as tiny as that of a child; he could do nothing with it. "You're a sex goddess—you can help me!" he pleaded with Jean. But Jean was no goddess, just a beautiful woman, and she could do nothing for him. In a frustrated rage, Bern attacked Harlow, bit her legs badly, then beat her unconscious with a cane.

Forced to stay together for the sake of Harlow's career, from which Bern needed income badly, their life became an impossible relationship. Bern could only watch helplessly as Harlow's love for him turned to hate. Neither did it help Bern to see Harlow, then doing the film *Red Dust* with Clark Gable, in steamy love scenes, including one where she was nude in the shower.

Besides his sex problems, Bern had another and equally bizarre dilemma that surfaced in the summer of 1932. Dorothy Millette, an aspiring actress, had lived with Paul Bern in New York as his common-law wife ten years before. Stricken with incurable amnesia at that time, Dorothy had been placed in a sanitarium in Connecticut, where Paul paid all her bills. Suddenly, Dorothy Millette's memory returned. And no matter how emphatically she was told, Dorothy could not comprehend that more than a decade had passed and Bern had moved on to Hollywood and Harlow. Dorothy wrote Bern that she was coming to see him. In Los Angeles, Bern pleaded with Dorothy that the scandal of bigamy would ruin Harlow's career and possibly jail him. It was no use. Dorothy only heard the part she didn't want to hear—that Bern didn't want to be with her. Bern finally convinced Dorothy to go to San Francisco, promising that he would join her. Dorothy went to San Francisco, but after a few days waiting and no Bern, she called and said she was coming to Los Angeles over Labor Day weekend. She was tired of waiting.

In the predawn hours of September 4, 1932, after a quarrel with Jean that sent her home to her mother, Paul Bern shot himself once in the head. His so-called suicide note read:

> Dearest Dear:
>
> Unfortunately this is the only way to make good the frightful wrong I have done you and to wipe out my abject humiliation. I love you, Paul. You understand last night was only a comedy.

Dorothy Millette, upon hearing the news of Paul's death, boarded a steamer in San Francisco and leaped to her death in the Sacramento River.

Harlow was saddled with Bern's enormous debts plus the high living expenses of her mother and stepfather. Despite suffering from the effects of burns on her eyes from set lights and kidney damage from the beating Bern had given her, Harlow kept making hit movies. They included *Hold Your Man* in 1935 with Gable, *Dinner at Eight* with Wallace Beery, and the musical *Reckless.* More pictures followed, along with the announcement of her engagement to actor William Powell. In 1936, Harlow had her biggest hit, *Libeled Lady,* with Spencer Tracy, Myrna Loy and William Powell, who gave his fiancee a 150-karat $20,000 star sapphire engagement ring for Christmas. Harlow was at the peak of her career, and with Powell, it looked like she had found the love she really needed.

Four months later Harlow became ill with an inflamed gall bladder. Powell urged her to take time off to rest. Harlow didn't, and on May 29, 1937, she collapsed in Gable's arms during the filming of *Saratoga.* Harlow's mother, Mama Jean, a Christian Scientist, saw her chance to put everyone in her debt. She was determined to heal Jean through simple prayer. Three days later Powell and some of Harlow's friends forced their way into Mama Jean's home.

"Doesn't she look better?" Mama Jean had pointed at her daughter. Harlow didn't look better—she was dying, and by the time Powell and the others got her to a hospital, it was too late. Those whom Jean Harlow loved had killed her.

**Ramon Novarro** (Ramon Samaniegos), 1899-1968. He died on Halloween and is buried in Calvary Cemetery.

On Halloween morning, 1968, actor Ramon Novarro's secretary, Edward Weber, opened the door to Ramon's bedroom and found the room drenched in blood. On the mirror was scribbled "Us girls are better than you fagits." On the bed was Novarro's body, hands tied behind his back, his once beautiful face beaten to a bloody pulp. In his hands was a pen, and on the sheet under his body was written the name "Larry."

Novarro was thought to be very spiritual. He was also gay. During the last few months of his life, he wrote over 140 checks to male prostitutes. At this time, a drifter named Paul Ferguson and his brother, Tom, heard the rumor that Novarro kept $5,000 in cash in his home. The pair paid Novarro a visit that night, and during a wild drinking spree, Paul Ferguson beat Novarro to death.

**Bob Crane**, 1937-1978. Buried at Oakwood Memorial Park, Chatsworth, California.

Because of a shaky financial position in the 1970s, Crane turned to working dinner theaters across the country, where he could earn $200,000 a year for about 30 weeks of work.

In the early morning hours of June 29, 1978, in his suite at the Winefield Apartment Hotel in Scottsdale, Arizona, Crane was killed by two severe blows to the head that caused massive skull fractures and brain damage. The blows were inflicted by a blunt instrument that was never recovered, and no one was ever charged with the murder. Much of the evidence that could have provided clues to the murder, including fingerprints, was reportedly mishandled by the Scottsdale police.

Crane was known to have many girlfriends and "drop-ins" who were in and out of his apartment. The police said they found over 50 videotapes of a sexual nature, showing Crane in sex acts with many different women. Crane was also known to have kept an album containing a large collection of pornographic stills of his frolicking. The album disappeared the night of his death. Some authorities speculated that only a man could have inflicted the brutal blows it took to shatter Crane's head. They speculated that the killer could possibly have been a cuckolded husband or an angry boyfriend, who probably removed the tape and stills of Crane having sex with his wife or girlfriend. We'll probably never know who killed Bob Crane.

In 1981, Crane's business manager, Lloyd Vaughn, was sentenced to one year in jail and five years' probation for embezzling $75,707 from Crane's estate.

**Sam Cooke,** 1930-1964. In the Garden of Honors, Forest Lawn, directly across from Sammy Davis Jr., his marker reads "Until the day break and the shadows flee away, Song of Solomon 2:17."

Sam Cooke was born in Chicago. His father was a minister, and Sam began his musical career singing soul with a group called the "Soul Stirrers." Cooke quickly moved from gospel to soul and then pop. His first single, "You Send Me," sold 1,500,000 copies in 1957, and he quickly became to black teenage girls what Elvis was to whites. Singing with RCA, he widened his appeal even more and began attracting a larger mixed audience. Called the "Father of Modern Soul," Cooke's hits included "Wonderful World," "Cupid," and "Another Saturday Night."

On the night of December 10, 1964, Cooke took a 22-year-old woman to a seedy motel, where he allegedly tried to rape her. What happened next is not clear, but claiming self-defense, the wife of the motel manager shot Cooke three times and finally clubbed him to death.

Thousands of people turned out at the A.R. Leak's Funeral Home the day of the funeral, screaming and crying. They were jostled and pushed as they attempted to view Cooke's body, finally shattering a glass door.

According to Cooke's friends, he was a gentle, considerate person who was "set up" and then murdered. To his thousands of fans, he remains a hero to this day.

## In Bloody Brentwood

On the evening of June 12, 1994, outside a condo at 875 South Bundy Drive, two people were viciously murdered. They were **Nicole Brown Simpson,** wife of actor/athlete, O.J. Simpson, and **Ronald Lyle Goldman,** an aspiring actor working as a waiter at Mezzaluna, a restaurant that Nicole frequented. Goldman was at Nicole's condo by unfortunate coincidence, merely to drop off a pair of sunglasses Nicole's mother had left at the restaurant earlier that night.

The coroner ruled the deaths were due to "multiple sharp force injuries," medical terminology to describe being violently stabbed to death and having your throat slashed.

Nicole was buried June 16, 1994, at Ascension Cemetery, 24754 Trabuco Road, Lake Forest, California. Ron was laid to rest on June 16, 1994, at Valley Oaks Memorial Park, 5600 Lindero Canyon Road, Westlake, California.

Nicole's ex-husband, O.J. Simpson, was charged with the murders. After over a year of testimony, he was found not guilty after less than four hours of jury deliberations. O.J., after being exonerated, vowed to find the killer or killers of Nicole and Ron. The district attorney's office of Los Angeles has closed the investigation, saying that all the evidence they had points to Mr. Simpson. However, they were unable to convince the jury. To date, no one has been held accountable for the slayings.

There remains much conversation and conjecture about these hideous murders. Will the crime ever be solved, or will Nicole's and Ron's spirits never be at rest?

**Robert Weiss** and **Jackie Dashiel Weiss** both died mysteriously within months of each other. Jackie, a well-known and respected newspaper woman, had retired recently from her job as editor of the Women's Section of the *Los Angeles Herald Examiner* due to a serious fall that incapacitated her. Bob had taken early retirement from his position of physicist at Hughes Aircraft. The couple was well known and active in civic and social functions in Los Angeles; their deaths stunned the city.

Compassionate and involved people, they worked with youth groups and often shared their home with people who needed help. Their compassion resulted in their undoing. They invited a young man who needed a home and help to stay with them. Things were becoming unpleasant and months later they asked him to leave. He refused. One morning, Jackie was preparing to keep a doctor's appointment when the young man took a drink of water up to her. Moments later when Bob went up to help her, he found her dead. The cause of death was unknown.

A scant three months later, during a scuffle, the young man strangled Bob. Before the incident, the young man had left the living room to get gloves, which suggested the murder was premeditated. He originally claimed that an intruder was responsible, but all the evidence proved he was the murderer. Eventually, he admitted it and was convicted of manslaughter. The big question is, did he kill Jackie too? What a loss.

# 4

## Body Parts

Much mystery and macabre adventures surround the death and burial of famous people. Here are a few of the more bizarre tales, as we know them.

**Franz Joseph Haydn's** head was stolen in 1809, and it wasn't returned until 1954, 145 years later. Haydn, the world famous composer, wrote timeless masterpieces including *The Creation* and *The Seasons*. Little did the beloved, gentle genius know his head would be bartered, stolen, hidden, studied and passed from hand to hand for years following his death.

Haydn died May 31, 1809, at the age of 77 in Vienna, a city that had just been occupied by Napoleon. Fearing retaliation from the French, a very quiet funeral was held for Haydn in a parish church, and he was buried in the Hundstrurmer Cemetery on June 1. Soon a group of Viennese phrenologists approached Joseph Rosenbaum, a close friend of Haydn, and bribed him to produce his friend's head for study. Rosenbaum complied, bribed the cemetery employees to dig up his friend, and cut off Haydn's head.

Nothing was heard of the missing head until 1820 when Prince Nicolaus II Esterhazy, Haydn's patron and Rosenbaum's employer, had Haydn dug up for removal to a mausoleum on his estate at Eisenstadt. Upon discovering the head was missing, the furious prince had the police search the then-implicated Rosenbaum's house for the head, which was successfully hidden under Frau Rosenbaum's sickbed. Rosenbaum suggested that if a suitable reward were offered, the head might reappear. The prince complied and offered a reward, which he never intended to pay. He did receive a head in return, but it was not Hadyn's.

On his deathbed, Rosenbaum confessed he had Haydn's real head and bequeathed it to the Vienna Society of the Friends of Music. But unknown to the dying Rosenbaum, his doctor had stolen the head and sold it to a noted Austrian professor who, in his will, left it to the Pathological Museum of the University of Vienna.

Hearing that Haydn's head was now at the Vienna Museum, the Vienna Society of the Friends of Music were furious. They sued for the return of the thrice-stolen head. Then the Prince joined the suit, claiming the head belonged with Haydn's body, where it came from originally. The Friends of Music won, and the head was placed in a glass case in their museum from 1895 to 1954, where it could be both viewed and handled by the public. Finally, Prince Paul Esterhazy, a Hungarian citizen under arrest by the Hungarian Communists, persuaded the Friends of Music to return the head to the Esterhazy family estate of Eisenstadt, which was in a Soviet occupied part of Austria.

On June 5, 1954 Haydn's skull was blessed by the cardinal archbishop of Vienna in front of the president of Austria and other dignitaries. It was then placed in an urn and carried in a procession through crowded, flag-draped streets to Eisenstadt, where the prominent sculptor, Professor Justinus Ambrosi, placed it gently in a new copper casket next to Haydn's body. Haydn was then reinterred under a tombstone with the following inscription:

> I shall not die, but live,
> And declare the works of the Lord.

**Richard "The Lionhearted" Coeur de Lion's** heart, and its true, final resting place, has been disputed since 1200 A.D. Richard, who died from an infected arrow wound on April 6, 1199, had left explicit instructions about the disposition of his corpse. His body was to be buried in a Normandy abbey at the foot of the tomb of his father, Henry II. His heart would be interred in the French city of Rouen. History further shows that Richard ordered his entrails to be buried in Poitou as revenge against their people who had rebelled against him.

Richard's exceptionally large heart was placed in a silver casket and interred with honors in the Rouen Cathedral as a reward for the city's loyalty to him. Years later the casket, with Richard's heart inside, was used as part of the ransom of St. Louis from the Saracens in 1250. The heart then disappeared for several centuries until

1838, when a lead box was found in another part of the Rouen Cathedral with the inscription "Hic jacet cor Ricardi Regis Anglorum." When it was opened, the lead box was found to contain the famous "Lionheart," which now resides in a museum in Rouen. Or does it?

The English, quite miffed at being left out of "divvying up the remains," brought up the point that their beloved King Richard "The Lionhearted" had a fondness for All Hallows Church in London and had expressed the wish that his heart be buried there. And so it was that some time in the 19th century, church officials began showing a receptacle in the chapel that Richard had built at All Hallows, which they claimed contained Richard's "Lionheart." Edward I, then King of England, even got the pope to grant an indulgence for all those who contributed to the upkeep of All Hallows Chapel.

**Abe Lincoln's** remains were moved 17 times over 36 years before ending up at his final resting place in 1901, underneath two tons of concrete and steel. It all began with a 12-day, 1,700-mile journey from Washington, D.C., to Springfield, Illinois. The trip by rail began on April 21, 1865. Along the way, there were several stops, many speeches, and over 1 million people who came to pay their last respects to their president, who had been gunned down by an assassin, John Wilkes Booth.

At Springfield, Abe's widow, Mary, escorted his coffin to the Oak Ridge Cemetery at the edge of town where, after a fitting ceremony, it was placed under armed guard in a temporary vault until a new mausoleum could be built.

Lincoln's remains never left the boundaries of the Oak Ridge Cemetery for 36 years but were moved at least 17 times. The coffin was opened five times for identification of its contents. One incident was the result of an attempt to entomb Abe in the Lincoln Memorial, which took nine years to build. When the movers attempted to put Abe's coffin in the newly built sarcophagus, the sarcophagus was found to be too small, requiring the removal of Lincoln's remains to a newer, smaller coffin.

At last, with Lincoln in place at his monument, it looked like his moving days were over. That was until master engraver Benjamin

Boyd was given a ten-year paid vacation at the state prison in Joliet, Illinois, for making counterfeit plates of U.S. currency. This put Boyd's boss, "Big Jim" Kinelly, between a rock and a hard place—he had plenty of street hoods to push his "funny money," but his inventory was being depleted at an alarming rate, and his engraving plates were now in the hands of the Secret Service. He needed Boyd, an engraver who was so good, the Treasury at one time had been forced to withdraw and redesign the five-dollar bill because no one could tell the fake from the real.

Big Jim's plan was simple: steal Lincoln's body, hold it for a $200,000 cash ransom, and demand to get Boyd sprung from prison as part of the deal. The Secret Service learned of Big Jim's plan, which was scheduled to take place on the night of November 7, 1876, an election day. The Secret Service managed to infiltrate the counterfeiter's gang with an informer, petty thief Lewis C. Swegles. He was charged with the job of sneaking out of the monument as soon as Big Jim had broken into the catacomb and alerting the Secret Service. But on that night Swegles had trouble sneaking out until he left on the pretext of going for the horse and wagon. Guns drawn, the Secret Service and their hired Pinkerton agents stormed the monument and a gunfight broke out. Luckily, no one was hit, as Big Jim and his men had withdrawn to a safe place outside to wait for Swegles and the wagon. Big Jim and his men would eventually end up in prison on other charges. But the fear of Lincoln's body being stolen caused the authorities to continually move, hide, shift and rebury him. Finally, in 1901, having had enough of seeing his father moved about like furniture, Abe's son had the coffin encased in steel, ten feet under the floor, and capped with tons of concrete. Abe was finally at rest.

Then there is the story of Boone's Bones. In 1820, the great American frontiersman **Daniel Boone** died on his farm at Tuque Creek, near Charette, Missouri. There he lay in a peaceful state until 1845, when the owners of a new cemetery in Frankfort, Kentucky, got the brilliant idea that someone as famous as Daniel Boone would be great publicity for their graveyard. After all, wasn't Daniel really a son of Kentucky? Agents were dispatched to meet with Harvey Griswold, the current owner of Boone's farm, and returned in triumph with Boone's bones. But were they his?

"Foul!" cried the people of Missouri, who then added ominously, "Griswold sold you the wrong bones." The feud over who has the real bones continues today. In 1983, the Kentucky state forensic anthropologist gave his opinion after examining a plaster cast of the skull interred in Kentucky. He declared that it did not resemble a Caucasian cranium at all but appeared to be that of a black slave, many of which were known to have been buried on the farm in Missouri where Daniel Boone was laid to rest.

The mystery of **The Two Goyas** occurred when the remains of Spain's famous painter of masterpieces such as the *Naked Maja* and *The Disasters of War* were transported to Madrid in 1899. Goya was to be buried beneath a dome on which he had painted his beautiful frescos in the Church of San Antonio de Florida a century before. Upon opening Goya's grave in Bordeaux, where he had first been buried, the authorities found two skeletons and only one head. Who was who? Being practical people, the Spaniards wisely transported all the remains to Madrid and placed them in a single magnificent sarcophagus marked "Francisco Goya. Let God sort them out" was their final thought.

**The Many Ashes of D.H. Lawrence.** What happens when you are surrounded by so many crazed, dysfunctional and hysterical relatives, friends, patrons, acquaintances and governmental boobs that your ashes must finally be mixed in a ton of concrete to stop their incessant wandering? That's what happened to the British novelist D.H. Lawrence, author of the steamy *Lady Chatterly's Lover* and *Sons and Lovers*. The story of what happened to Lorenzo's ashes (Lorenzo was D.H.'s nickname) has so many variations, culled from letters, memoirs, autobiographies, interviews and ravings, that all we can do is list them here. You can reach your own conclusion.

The story of the ashes began quietly with Lawrence's death near Vence in the south of France on March 2, 1930. His German wife, Freida, buried him in the small, local cemetery. So far so good, and not a bad place to leave him, but Freida had a dream. She wanted to move D.H. to their ranch in Taos, New Mexico. They had fallen in love with Taos and purchased the ranch after being introduced to the beauty of New Mexico as an artist's colony by aspiring cultural mavens Mabel Dodge Brett and Willa Cather.

Freida spent the next three years in litigation over D.H.'s not too substantial estate in England before returning to her beloved ranch in Taos in 1934. This time she returned with her new husband, the dashing but loony ex-army officer Angelo Ravagli, who had been a friend of the Lawrences' in Italy. Angelo immediately began building a little shrine for D.H.'s remains, high up on a sunny hill on the ranch.

By March 13, 1935, Angelo and Freida were in Marseilles, having D.H.'s remains cremated at the St. Pierre Cemetery in preparation for his long trip home. While Freida argued with the American consul in Genoa for permission to bring D.H. home to America, Freida's daughter, Barbara, was doing the same thing in Paris. On April 4, 1935, ashes in hand, Angelo set sail. He traveled from Villefranche to the United States on the *Conte de Savoia*. On April 11, U.S. Customs and Immigration in New York refused to allow entry of D.H.'s ashes. The government considered the writer an affront to public morals since they had already banned his books. Finally the intervention of the famous photographer Alfred Steiglitz, another of Mabel Dodge Luhan's stable of artists, convinced government officials to let D.H. in. However, it would be three nervous days before customs could find the urn. It was lost in one of their warehouses.

Angelo now began another great adventure—his train trip across America to Taos. He didn't say how long it took him, but he finally arrived at the railroad station in Lamy, the closest station to Taos. He was met by Freida and friends who had come by car to pick him up. They immediately left for Taos, only to return sometime later. They had covered 20 miles on their way home before realizing they had forgotten good old D.H., who was still in his urn, sitting on the station platform.

Since it was too late to return to Taos, they proceeded to the La Fonda Hotel in Santa Fe for a festive dinner party. After dinner, in the early hours of the morning, they decided to visit a friend, an eccentric, hysterical and high-strung Russian artist-in-residence, Nicolai Fechin, and his wife. Finally tiring of the party at Fechin's, Freida and the others continued to Taos, only to discover—you guessed it—they had left the urn at Fechin's.

Freida later claimed it was only there for a day. According to others, it was there for a week. During this time Madam Fechin, who was extremely emotional, made a little altar under an icon for D.H.'s ashes and surrounded it with burning candles. After a while a great peaceful radiance supposedly came from the urn, and she declared she understood D.H.'s essence completely. Freida had some trouble getting the urn back, as Madam Fechin thought it was a gift.

But there are more stories from the various players in this drama. Angelo confessed to the Baron Prosper de Halleville that he dumped D.H.'s ashes during his journey and refilled the urn, fearing he would have trouble with the authorities getting them to Taos. Also, writer Witter Bynner claimed that during the dinner party in Santa Fe at La Fonda, he spilled the ashes in the food and refilled the urn from the fireplace. And Dorothy Brett, who claimed, along with Mabel Dodge Luhan, that she had loved D.H. and that his wish was to be free, wanted his ashes scattered to the wind over his ranch. Dorothy Brett even told some people she had scattered D.H.'s ashes herself, replacing them with piñon ashes from her stove.

Freida then learned that Dorothy Brett had called her shrine "a horrid chapel, ghastly Villa d'Este, with grass steps, fir trees, huge poles and a cattle guard, a station toilet." Further, Mabel threatened to take the ashes herself and scatter them to the wind as D.H. would have wanted her to. So Freida had the ashes mixed into a ton of concrete, which supposedly now sits as the altar in D.H.'s shrine today. D.H., wherever you are, you must be glad it's over.

**John Belushi's** family, in 1983, had to have his grave moved to an isolated part of a picturesque New England graveyard because of the dozens of fans who descended on the site and stole or damaged many of the other stones there.

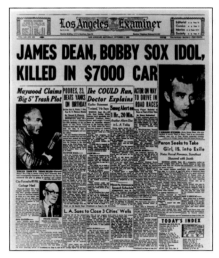

James Dean — *Rebel Without a Cause.*

**Groucho Marx** had his ashes stolen from Eden Memorial Park in the Mission Hills area of Los Angeles in 1982. They were left the same day at Mt. Sinai Memorial Park in Glendale.

**James Dean's** headstone was stolen twice from a cemetery in Fort Wayne, Indiana. The second time it was returned with a note. "You have heroes," someone wrote. "How would you like to see their graves messed up?"

Gone too soon — Natalie Wood and James Dean.

Elvis Presley — The King of Rock and Roll.

# 5

## The Out-of-Towners

**Elvis Presley,** 1935–1977. "The King of Rock and Roll" was born in Tupelo, Mississippi, and died of a heart attack at his Graceland mansion in Memphis, Tennessee, at the age of 42. His death was front-page news throughout the world, and his obituary in the *London Times* was the longest ever given an entertainer.

For the funeral, 80,000 grieving fans jammed the grounds at Graceland, and over 30,000 of them were able to view Elvis in his coffin. It was described as a nightmarish scene of hysteria, which was desecrated by a drunk driver who drove his out-of-control car into the crowd, killing two people. At the cemetery, Elvis's grave was covered with hundreds of floral arrangements, including many shaped like guitars and hound dogs.

Underneath the hair grease and rhinestone jackets, Elvis had always been a nice, religious, patriotic young man from a family of modest means. He was working as a truck driver when he recorded his first song, "Blue Moon of Kentucky," in 1954. Then in 1956, Elvis had his big breakthrough recording, "Heartbreak Hotel." He was off and running and he never looked back. Elvis recorded 83 hits over the next 16 years, which sold 500 million copies. Simultaneously, he starred in 33 movies, and his fans were estimated at 73 million worldwide. Presley gave rock and blues a gloss of country and western, a touch of gospel, a rockabilly beat and some body moves of insinuating sexuality that caused one Baptist pastor from Des Moines to label him "morally insane."

Somewhere along the way to the top, Presley acquired Colonel Tom Parker as his manager. Parker was a hucksterish Dutch-born carny man who at one time traveled the circuit with "The Great Parker Pony Circus" of miniature horses and was known to have painted sparrows yellow so he could sell them as canaries.

Presley broke into movies in a supporting role in *Love Me Tender* in 1956. His movie charisma was immediately apparent, and he next starred in *Loving You* in 1957 and in what many consider to be his best picture, *Jailhouse Rock* that same year. And he just seemed to get better in films with a continuing string of hits, including *King Creole* and *Flaming Star*. Following his army tour, where he met 14-year-old Priscilla Beaulieu, Presley's pictures became more bland, and he produced fewer hit records.

In 1961 he quit doing live tours, and in 1967 he married Priscilla. They had one daughter, Lisa Marie, and were divorced in 1973. Elvis continued to crank out mediocre films and began to battle with seesawing weight problems brought on by heavy drug use. When he returned to making live appearances the last few years before his death, his fans were shocked to see him so bloated and overweight that at times he would split the seams of his trousers during a performance.

Presley's remains were returned to Graceland. Presley's father had him interred on October 2, 1977, after vandals tried to steal the body. He is buried near his mother, Gladys, father, Vernon, and grandmother Minnie Mac. His twin brother, who was stillborn, is buried in Tupelo, Mississippi. Elvis was, and still is, a legend.

**Timothy Leary,** who died on May 31, 1996, may be the farthest out out-of-towner of them all. Leary, the evangelist of LSD, paid Houston-based Celestis Corporation $4,800 to launch his ashes into space, where they will orbit the earth until they burn up on re-entry.

Leary, who was 75 when he died, was an ex-Harvard professor who gained instant fame with his mantra in the 1960s, "Turn on, tune in, drop out." Leary's open endorsement of drug use, including his favorite, LSD, was the beginning of bringing drugs away from the needle-shooting junkies in the back alleys and into the hands of young people and adults in mainstream America. There they found acceptance, if not respectability.

"He was the guru of weirdness and good tidings," said Todd Gitlin, a New York University professor and author of *The Sixties, Years of Hope, Days of Rage*. And a 1960s band, The Moody Blues, wrote about Leary in their song "Legend of the Mind," "Timothy Leary's dead. Oh, no, no, no . . . He's outside, looking in."

Leary spent his time in the sixties experimenting, on himself and others, with drugs. He was seen giving his support to the Chicago Seven during their trial, chanting with John Lennon and his wife, Yoko, and dropping out with Kerouac and Allen Ginsberg.

Not everyone, or even many, liked Leary and what he was selling. Richard Nixon called him "The most dangerous man in America." And Daniel Addario, chief inspector of the San Francisco district attorney's office said, "He was an evil son of a bitch." Not all of Leary's life went smoothly. Of his five wives, one committed suicide, as did his only daughter. G. Gordon Liddy, who at that time was a local law officer, busted Leary on drug charges in 1966 and again in 1970. Leary was sent to the state prison at San Luis Obispo to serve up to 20 years for marijuana convictions. He escaped from prison shortly thereafter but was recaptured in 1973 and spent the next three years behind bars.

For the next two decades, Leary dabbled at stand-up comedy, writing, traveling the lecture circuit and palling around with his Hollywood friends. Suffering from terminal prostate cancer, Leary spent his last days writing a book, *The Ultimate Trip, A Manual for Designer Dying*, and tending his site in cyberspace on the World Wide Web. There he kept people up to date on the progress of his illness, including the exact amounts of marijuana, cocaine and nitrous oxide he consumed daily. His philosophy was "To try to enjoy every moment and do everything in public."

For his last night of partying, Leary and his pals, such as Trudy Truelove, put on dog collars with flashing lights and went off to the Beverly Hills Hotel for the 50th annual banquet and awards ceremony of the Los Angeles Advertising Women. Leary was there to pick up a humanitarian award for his friend Susan

Timothy Leary — Turn on, tune in, drop out.

Sarandon. But it wasn't destined to be a pleasant experience. Leary found himself sitting across from TV's Art Linkletter, whose 20-year-old daughter, after several bad experiences with LSD, had leaped to her death from an apartment building window. Linkletter despised Leary and had spoken out publicly about his hatred of both recreational drugs and Leary many times.

Neither man spoke to the other, but Linkletter would later say, "I was so glad to see him because he is suffering so. It was pretty good evidence about what happens to you when you live that kind of life."

Back home, Leary was despondent about his address to the group, a stream-of-consciousness mind wandering that turned into a shamble of disconnected words. Of Linkletter, Leary could only say, "He wouldn't look at me. He wouldn't look at me." But Leary's friends told him he was great, so Leary cheered up, took a hit of nitrous oxide, and was off to Spago with his wheelchair and friends for a late supper.

A footnote to Leary's story: Independent film producer Paul David produced a documentary of Leary's last days. On August 26, 1996, Los Angeles newspapers reported the gruesome final scene of the film, showing surgeons removing his head from his body and placing it in a glass cabinet to be frozen cryonically.

"That never happened," according to Leary's stepson, Zachary. According to the younger Leary, his stepfather's body was intact when it was cremated. Another scene during the closing credits of the film shows Leary, before his death, being fitted for a death mask. David refused to say whether the scene is real or not.

"It's intended to give people something to talk about," he said.

**Joel McCrea** (Joel Albert McCrea). Buried on his ranch on Route 10, Camarillo-Vesisona, Ventura County, California.

McCrea was a native Californian who drifted into working in the movies while attending Pomona College. DeMille gave him his first starring role in *Dynamite* in 1929. Tall, lithe and handsome, he played drama, comedy and adventure roles during the 1930s, including *Dead End* and *Union Pacific*. In the 1940s, he made *Foreign Correspondent* for Hitchcock, plus some comedies and dramas, but it was Fox's *Buffalo Bill* in 1944 that made him a big star. Most of his subsequent films were westerns, including the classic *Ride the High Country* for Sam Peckinpah. McCrea also dabbled in TV and radio while developing his ranch and cattle business. On his tax returns he listed his occupation as "rancher." When he died in 1990, he was still married to his actress wife, the charming Francis Dee, whom he wed in 1933.

**Percy Kilbride,** 1888-1964. Percy was best known as "Pa" in the seven *Ma and Pa Kettle* movies he made with Marjorie Main. He chose to be buried in a military cemetery, San Bruno/Golden Gate, near San Francisco.

He was a private in Company B of the 317th Infantry in World War I. His other connection with the military is his famous sailor-neighbor, Admiral Chester William Nimitz, 1885-1966, who is buried near Percy at Bruno/Golden Gate. In 1941, Nimitz, following the attack on Pearl Harbor, became commander in chief of the Pacific Fleet and finished the war as Chief of Naval Operations, the highest rank in the Navy.

**Wyatt Earp,** 1848-1929. Wyatt is buried in Hills of Eternity, a Jewish cemetery in Colma near San Francisco.

One account says he was buried at Hills of Eternity by his wife, Josephine, who was Jewish. Another contends Josephine was his sister and was married to a Jewish man, Max Weiss. The marker lies flat on the ground, as the three previous upright stones were stolen. For many years Wyatt was the bread and butter of the "pulps" and then of Hollywood producers, who probably pushed more film through the camera documenting the "adventures" of this man than any other true-life human being.

Earp first appeared as a lawman in Ellsworth, Texas, where a desperado named Ben Thompson had just unloaded his shotgun into the sheriff. Earp had said to the mayor, "It's none of my business, but if it was me, I'd get me a gun and arrest Ben Thompson or kill him." Earp was hired on the spot and began his first job as a lawman. His job ended that same day with the arrest of Thompson, who pled guilty and was fined $25 for disturbing the peace.

During his career as a lawman, Earp left us a legacy of names: Boot Hill; Dodge City, Queen of Cowtowns; Big Nose Kate; Bat and Jim Masterson; Chalk Breeson and his Long Branch Saloon; Dora Hand and her saloon ladies, "The Fairybelles"; Tombstone; Jim, Virgil, and Morgan Earp. Then there was Doc Holliday and the OK Corral where, on October 26, 1881, Wyatt, Virgil, Morgan and Doc, the one-time dentist and gambler, faced off with the Clanton gang: Ike, Billy, Frank and Tom McLowery and Billy Claiborne. It was a gunfight that lasted 30 seconds, with each side firing 17 shots. The final score: outlaws, three hits; good guys, eleven (three in Frank, two in Tom, and six in Billy). Years later, when Doc lay dying from tuberculosis, his last words were, "Well, I'll be damned."

**Arthur Kennedy,** 1914–1990. A versatile character actor and occasional lead, Kennedy was nominated for Oscars four times, including one nomination for *Some Came Running* opposite Frank Sinatra in 1958. Kennedy died in a hospital in Branford, Connecticut, and is buried on his family's farm in Nova Scotia.

**Ava Gardner,** 1922–1990. A lovely green-eyed brunette, Ava came from a poor family and spoke with a thick, Southern accent. Despite this, she learned to act and control her voice. She received a 1954 Oscar nomination for *The Barefoot Contessa* opposite Humphrey Bogart. In 1957 she divorced her husband, Frank Sinatra, after

Ava Gardner — A sex goddess on and off the screen.

playing the role of Lady Brett Ashley, an American expatriate living in Spain. Ashley was the woman with an incurable thirst for men in Hemingway's *The Sun Also Rises.* After her divorce, Gardner took up Lady Brett's lifestyle herself and moved to Spain to enjoy the good times with the jet-setters and bullfighters. Her other husbands were Mickey Rooney and band leader Artie Shaw. Gardner died in London and is buried in Smithfield, North Carolina, her hometown.

**Terry-Thomas,** 1911–1990. Thomas was a gap-toothed comedic actor who frequently played addled aristocrats or scheming villains. He is best remembered in America for his role as the dastardly villain in *Those Magnificent Men in Their Flying Machines* in 1966. Terry-Thomas suffered from Parkinson's disease and died in a nursing home in England.

**Gary Merrill,** 1915–1990. A charming leading man, Merrill's best performance was opposite his soon-to-be ex-wife, Bette Davis, in *All About Eve.* His screen career never really took off, except for the three Davis vehicles in which he starred with his wife. He and Davis divorced in 1960, and Merrill was kept busy and prosperous doing voice-overs for radio and TV commercials.

**Paulette Goddard,** 1911–1990. A former Ziegfeld girl, Paulette got her big break in pictures when Charlie Chaplin fell in love with her and cast her in his 1936 hit, *Modern Times.* The two later married and divorced, and Goddard went on to enjoy a career that spanned from the 1930s through the early 1950s. Goddard possessed an earthy, intelligent quality and received an Oscar nomination for *So Proudly We Hail* in 1943. Her other husbands included Burgess Meredith and novelist Eric Maria Remarque. An extremely wealthy woman, Goddard left generous endowments to New York University. She died at her home in southern Switzerland.

**Rex Harrison (Sir),** 1908–1990. Harrison is, of course, best remembered as Professor Henry Higgins in the Oscar-winning *My Fair Lady,* a part he created on Broadway. Sophisticated and charming, the debonair Harrison played in a long series of drawing-room comedies, including Noel Coward's *Blithe Spirit.* Harrison had a long career, which continued through the 1980s. His six wives included Lilli Palmer. The press dubbed him "Sexy Rexy" after the suicide of Carole Landis, with whom he was having an affair. He was knighted by Queen Elizabeth in 1989. His two books include an autobiography, *Rex,* published in 1974; and another about the art of comedy, *A Damned Serious Business.* Harrison died in his Manhattan apartment, and a memorial service was held at the Church of the Transfiguration in New York.

**Margaret Lockwood,** 1916–1990. Lockwood was a British beauty best remembered in America for playing the plucky, young heroine in Hitchcock's *The Lady Vanishes* in 1938. Most of her other movies were period pictures made in England. She passed away in the Cromwell Hospital in London.

**Mary Martin,** 1913–1990. Martin was a high-energy Broadway musical star whose motion pictures were less than memorable. However, she had a brilliant Broadway stage career, starring in such hits as *South Pacific, Peter Pan,* and *The Sound of Music.* She

Mary Martin with Carol Channing — Hello Dollies!

passed away at her Rancho Mirage home in California and was buried in New York. Martin's son, actor Larry Hagman, is famous for his TV roles as J. R. Ewing in *Dallas* and as Barbara Eden's "Master" in *I Dream of Jeannie.*

**Joan Bennett,** 1910–1990. Joan was the younger sister of Constance Bennett. She made her film debut as the damsel-in-distress in the wildly successful *Bulldog Drummond* opposite Ronald Colman. She made many films in the 1930s and 1940s, including playing the glamorous mother to Elizabeth Taylor in *Father of the Bride* in 1950. She died in Scarsdale, New York, and was cremated and buried in Old Lyme, Connecticut.

**Ben Johnson,** 1920–1996, died of a heart attack in Mesa, Arizona. Johnson was the real thing: a cowboy from Pawhuska, Oklahoma, who grew up punching cattle for his rodeo champion father. He joked that he got to Hollywood "in a carload of horses," escorting stock bought for Howard Hawks' 1943 film, *The Outlaw.* Rugged, crusty and a Western gentleman, he turned down the script for Peter Bogdanovich's *The Last Picture Show* because, he said, "It was the worst thing I ever read. Every other word . . . was a dirty word. So I turned it down."

Bogdanovich let Johnson rewrite the script, and Johnson won the English Academy Award, an Oscar, a Golden Globe, and The New York Film Critics award. He played the cowboy and town tycoon without having to say a single dirty word.

Johnson attracted director John Ford's attention in 1948, when he saved the lives of several actors involved in an accident while filming *Fort Apache.* Ford immediately starred him in *Three Godfathers* and *She Wore a Yellow Ribbon.* During his career, Johnson appeared in some 300 films, including six with John Wayne. He left the picture business briefly in 1951 to go rodeoing, and in 1953 he won the world championship in team roping. He returned to making movies with the comment, "At the end of the year I didn't have $3. All I had was a wore-out automobile and a mad wife." On receiving his star on the Hollywood Walk of Fame, he said, "I don't know why in the hell you waited so long to give me the star. You waited till I got so old I couldn't hardly enjoy it." His wife, Carole, died in 1995.

**Guy Madison** (Robert Ozelle Moseley), 1922–1995. Buried at Desert Memorial Park, Cathedral City, California. Guy Madison is best remembered for the long-running Western TV series in the late 1950s, *The Adventures of Wild Bill Hickock.* During his career, he made more than 85 movies. "We shared a lot of campfires together. It's another empty saddle, and I will really miss him," said his neighbor and pal, Rory Calhoun. He was divorced from actresses Gail Russell and Sheilah Connolly.

**Gilda Radner,** 1946–1989. Buried at Long Ridge Cemetery in Fairfield, Connecticut. Radner was best known as one of the original "Not Ready for Prime Time" players on *Saturday Night Live,* where she won an Emmy for the 1977–78 season.

In 1980 she starred on Broadway in her one-woman show, *Gilda Live.* She met and married actor Gene Wilder during the filming of *Hanky Panky* in 1982. They made two more movies together before her death from ovarian cancer. Her autobiography, *It's Always Something,* was published in 1989. She was greatly loved by her associates. Gene Wilder remains active in fund-raising efforts to support the fight against cancer.

**George Peppard,** 1928–1994. Buried at North View Cemetery in Dearborn, Michigan. Peppard was a good-looking, steely eyed leading man who starred in *Breakfast at Tiffany's* with Audrey Hepburn. He made several more movies in the 1960s but is best remembered for his TV roles, including *Banacek, Doctor's Hospital,* and *The A-Team.*

**Cameron Mitchell,** 1918–1994. Buried at Desert Memorial Park, Cathedral City, California. Mitchell was an all-purpose leading man who was as much at home on Broadway as in the movies. On stage he was Happy, one of Willy Loman's sons in *Death of a Salesman.* His motion picture career lasted from the 1940s through the 1970s and included *Monkey on My Back* and *Hombre.* On TV he starred in the series *High Chaparral* and *Swiss Family Robinson.*

**Martha Raye** (Margaret Theresa Reed), 1916–1994. Buried at Fort Bragg National Cemetery, Fort Bragg, North Carolina. Raye, with her rubber face and large mouth, was one of the few female clowns in the movies. She was also a gifted singer and made her film debut with Bing Crosby in *Rhythm on the Range* in 1936. Through the 1930s and 1940s, she played the man-crazy second banana in dozens of movies, including *Four Jills in a Jeep* in 1944, which was a fictionalized version of Raye's experiences entertaining the

Danny Thomas with Debbie Reynolds — His legacy is the St. Jude's Hospital for Children.

Martha Raye, the GI's favorite lady, with Rosemary Clooney.

troops in World War II. From 1954 to 1956 she had her own TV series, *The Martha Raye Show.* In 1962 she had the second lead with Jimmy Durante in *Billy Rose's Jumbo.* She was the first female to receive the Jean Hersholt Humanitarian Award. A stroke in her later life never dampened her enthusiasm.

**Hal Roach,** 1892–1992. Woodlawn Cemetery, Elmira, New York.

Roach was the leading producer of comedies from the 1920s through the early 1940s. Harold Lloyd was his first star, and in 1921 he brought out the *Our Gang* series. He followed that with comedy shorts featuring Will Rogers.

His biggest success of all was when he teamed Stan Laurel and Oliver Hardy together for a series of films in the late 1930s. He produced several features, including *Topper* and *Of Mice and Men.* After Roach's return from World War II, he initiated the revival of a market for featurettes, after which he retired. He was given an honorary Academy Award in 1984. He lived to see his 100th birthday.

Hal Roach— Hearty Hollywood pioneer.

**Danny Thomas** (Amos Jacobs), 1914–1991. Buried at St. Jude's Hospital, Memphis, Tennessee. Originally a nightclub comedian, Thomas is best known for his TV work, including his Emmy-

Joseph Cotten and wife, Patricia Medina — His autobiography was *Vanity Will Get You Somewhere.*

winning 1954 series, *Make Room for Daddy*. He was the real-life father of *That Girl* star Marlo Thomas. And his lasting legacy is the St. Jude's Hospital for Children, which he built and which his estate continues to support.

**Diane Varsi,** 1938–1992. Interred at Mt. Tamalpais Cemetery, San Rafael, California. Varsi, who married twice before she was 21, earned her Academy Award nomination for *Peyton Place* in 1957. She made only three more movies, including *Ten North Frederick,* before retiring in 1960. In the late 1960s and early 1970s she tried to resume her film career but was only able to find work in a series of low-budget pictures.

**Joseph Cotten,** 1905–1994. At Blanford Cemetery in Petersburg, Virginia. Cotten, with his distinctive voice, was one of Hollywood's finest and most versatile actors. He made his film debut with Orson Welles in *Citizen Kane* and subsequently made dozens of films. Some of his finest performances were in other films with Welles, including *The Third Man* and *Touch of Evil.* Cotten was married to the beautiful English actress Patricia Medina. His autobiography, *Vanity Will Get You Somewhere,* was published in 1987. Patricia is presently writing her own autobiography.

**Pat Buttram,** died in 1994. Buried at Nicholas Funeral Home, Highway 5, Statelyville, Alabama. Buttram was best known as Gene Autry's gravel-voiced sidekick in 1930s oaters such as *Round-Up Time in Texas*. He was also well known in Hollywood as a very funny man and was often called on for "roasts" and other social functions.

## Out-of-Town Rockers

**Jim Morrison,** 1943–1971, of the Doors, died of heart failure in his Paris apartment and is now interred in the famous Père-Lachaise Cemetery in Paris, near Oscar Wilde and Gertrude Stein. Despite the presence of a TV camera and guards with dogs, Morrison's grave is visited by over a million fans yearly, many of whom are teenagers who come to drink, do drugs, and deface his and other markers with lipstick and spray paint. Morrison's cemetery lease expires in 2001—none too soon, say the cemetery officials. At that time, his family will probably take him to Venice, California.

**Jimi Hendrix,** 1942–1970. Hendrix died of suffocation due to acute barbiturate intoxication and is buried in Greenwood Memorial Park in Renton, Washington. Always flamboyant, Hendrix was a psychedelic product of the sixties who loved two things: women and making music on his "axe." Jimi's music wasn't black and it wasn't white—it was Jimi. Known as a musician's musician, he was admired by his contemporaries, such as Mick Jagger and John Lennon. They admired his unique sound, which may have come in part from the fact he was a mixture of black, white, Cherokee and Mexican heritage. Hendrix was as popular in England as he was at home, and his early death took away a fine musician.

**Buddy Holly,** 1936–1959. Holly was only 22 when he was killed in an Iowa plane crash with Ritchie Valens and the "Big Bopper," J.P. Richardson. Holly's death was an enormous loss to the music world. Not only was he a brilliant musician, mixing lead/rhythm, bass and drums in his group, The Crickets, but also he had written several songs destined to become classics. Many of us remember "Peggy Sue," "That 'll Be the Day," "Early in the Morning," and "It's So Easy." Buddy is buried in his hometown of Lubbock, Texas, under his real name, Buddy Holley.

**Jerry Garcia**, 1942–1995, and his band, The Grateful Dead, were another product of the psychedelic sixties. They were famous for their nonstop touring, doing over 3,000 concerts during the life of the band. They were even better known for the loyalty of their fans, known as Deadheads, who often followed them from concert to concert all over the country. Patrick Carr of *The Village Voice* wrote, "Where are your children, parents? They're out on an evening with the Grateful Dead, blitzed out on acid and changing overnight." Some of Garcia's ashes were placed in the Ganges River in India. The rest were scattered over the Pacific Ocean.

**Bill Haley**, 1926-1981, was the "Rock Around the Clock" singer, with his band, The Comets. His ashes are at home with his family in Harlingen, Texas.

**Marvin Gaye**, 1940-1984, the soul singer, was killed by his father. His ashes were sprinkled in the Pacific Ocean.

**Kurt Cobain**, 1967-1994, had his ashes taken to a Buddhist monastery in rural New York by his wife, Courtney Love.

**Janis Joplin,** 1943-1970, another psychedelic singer from the sixties, was born in Port Arthur, Texas. She was immensely popular for her mix of bluegrass, blues, soul and rock. She sang with several bands, including Big Brother and the Holding Company. After she died of a heroin overdose, her friend, actor/songwriter/singer Kris Kristofferson, was moved to write, "Just say she was someone, so far from home, whose life was so lonesome, she died all alone."

Barbara Stanwyck with Robert Taylor. She was a one-man woman — his.

# 6

## Where Are They Now?

"Buried at residence or at sea" is a term used by the Los Angeles County coroner when the deceased's remains are sent to their residence. This is probably done to insure the privacy of the deceased's final resting place. All of those listed below were cremated.

**John Payne,** 1912–1989. Residence located at 6363 Delaplane Road, Malibu. Payne was a versatile leading man who starred in musicals, comedies, dramas and action-adventures. His best-remembered pictures include *Sun Valley Serenade* with Sonja Henie in 1941 and *Miracle on 34th Street* in 1947. He was married to Anne Shirley and Gloria DeHaven and to Alexandra Lucas when he died. His ashes were shipped to his home state of Virginia for interment.

**Barbara Stanwyck,** 1907–1990. Residence located at 1055 Loma Vista Drive, Beverly Hills. Stanwyck played tough, hard-edged but likable leading ladies in motion pictures and TV. Orphaned at an early age, she struggled through a difficult marriage before divorcing vaudeville star Frank Fay, who was bitter at her success in motion pictures. She received her first Oscar nomination in 1937 for *Stella Dallas* and then starred in DeMille's *Union Pacific* in 1939. Her best-remembered pictures were *Double Indemnity* in 1944 and *Sorry, Wrong Number* in 1948. Over her film career, she starred in dozens of pictures. She won an Emmy for her TV role as the frontier matriarch in *The Big Valley*. She married handsome leading man, Robert Taylor, whom friends say she continued to love after their divorce until her death.

**Martin Ritt,** 1920–1990. Residence located at 13515 Bombay Drive, Pacific Palisades. Ritt was a director working on TV when he was blacklisted in 1951. He is best remembered for directing Paul Newman in *Hud* in 1963, for which he received an Oscar nomination.

**Vincent Price,** 1911–1993. Buried three miles out to sea off the coast at Santa Monica. Price was an articulate, well educated, extremely sophisticated actor and a gourmet cook with a soft, pleasing voice. He acted with a bit of tongue in cheek as the "King of the Horror Movies."

A Yale graduate with a master's degree from the University of London, Price played in period pictures in the 1930s and 1940s. He was a slick, sophisticated murderer in *Laura* and a delicious Richelieu in *The Three Musketeers*. In the 1960s he joined Roger Corman as the premier interpreter of Poe in such films as *The Mask of Red Death*. As the years passed, premium parts came less often, but Price, always in good humor, spent his time enjoying life. Over the years he built up an important collection of paintings and wrote several books on art and cooking. He was always a professional and encouraged Tim Burton to make the animated short *Vincent* about a youth who was infatuated with Vincent Price. His last role was in Burton's *Edward Scissorhands.*

Anthony Perkins — "People don't amount to a hill of beans in this crazy world."

**Anthony Perkins**, 1932–1992. His ashes were divided in half. One half went to his residence at 2840 Seattle Drive, Los Angeles; the other half went to an unknown location. Perkins, of course, is best remembered for his portrayal of Norman Bates in 1960's *Psycho.* He was also active on stage and co-wrote *The Last of Sheila* with his friend Stephen Sondheim. While he was dying of AIDS in 1992, he left behind several quotes from *Casablanca*, including Bogart's

Vincent Price — Versatile actor, artist, author, *bon vivant*.

observation that the problems of a few people "don't amount to a hill of beans in this crazy world."

**Alex North,** 1910-1991. He was buried at sea, three miles off San Pedro, by the Neptune Society. North is the only music composer to ever receive a special Academy Award for

lifetime achievement. His scores include *Under the Volcano* in 1984 and *A Streetcar Named Desire* in 1951.

**Tony Richardson,** 1928-1991. Residence located at 1478 North Kings Road, Los Angeles. This stylish British director made such films as *A Taste of Honey* in 1961 and *Tom Jones* in 1963.

**Lee Remick**, 1935-1991. Residence located at 570 North Bundy Drive, Los Angeles. Remick was an extremely talented, breathtakingly beautiful actress who made her film debut at 21 in Elia Kazan's *A Face in the Crowd.* Her best pictures included *Anatomy of a Murder* and *Days of Wine and Roses,* for which she earned an Oscar nomination in 1962. In addition to her film work, Remick was very active in TV. She starred in the miniseries *Ike* in 1979.

Lee Remick — Breathtakingly beautiful and getting her star on Hollywood Blvd.

**Alexis Smith,** 1921-1993. Buried at sea, three miles off San Pedro by the Neptune Society.

Smith was a gorgeous redhead who appeared in dozens of movies, on stage, and on TV from the 1940s until her death. Her most memorable movies include Capra's *Here Comes the Groom* in 1951 and *The Young Philadelphians* in 1959. In 1971, Smith took to the stage, singing and dancing in Stephen Sondheim's Broadway musical *Follies*, for which she received a Tony. During the 1980s, she appeared on several nighttime soaps including *Dallas*. One of her last performances was as the love interest of Robert Young's Dr. Marcus Welby in a TV special filmed in Europe. She was married to actor Craig Stevens.

**Dinah Shore,** 1917–1994. She was cremated, with 25% of the ashes going to Hillside Memorial Park; 25% going to Shirley Shore at 916 North Oxford Way, Beverly Hills; and 50% to a friend, Murry Niedorf, 17846 Cathedral Place, Encino. This Southern songbird from Tennessee was a five-time Emmy winner for her Sunday night *Dinah Shore Show* in the 1950s. In 1970, she returned to NBC with *Dinah's Place*, a talk show. She then moved to CBS with *Dinah,* another talk-variety show, and was at it again on TNN in 1989 with *A Conversation with Dinah*. Always a singer, she took her name, Dinah, from the song of the same name, "Dinah, Sweet As Apple Cidah."

She was married to actor/artist/sculptor George Montgomery for 18 years and briefly to Maurice Smith. A ten-time Emmy winner, she was an avid golfer, with a Palm Springs tournament named in her honor, and the author of two cookbooks, including *Someone's in the Kitchen with Dinah.*

Dinah Shore with George Montgomery and Betty White. Something was always cooking with Dinah!

**Tom Ewell,** 1909–1994. Residence located at 105 Aspen Way, Rolling Hills Estates. Ewell will always be remembered as the fellow standing with a grin on his face, watching Marilyn Monroe's skirt billowing up in that classic scene from *The Seven Year Itch*. His other big hit was as the wandering rake in *Adam's Rib* in 1949. On television, he played the boozing buddy on *Baretta* in the 1970s.

**Lana Turner,** 1921–1995. Residence located at 2170 Century Park East #2006, Century City, Los Angeles. Turner, who was *not* discovered at Schwab's drugstore, was best known as the "sweater girl" to our GIs in World War II. While she appeared in dozens of movies, her best role was in *The Postman Always Rings Twice*. In 1957 she received an Oscar nomination for the steamy *Peyton Place*. Her TV appearances included *The Survivors in* 1969–70 and *Falcon Crest* in 1982–83. Her stormy off-screen life included marriages to Artie Shaw, millionaire Bob Topping, and TV Tarzan Lex Barker. In 1958, her longtime boyfriend, mobster Johnny Stompanato, was stabbed to death by Turner's daughter, Cheryl Crane, who feared for her mother's safety during a screaming argument with Johnny. Many people still question just who did murder Stompanato. Lana was cremated and her ashes are with her family.

**Ida Lupino,** 1914–1995. Located at the residence of Mary Ann Anderson, 535 South Orchard Avenue, Burbank. Lupino was a petite beauty from England who began her film career in America playing ingenues in the 1930s. In the 1940s she made over a dozen films, including *Road House*, in which she also sang the ballad "Again." She began directing in 1949 and made several modestly budgeted films, the best of which was *The Hitch-Hiker.* In the 1950s she made films only sporadically, as she was busy in TV with her then-husband Howard Duff on *Four Star Playhouse,* where she worked on both sides of the camera. They also made *Mr. Adams and Eve* in 1957–58. Working as a director, she filmed such series as *Have Gun Will Travel, The Donna Reed Show* and others. She returned to acting in motion pictures in the 1970s for a few token appearances before she retired. Her husband from 1938 to 1945 was Louis Hayward.

Henry Mancini with his wife, Ginny. "Moon River" and "The Theme from the Pink Panther" were among his hits.

**Henry Mancini,** 1924-1994. Located at the residence, 261 Borado Drive, Los Angeles. Mancini was an astoundingly prolific composer who scored dozens and dozens of films and TV shows. He received his first Academy Award nomination for *The Glenn Miller Story* in 1954. His jazz themes for the TV series *Peter Gunn* and *Mr. Lucky* both were hits on the record charts. He received other Oscar nominations for "Charade" and "Dear Heart," while "Days of Wine and Roses" and "Moon River" from *Breakfast at Tiffany's* won Oscars. Of course his most memorable work was his theme from *The Pink Panther.* His autobiography, *Did They Mention the Music?* was published in 1989.

**David Wayne,** 1914-1995. Located at the residence of the executor, 600 South Lake #301, Pasadena. Puckish Wayne began his career on the stage in 1936, and in 1947 he won a Tony for *Finian's Rainbow.* He played Ensign Pulver in *Mr. Roberts* and won his second Tony for the role of Sakini in *Teahouse of the August Moon* in 1954. Through the late 1940s and 1950s, Wayne was active in motion pictures, playing both comedy and drama roles in movies such as *How to Marry a Millionaire* with Marilyn Monroe and *The Last Angry Man.* In the 1970s he made a few movies, including Billy Wilder's remake of *The Front Page.* His TV career also began in the 1970s. He appeared in episodes of several series and starred as inspector Richard Queen in *The Adventures of Ellery Queen.*

**Claude Akins** died in 1994. Residence located at 1927 North Midlothian, Altadena, California. Akins was a big, "good ol' boy"

Elizabeth Montgomery — Bewitching.

Southern actor who played supporting roles, mostly in Western films such as *Rio Bravo* with John Wayne. He also enjoyed a run on TV as a trucker in the series *Movin' On* and as a sheriff in *The Misadventures of Sheriff Lobo.*

**Elizabeth Montgomery,** died 1995. Residence located at 1230 Benedict Canyon, Beverly Hills. She was the daughter of actor Robert Montgomery and appeared on TV in several of his productions. She is best known for playing Samantha in the TV sitcom *Bewitched* with Dick York and Agnes Moorehead.

# 7

## Pet Cemeteries

**Los Angeles Pet Memorial Park** is located at 5068 North Old Scandia Lane in Calabasas. Nestled in the foothills northwest of Los Angeles, this 10-acre pet cemetery was started in 1928 in the corner of a cattle grazing range. It had the dubious literary honor of becoming the fictional "Happier Hunting Ground" in English author Evelyn Waugh's 1948 satirical novel, *The Loved One*. Los Angeles Pet Memorial Park is now the final resting place for about 40,000 animal friends. Hopalong Cassidy's horse Topper is here, along with Humphrey Bogart's dog Droopy, Charlie Chaplin's cat Boots, and Rudolph Valentino's dog Kabar. Tonto's "Gettum-up, Scout" horse from *The Lone Ranger* TV series is here, as is the beloved speckled pooch Petey from the *Our Gang* movies.

◆

**Pet Haven** Cemetery is located at 18300 South Figueroa Street, Gardena, in the unincorporated Harbor Gateway strip. Pet Haven is the final resting place of over 30,000 animals. It was created in 1948 by a pet owner who was upset that the Los Angeles Pet Memorial Park in Calabasas had insufficient water for him to grow grass on his dog's grave. Gangster Mickey Cohen's dog Mickey Jr. is here, along with Lady, Little Joe's horse from the *Bonanza* TV series. The tombstones carry such epitaphs as "Nasty—Our Faithful Friend," and "Sandy—1972–1988—I Know You Gave Me the Best 16 Years of Your Life."

◆

If you're ever passing through Victorville, be sure to stop off at the Western fort-like Roy Rogers Museum. Here you'll find all the memorabilia, from saddles to boots, that cowboy singer/actor **Roy Rogers** has collected throughout his singing and movie career as "King of the Cowboys." You'll find a lot of his wife and leading

Roy Rogers and his pal, Trigger.

lady's belongings here also. **Dale Evans**, "Queen of the West," was right there with Roy, singing along and acting with him on the silver screen. A special treat here at Roy's museum are the stuffed figures of his beloved horse, Trigger; their German Shepherd, Bullet; and Dale's pinto, Buttermilk. Dale has been known to say, "I sure hope I don't go first. Roy will have me stuffed."

# 8

◆

## Welcome to the Afterworld, Online

Electronic graveyards, cannibalism instructions and casket shopping are now on the Internet. So are online obits, dead pet memorials and where to get help turning people and pets into mummies. Says Joel Gazls-Sax, who reviews online cemetery sites for the World Wide Web Post-Mortem page using a four-tombstone rating system, "I don't think it's because Americans are suddenly more morbid. I think it's just a natural interest that has spread to the Internet."

Online, there are tips for burial at sea (such as avoiding waters used by commercial net-dragging trawlers); an E-mail celebrity dead pool; and the Carlos A. Howard Funeral Home, "the first full-service mortuary on the Internet," which advertises the $1,192 Onyx Regal Velvet coffin with pin striping, adjustable bedsprings and mattress. However, the most popular attractions are the cyber cemeteries, where the dead are interred electronically. At the Virtual Pet Cemetery, Buster Brown is memorialized as a little brown mutt who "slept on my bed at night and puked on my pillow." Meanwhile, on the Dead Pet Home Page, a dog named Nero is in animal heaven "chasing cars made of smoked ham and mailmen made of salami."

At the Virtual Memorial Gardens, which contains epitaphs for about 1,000 humans and pets, hundreds of net users explore every day, according to Lindsey Marshall, a British university professor who maintains this free service. And at The Cemetery Gate, mortician Bruce Armstrong puts obituaries online for $25 and offers a free list of resources on grief, including E-mail support groups. "In today's mobile society, where people don't always live near their loved one's actual grave site, it's important to still have a focal point to think about the person who died," Armstrong says.

The World Wide Web also offers tours to world-famous burial grounds. At the World Wide Cemetery, you can call up photos of Paris' Cemetiere de Père-Lachaise, where Jim Morrison of the Doors is buried, while other cyber sites take viewers to the Vietnam Memorial in Washington, New Orleans cemeteries, a tribute to Wolfman Jack, and the Tomb of the Manicurists Egypt.

For the extremely adventurous, there is also the Dark Side of the Web, a clearinghouse of the ghastly. You'll find a mortuary where you can view autopsy photos of Mussolini and his mistress and the Cannibalism Page, with graphic and disturbing instructions for "the preparation of humans for consumption."

For your viewing pleasure, here are some of the biggest hits of the cyber afterworld:

**Paul is Dead?** A rehashing of the "evidence" that fueled rumors of Paul McCartney's untimely death in the 1960s.

**Summum Mummification.** Corky Ra's site where he describes his bizarre encounters with alien beings and promotes a service that mummifies dead pets and humans.

**The Natural Dead Center.** A do-it-yourself funeral guide with primers on biodegradable body bags, burials at sea and backyard interments, which carry the caution that such burials at home can decrease the value of property as much as 50%.

Paul is dead?

# 9

◆

## Opening Pandora's Coffin
## Southern California's "Cemeterygate"

What happens when there are more bodies than places to put them? Up until now, the answer to that question was easy at some Southern California cemeteries. At **Paradise Memorial Park** in Santa Fe Springs, groundskeeper Victor Fortner, 48, faces 69 felony counts of illegally digging up remains, grand theft, fraud and embezzlement. According to investigators, Fortner instructed cemetery workers to dig up caskets at the sold-out cemetery and replace them with those of the newly deceased. In some graves, the investigators found six or seven bodies buried after the operators of the park allegedly sold the plot over and over.

They also found where the remains went. A 7-foot-high, 50-foot-long pile of bones was found unceremoniously dumped behind a shed, while the deceased's headstones were found stacked inside another shed. Fortner has acknowledged that he dug up coffins, but he said he didn't realize it was illegal, according to Sheriff's Sergeant Scott Clark. "Nothing like this has ever happened in California," said Ray Giunta, former executive director of the State Cemetery Board, "They had trust fund problems, but never the disinterment of bodies!"

"I've taken five or six families to the same grave at the Paradise Memorial Park," said Mike Mintz, a private cemetery consultant who has taken over the grounds on behalf of the state. "Five, six, seven people were buried in the same grave on the same day."

A few days earlier, Betty Campa had stood at the Paradise grave of her grandfather, who was buried in the cemetery in 1933. "Here I think I'm talking to my grandfather and I'm talking to someone else," said Campa, 66. She clutched a paper showing her grandfather had been disinterred in 1992, his bones tossed on the pile, and six others buried in his grave, including Beatrice, Alberta, Mary, and Hubert.

In June of 1995, the now-defunct State Cemetery Board began investigating complaints that 67-year-old Paradise was so run down as to be a health hazard. As word spread of problems in Paradise, investigations were also underway at Lincoln Memorial Park in Carson and Angeles Abbey Memorial Park in Compton, according to the State Department of Consumer Affairs, which now regulates state cemeteries.

"Trouble in Paradise" began when a grand jury handed down criminal indictments on January 1, 1996. Victor Fortner was charged with 69 felony counts. At the time of his arrest, he was held on bail of $568,000. His sister, Felicia Fraction, and his mother, Alma Fraction, were both held on individual bail of $108,000. They were charged with three counts of embezzling maintenance funds from the cemetery.

◆

Meanwhile, over at a dysfunctional cemetery called **Lincoln Memorial Park** in Carson, which also dates back to the 1920s, some relatives have spent as much as three weeks trying to find the remains of loved ones. Their headstones were found in garbage bins and were being used as roadside curbs. Investigators found coffins buried only three inches below ground. Another bizarre discovery showed burial plots scattered helter-skelter all over the grounds instead of being in traditional rows. Even the headstones were not facing in the same direction as they do at traditional cemeteries. At Lincoln, some of the headstones were placed between rows, facing at 90-degree angles, while others were simply jammed against roads or placed in odd corners of the 20-acre lot.

State officials have speculated that Lincoln's burial plots were probably sold out only recently. The owners may have resorted to reselling plots to pay for upkeep after they embezzled much of the maintenance trust fund, alleged Ray Giunta, former executive director of the cemetery board. Lincoln is owned by the Hollywood Cemetery Association, which also owns Hollywood Memorial Cemetery.

"Alas, poor Yorick," said Shakespeare's Hamlet as he held aloft the skull of his old friend whose bones were dug up to make way for the recently deceased Ophelia. And in his own epitaph,

Shakespeare must have had a premonition of some possible fate, because he wrote:

> Good friend, for Jesus' sake forbear;
> To dig the dust enclosed here.
> Blest be the man that spares these stones,
> And cursed be he that moves my Bones.

◆

## Who's Going to Mow the Lawn?

Over at **Sunnyside Cemetery** in Long Beach, the cemetery's owner, 43-year-old Dean A. Dempsey, has been charged with three felony violations of the State Health and Safety Code. Maria Chacon Kniestedt of the State Department of Consumer Affairs began investigating Dempsey in 1994, after complaints that the grounds at Sunnyside were an unkempt mess. The board then moved quickly to seize the park's bank accounts. Bail for Dempsey was set at $680,000, and he is charged with embezzling $500,000 from Sunnyside's endowment fund.

Officials from Consumer Affairs allege that Dempsey began raiding the fund in 1988, just a year after he purchased Sunnyside for $100. He allegedly used the money paid by those buying graves to settle personal debts, Kniestedt said. These debts included bar tabs and payments on a leased Mercedes. However, in a 1994 interview, Dempsey denied any wrongdoing, saying the park's endowment fund was not generating enough interest to pay for upkeep. He used the money, he said, only to pay for maintenance of the grounds.

◆

## And Now a Word from the Ex-Cemetery Chief

*Et tu*, Ray Giunta? A state auditor's report revealed that Raymond Giunta, the former chief of the State Cemetery Board and a past crusader against mismanagement of California cemeteries, illegally accepted more than $10,000 of a cemetery's endowment fund and used some of the money for personal expenses.

According to state auditor Kurt R. Sjoberg, the investigation began in April of 1995, after an anonymous tipster called the state's "whistle-blower" hotline. Investigators found that the funds in question once belonged to the Arlington Cemetery in Sacramento County, whose bank accounts had for years been under state control. Arlington was purchased in November of 1994 by a private party. On December 29, 1994, Giunta (who, as executive director of the Cemetery Board, had control of trust funds from all cemeteries taken over by the state) mailed the new owner a cashier's check for $10,237.66, the amount in Arlington's endowment account at the time of the sale.

After the new owner received the check, he endorsed it back to Giunta. Giunta agrees that the owner endorsed the check over to him. He claims he was being hired to help fix up and modernize the cemetery. He says investigators knew that the money was not in restricted accounts and that the owner also set up a separate endowment fund, which now has a balance of $25,000.

And to cap it all, after the state seized Paradise Memorial Park, a yet-to-be-named employee of the Cemetery Board illegally wrote checks on the cemetery's endowment account to himself, totaling $3,840.

Who is going to mow all these lawns?

# 10

## The Monster Mortician

David Sconce is a genuine monster whose life is a horror story, the kind that makes big, best-selling books. Moreover, unlike best-selling stories, which concern other people and usually take place at a distance, his crimes touch on circumstances that will affect each of us at the end of our lives or at the death of our loved ones. When a body is turned over to the mysterious ministrations of a mortician, what happens? This is the tragic story of what befell David Sconce's "clients."

For weeks the clear desert air over the sleepy little community of Hesperia was fouled with the sickening, acrid smoke pouring from the Oscar's Ceramics Plant on Darwin Road. Neighbors complained daily to the authorities about the stench. One complainer, who had been in a Nazi concentration camp, insisted it was the smell of burning flesh. Then on January 20, 1987, police and fire authorities raided the plant. They found evidence that would eventually reveal that David Sconce was truly a "monster mortician." Oscar's Ceramics was not making panels for space stations as the owner claimed. Instead, its two large kilns were filled with burning human bodies soaked in diesel oil. The burning created the stench that attracted the authorities.

"They were just stacked in there like cord wood," the Hesperia Fire Marshal said. "All of a sudden, this foot fell out, still burning. Then another foot fell out."

Now the people of Hesperia knew what the unmarked white trucks, coming and going around the clock, had been delivering— human fuel for an illegal crematorium. And no imagined scene from hell could equal what was created from the burning of the bodies in the kilns at Hesperia:

Human bones and ashes partially filling 55-gallon garbage cans.

The thick, dark liquid of human body fat mixing with diesel oil on the floor and running out the back door to an overflowing pit, then pouring like a stream into the desert brush 70 yards away.

A leaking coffin filled with eyes and vital organs floating in a preservative, waiting to be processed for sale.

Gold teeth that had been removed with pliers, ready to be melted down.

This discovery was the beginning of an investigation that would last for months. Soon it was revealed that some members of the respected, fourth-generation, church-going, wealthy Lamb family of Pasadena were in reality ghouls—stealing and selling gold teeth, money, eyes, and body organs from the deceased left in their care. In all, 67 counts were filed initially, including co-mingling of ashes, mass cremation of bodies, forging organ-donor consent forms and more. Those charged were Laurianne Lamb Sconce, her husband, Jerry "Coach" Sconce, and their son, David.

David Sconce was by far the most appalling. A true monster, he walked casually among us. He committed crimes so sickeningly hideous, in such a matter-of-fact way, that he truly deserves his place in history with the other ghouls who commit crimes so heinous they're almost impossible to believe.

We can scarcely imagine what goes on in the mind of a man who:

— Has the license plate "I BRN 4 U" on his truck.
— Calls pulling gold teeth from cadavers "popping chops."
— Planned the murder of his grandparents by poisoning their Sparkletts water bottle.
— Solicited the murder of the district attorney.
— Plotted to stuff plastic explosives in a body going to a competitor's crematorium so it would blow up.
— Had funeral home executives beaten and half blinded with chemicals, one so badly he died of a heart attack.
— Is charged with the murder of a funeral home competitor, Tom Waters, who died a horrible, ghastly death, possibly from being poisoned by Sconce.
— Sold eyes and body organs stolen from the dead.
— Planned to murder his jail house bodyguard.
— Threw teeth, braces, bones and artificial joints underneath a house he rented.

- Stole a Corvette from a new car lot, photocopied his own Corvette's registration, and gave the car to an employee as a gift.
- Burglarized a girlfriend's home twice because she stopped dating him.
- Used a two-by-four to pound more bodies into his ovens.
- Could pick up a body and toss it like a spear into the ovens.

Sconce stated his philosophy toward the dead by saying "It's just an abandoned house." His outlook was one of ghoulish humor.

- Dead fat guys are to laugh at.
- Gave his mother a button that read "Dead people are cool." She pinned it on a doll on her desk.
- Old, decrepit people are $55, the cheapest burn.
- When smelling a truckload of bodies that had been decomposing for three days in the desert, he said, "Smells like money to me."
- Sewed breasts on a male cadaver.
- Had a ritual of cutting a "T" on bodies and sticking tubes in.
- Said he felt like God when he went into a body to pull the organs out.
- Was heard to say, "I love it. I love squishing through intestines." To him, this was an aphrodisiac.

In 1989, as a result of a plea bargain before Superior Court Judge Terry Smerling, Sconce pleaded guilty to 21 counts involving the theft of body parts and performance of mass cremations. In return, the court agreed to drop the other charges, which included conspiracy to commit murder. Sconce was sentenced to five years in prison. Then in 1991, while Sconce was serving his time, another Superior Court judge, Paul Boland, ruled that Judge Smerling did not have jurisdiction to dismiss the conspiracy charge against Sconce.

Sconce was released from prison in 1994 after serving five years. He immediately dropped from sight. At the same time, however, rumors began to circulate that he was planning to finance his activities by forging fake casino chips in his parents' home in

Bullhead City, Arizona. He planned to use the bogus chips across the river at the casinos in Laughlin, Nevada.

In October of 1995, while serving another five-year term for manufacturing counterfeit bus passes, Sconce was extradited to California from Arizona to stand trial on a charge that he conspired to murder Elie Estephan to collect on his $250,000 life insurance policy. Sconce has since been denied a request that he would plead guilty to the conspiracy charge in exchange for probation. His trial is scheduled in 1996.

Sconce's mother, Laurianne Lamb Sconce, was convicted in April 1985 of seven counts of unlawful removal of body parts, forgery and misappropriation of a trust account. Her husband, Jerry "Coach" Sconce, was found guilty of a trust fund management violation. In further actions, attorneys representing the victims' next of kin sued the mortuary employees, including the Sconces, who agreed to a settlement of $15.7 million.

# 11

◆

## Gaucheries

The following is an excerpt from Matt Weinstock's column in the now-defunct *Los Angeles Daily News,* 1946.

> When the last McKinley is uttered
> When the last, last tears have been shed,
> And the last, last candle has guttered
> O'er the defenseless dead;
> O waft me on wings of faires,
> Uprising to greet the dawn
> To the singing of caged canaries,
> As featured at Forest Lawn
> Where a family grave is rented
> 'Neath a sky with never a rift,
> And the corpse of the late lamented
> Is wrapped as a Birthday Gift.
> —Arthur Wimperis

Weinstock went on to remark: "If, as hinted in All-Year-Club folders, life in Los Angeles can be beautiful, death is an exquisite, almost unbearable delight. As nowhere else in the world, newspaper, radio, billboard, and streetcar ads exhort on the package deal. 'Why live' they seem to state, 'when we can bury you for practically nothing?'

"Forest Lawn employs more than five hundred persons, who gather monthly at meetings which have been described as 'pious, punctual, perfect.' Attendance is compulsory. Employees are offered cash prizes for suggestions that might better the services. The 'find' in this category was a man who, in 1944, came up with the payoff idea that grave sizes be reduced from 33 1/3 square feet to 30 square feet. This suggestion was immediately put into practice."

◆

**San Quentin's Boot Hill** is the third location for this prison's cemetery, which was in use from the early 1920s to 1952. The occupants, who died while in prison, were buried with plain wooden markers that bore only their assigned prison number, but no name. Boot Hill's two most famous occupants were "Bluebeard" Watson and William Kogut. Watson was sent to San Quentin's death row after having hustled a number of his 20 or more wives off to unscheduled meetings with their Maker. Watson, who operated his own version of a newspaper personals column, "Seeking a Wife," urged his respondents to keep their communications confidential.

William Kogut, who was sent to death row for murdering a man in a gambling hall brawl, decided to cheat his executioner in a bizarre way. He fashioned an explosive gun-like device by stuffing explosives and a pack of playing cards into a container. Kogut then pointed the device at his head, heated it up, and fired. The device worked and the cards shot out at high speed, killing him.

"They found the ace of diamonds embedded in his brain," according to Associate Warden Dick Nelson.

No mention was made of what happened to the other cards that make up the "Dead Man's Hand," aces and eights. It was this hand that Wild Bill Hickock was holding on the afternoon of August 2, 1876, when Jack McCall, a cross-eyed, whiskey-headed coward, shot Wild Bill in the back.

◆

## "Oh Bury Me Not . . ." Strange Requests and Stranger Answers

Greg and Richard Zook, who own a mortuary in Monrovia, say it's a profession that inspires many wisecracks. "I bet a lot of people are dying to come see you" is a common one. Some of the unusual requests made of the Zooks in their 25 years in business include one from a family who asked to have the ashes of their loved one mixed with those of their pet.

Another family told the Zook brothers their deceased relative did not like lying on his back. "After the viewing of the body was completed, we arranged his body so he was lying on his side prior to burial," Richard Zook said.

People request that many strange or symbolic items be placed inside their caskets, including baseball gloves, golf clubs and a bottle of Jack Daniels. One time, a son looked at his father in the casket and said, "Something is missing." It was the ever-present toothpick between his father's teeth. The Zooks were happy to oblige. But they refused one family's request to bury their loved one in the nude.

"It wouldn't have been a problem," Greg Zook said, "except they also wanted an open-casket viewing."

The Los Angeles County Peace Officers' Memorial

# 12

◆

## Taps

**The Unknown Soldier** came about when World War I ended and the Allies—Belgium, France, Great Britain, Italy and the United States—found that many of the soldiers killed in battle could not be identified by name. In order to honor the memory of these fallen soldiers in some special way, each of the Allies chose a symbolic unknown soldier and buried him near their national capital in a monument honoring all the unknowns.

Belgium placed its unknown soldier in a tomb at the Colonnade of the Congress in Brussels. France buried its beneath the Arc de Triomphe in the center of Paris. Great Britain buried its unknown soldier in Westminster Abbey. Italy's lies in front of the monument to Victor Emmanuel in Rome.

The United States' unknown soldier was one of four unidentified war dead taken from cemeteries in France and brought home to America. American Sergeant Edward Younger chose one of these soldiers, and he was brought to Washington, D.C., to lie in state. On Armistice Day, November 11, 1921, the unknown soldier was buried in Arlington National Cemetery. The tomb bears the inscription "Here rests in honored glory an American soldier known but to God." Congress later directed that an unknown soldier from each of the three subsequent wars, World War II, and the Korean and Vietnam, be buried near the Tomb of the Unknown Soldier.

They rest there now, near the head of the tomb. An honor guard from the Honor Guard Company of the First Battle Group, Third Infantry, stands guard at the tomb at all times.

◆

The moving **Vietnam Memorial**, which was displayed at Green Hills Memorial Park south of Los Angeles during the 1996 Memorial Day weekend, is one of the three half-size replicas of the original monument in Washington, D.C., currently touring the country.

The replica was built with funds raised by the cemetery, local veterans groups and community efforts. As with the original, the names on the memorial are recessed so that visitors can rub a pencil on paper to make an imprint of a name.

Keith Martin, an infantryman wounded in Vietnam by a mine explosion that killed three other soldiers, came to stare at the row of names. "I never found out who the men were who died that day," Martin says. "All the names blend together. It's like I know them all."

On a recent Sunday, visitors to the memorial left cards, flowers, flags, photos and other offerings. The hushed silence was broken only by wind on the flags and the sound of children playing in the distance. A service and military flyover was to take place the following Friday.

Simba Wiley Roberts, who was wounded and narrowly escaped death as a member of a tank crew in Vietnam in 1969, sees the wall as a "Circle of Life."

"What completes the circle is me and you and anybody else who keeps their memories alive," he said.

◆

The **Los Angeles County Peace Officers' Memorial** is located at the Sheriff's Training and Regional Services Center in Whittier, California. On a recent Tuesday in May, law enforcement officers gathered to honor their fallen comrades at the 27th Annual Los Angeles County Peace Officers' Memorial service. This event drew more than 1,000 people, friends and families of fallen officers who were joined by police, sheriff's deputies, federal law enforcement officers and others, including Los Angeles District Attorney Gil Garcetti and Los Angeles Police Chief Willie Williams. "In law enforcement, they are all family," County Sheriff Sherman Block said. "They will forever remain a part of us." Standing in the bright sunlight, many people lifted sunglasses to dab at tears as a lone bag-pipe played "Amazing Grace" and the flags were lowered to half-staff.

"Yours is a call few of us would be capable of," said Jess Marlow, guest speaker and KNBC-TV anchorman. "Even when off duty, you are not beyond the call of duty. And certainly two of those you honor today affirm that."

The names of four officers killed in 1995 were added to the black marble wall that day, bringing the total fallen officers listed to 405. Nationwide in 1995, 161 officers died in the line of duty, and their names have been added to the 14,067 inscribed on the National Law Enforcement Officers Memorial in Washington.

Sheriff Block ended the ceremonies with the laying of a wreath of bright yellow mums at the memorial. "Each year our fervent prayer is that at the next memorial we will have no new names. But, unfortunately, that's not possible," he told the hushed crowd.

# Part II

◆

## Who's Who and Where?

IN MEMORY OF
## THE GRAND ARMY OF THE REPUBLIC
1861 — 1865

PRESENTED BY
GEN. W. S. ROSECRANS
CAMP & AUXILLIARY NO.2
SONS OF THE UNION VETERANS
OF THE CIVIL WAR
DEDICATED MAY 30,1957

Angeles Rosedale Civil War graves and memorial cannon—"With Malice Toward None."

# 13

◆

## Angelus-Rosedale

In 1994, John L. Hill II, owner of the Angelus Funeral Home, purchased the 100-year-old Rosedale Cemetery, located at 1831 West Washington Boulevard in Los Angeles. A well-maintained cemetery, Rosedale has many interesting monuments set along curving rows of palms in an older area of Los Angeles. The cemetery is managed by John L. Hill III, grandson of John Lamar Hill Sr., who founded the Angelus Funeral Home.

Incorporated on June 9, 1884, by the Rosedale Cemetery Association, it was the first cemetery in the Los Angeles area to adopt the memorial park concept, with decorative trees, shrubs, flowers and works of art. In 1887, the second crematory in the United States was opened at Rosedale, and by 1913, there had been 2,392 cremations. A non-denominational chapel was built in the early 1900s, as well as a columbarium modeled after the design of a Greek temple. In 1939, the crematorium and chapel were awarded a Certificate of Merit by the American Institute of Architects. Rosedale was also the first of the southland cemeteries available to people of all races and creeds.

For many years a Mortuary Car was available on the local street-car line that made its way along 16th Street (later called Venice Boulevard). The Mortuary Car provided transportation for both the deceased and those going to funeral services at Rosedale and the nearby Chapel of the Pines columbarium, which also has a crematory. The Mortuary Car service was stopped when the entrance to Rosedale was moved to Washington Boulevard.

One of the most touching scenes at Rosedale is the area set aside for the 450 veterans of the Grand Army of the Republic. Here a large black Civil War cannon bearing the inscription "With malice toward none" stands guard over the small, fading gravestones of the dead.

Many of the founders of Southern California are buried at Rosedale. They include Frederick Hastings Ringe, who named Harvard Street because he was educated at Harvard. Ringe at one time owned all of Malibu as a private estate. Interred here is the Shatto family, who once owned Catalina Island, and Phineas Banning, who built Los Angeles Harbor. Also at rest in Rosedale is Hatti Clark, one of Los Angeles' busiest prostitutes, who advertised "Guaranteed to give you as good a time as you'll get anywhere." Of national prominence is the grave of Jesse Benton Fremont, wife of General John Fremont. He is credited with raising an army in California during the Civil War to ensure that Mexico would not use that war as an opportunity to claim California for its own. Jesse also is credited with calling Abraham Lincoln "an ass" for not moving quickly enough to emancipate the slaves.

**John Lamar Hill Sr.,** 1887–1942. In the family vault.

Born in the small rural southern town of Oakland, Georgia, John went to work for the Pullman Company on the Southern Pacific Railroad as a porter. He made many runs to Los Angeles and San Francisco from Atlanta, during which time he became a member of the union, the Brotherhood of Sleeping Car Porters. Later, he became president of the union and in 1929 led them in a strike against the Pullman Company for better wages, which the union won. In 1925 John had joined two other Georgia businessmen in forming the Angelus Funeral Home. The business flourished and in 1932, famous architect Paul Williams was hired to design their new funeral home on East Jefferson Boulevard. A few years later,

Hattie McDaniel — Scarlett's Mammy and Academy Award winner.

Angelus became one of the largest funeral homes in the city.

**Hattie McDaniel,** 1895-1952. Near the cemetery office, just in from the curb, behind palm trees in Section D.

Hattie was best known as Mammy to Scarlett O'Hara in *Gone with the Wind,* a role for which she won a Best Supporting Actress Oscar in 1939. In addition to being the first black woman to win an Oscar, she was the first to sing on the radio. Hattie appeared in over 300 movies during her career, including *Judge Priest* in 1934 with Will Rogers, *Six Boats* in 1936, and *Since You Went Away* in 1944. On the radio, and later on TV, she played Beulah on the show of the same name. When she died in 1952, three thousand people came to her funeral, and 125 limousines accompanied her body to Rosedale, where she lies beneath a plain, flat stone.

**Maria G. Rasputin,** 1900-1977. Close to the main road.

Maria, daughter of Grigori Rasputin, a priest of the Khlysty sect, was adopted by the Czarist royal family in Russia because of the great affection and trust Czar Nicholas II and Czarina Alexandra had for her father. Grigori was able at times to halt the bleeding of their son, Prince Alexei, a hemophiliac. Maria and her younger sister, Varya, grand duchesses Olga, Tatiana, Marie and Anastasia were privately tutored.

When Maria was 16, her father was murdered and she stayed under the Czar's protection until his abdication in 1917. The Revolution forced Maria and Varya to flee to their original home in Siberia. Maria later married a White Russian officer, Boris Soloviev, in Saint Petersburg. She fled to Paris upon receiving the news that the Czar and his family had been executed. Boris died in 1926, leaving Maria with their two young daughters. For a short time, Maria worked as a maid and then a cabaret dancer in Bucharest. Later, she joined the Ringling Brothers Circus, and the Ringling Brothers brought her to America. She left the circus after being mauled by a bear and moved to Los Angeles. Maria said of her father, "My father was very kind, a very holy man. Always he think of others, never himself, only others. Many people were jealous of him."

Maria's father, Grigori Efimovich Rasputin, was one of the most frightening, mysterious and powerful figures in history. A semi-literate peasant, Grigori became a priest in the Khlysty sect of the Russian Orthodox Church, a group that believed in mixing religious fervor with sexual indulgence. Rasputin, with his almost hypnotic control over women, was able to convince dozens of them, many of royal blood, married or not, and of all ages, that the way to redemption was to let him "walk within them."

Rasputin's ability to control the hemophiliac bleeding of Prince Alexei allowed him to win the love and confidence of Alexei's parents, Czar Nicholas and Czarina Alexandra Feodorovna, who continually sought his advice on state matters. Rasputin maintained his power over the royal family and continued his attempts to get the Czar to end the war in Germany, which he feared would destroy his beloved Mother Russia. This so angered a group of royalty and naval and army officers that they plotted to murder him.

Led by Prince Yussupov, the plotters invited Rasputin to a night of debauchery with a band of gypsies at a club called the Villa Rode. Here they fed him food laced with cyanide of potassium, poisoned wine, and more food mixed with iron shavings, while they all sang gay gypsy songs and made love to the gypsy women. When it became apparent that Rasputin was not about to die, Yussupov pulled out a loaded revolver and shot Rasputin in the back. The murderers, shaken because Rasputin was so hard to kill, were about to remove the body when, to their horror, Rasputin stood up and started walking toward Yussopov. Several of them pulled pistols and began shooting Rasputin. Then they dragged him from the house and battered him with a steel press. While attempting to stuff his body through the ice in the River Neva, Rasputin came back to life once more and tore free his bound right hand. He made the sign of the cross before disappearing into the dark, freezing water.

Maria spent her last days in Los Angeles writing a book about her father, *Rasputin; The Man Behind the Myth,* co-authored by her friend Patte Barham, a well-known social figure and philanthropist.

**Lieutenant Colonel Allen Allensworth,** 1842–1914. This monument is recognized by a red, cylindrical stone.

Allen Allensworth founded the townsite of Allensworth in Tulare County in 1908, the only all-black community in California. The purpose of the community was to focus on building self-reliance and self-respect among black citizens of California. Allensworth, born a slave in Kentucky, became a U.S. Navy seaman and later the chaplain of the all-black 24th Infantry. When he retired, Allensworth was the highest ranking black man in the U.S. armed services.

**Andy Razaf** (Andreamenentania Razafkeriefo), 1895–1973. Facing the chapel on the right side, second row.

Razaf, a lyricist and composer, collaborated with Eubie Blake and pianist Fats Waller on such classics as "Ain't Misbehavin'," "Stompin' at the Savoy," "That's What I Like 'Bout the South," "The Joint is Jumpin'," "Keeping Out of Mischief Now," and "Honeysuckle Rose."

Razaf came to the United States from Madagascar, where his grandfather had been the U.S. consul. Razaf worked as an elevator operator in Tin Pan Alley, wrote poetry and played semipro baseball before teaming up with Waller. In 1925, he and Waller wrote the musical hit *Hot Chocolates,* which included the songs "Ain't Misbehavin'," "Black and Blue," "Honeysuckle Rose," and "I Got a Feeling I'm Falling."

**Francis Murphy,** 1836–1907. Marked by a brown stone near a black slate pyramid.

Murphy's stone reads "Gospel Temperance. 'With malice toward none and charity for all, I the undersigned, do pledge on my honor, God helping me, to abstain from intoxicating liquors as a beverage, and I will by all honorable means encourage others to abstain.' signed, Francis Murphy, Worldwide Apostle."

Francis Murphy, an Irishman, emigrated to the United States, where he fought in the Civil War. He had become an alcoholic, and after reforming, he lectured throughout the world on abstinence, encouraging people to sign the pledge on his tombstone. His plea is said to have reached 16 million people who pledged to stay liquor-free.

**Frank Chance,** 1877–1924. Near a brownstone pyramid in an unmarked grave.

Chance was the player-manager of baseball's Chicago Cubs from 1905–1914, during which time they won four pennants and two World Series. Chance's skills as a player precipitated the famous line penned by Franklin P. Adams of the *New York Evening Mail.* After the New York Giants had been beaten by the Cubs, due mainly to double plays by Chicago, Adams wrote, "These are the saddest of all possible words, Tinkers to Evers to Chance." However, all three of these players were elected to the baseball Hall of Fame in 1946.

**Art Tatum,** 1909–1956. At the back of the cemetery, Section 5, Row 178.

The grave marker is black marble with a piano etched in clouds and the words "Though the strings are broken, the melody lingers on." In the upper left-hand corner are musical notes and the words "Someone to watch over me." Tatum was, and still is, considered by many to be the most creative jazz musician ever to touch a piano. The great Oscar Peterson thought Tatum was untouchable as a jazz artist, and Fats Waller told his audience one night when Tatum walked in, "I play piano, but God is in the house tonight."

Tatum's very emotional touch on the piano keys brought admiration from classical musicians Horowitz and Toscanini and jazz greats including Coleman Hawkins and Charlie Parker. Tatum was blind in one eye and had only limited vision in the other. As a teenager he had his own radio show; then in 1933 when he cut his first record of "Sophisticated Lady" and "Tiger Rag" at the age of 24, Tatum found himself internationally famous.

Now a genuine living legend, Tatum formed his own band with blues singer Joe Turner. However, he soon found playing with a large group cumbersome and quit to play with a trio that included guitarist Tiny Gritnes and Slam Stuart on bass. Yet as a soloist, Tatum was at his finest. He blended some Waller and Earl Hines, the Duke and Debussy into his playing, then broke through it all to become probably the finest jazz pianist of all times. He was said to be at his best in smoky, after-hours joints late in the night. There his left hand chased the bass and the right played incredibly complex variations of melody.

Most of Tatum's music went unrecorded, except for some 100 songs he recorded for Norman Granz on Verve from 1953 through 1955. But for those who knew and loved him, the best Tatum played was just about dawn as the first rays of the sun began to touch the grimy windows of some smoke-filled dive.

Recently, Tatum's wife moved his remains to Forest Lawn in Glendale to allow room for her to be buried next to him. She graciously left his stone at Rosedale to mark where he was first buried.

**Anna May Wong,** 1907–1961. Her pink marble monument is near Tatum's. Its inscription in Chinese bears her mother's name, as they are both interred here in the same grave.

Anna May Wong — star of *Daughter of the Dragon.*

Anna May was an exotic Asian actress who was very popular in the 1930s. Her motion pictures included *Daughter of the Dragon* in 1931, in which she starred opposite Warner Oland, who played the infamous Dr. Fu Manchu. She made *Java Head* in 1934 in which Wong played a Mandarin princess married to a Caucasian sea captain whose roots were in a puritanical English seaport.

Ann Sheridan — A hot-headed redhead.

# 14

◆

## Chapel of the Pines

This is one of Los Angeles' oldest crematoriums, established in 1903 in a columbarium. It is included here because it is just around the corner from Angelus Rosedale Cemetery, at 1605 South Catalina Street.

Located in a handsome, domed building that looks more like an observatory or a lodge hall, Chapel of the Pines is a circular building with pews in curved rows facing the elevator that carries the deceased below to the crematory. Around the carved walls are vaults for the individual cinerary urns, and in front is a garden, where the deceased's ashes can be co-mingled with the ashes of others. Over 190,000 cremations have taken place here, and it currently is performing 3,000 cremations a year.

**Nigel Bruce**, 1885-1958. Located in a small compartment.

Bruce is best known for playing the bumbling Dr. Watson to Basil Rathbone's Sherlock Holmes. They starred in 14 pictures between 1939 and 1946, including *The Hound of the Baskervilles* and *The Adventures of Sherlock Holmes,* both made in 1939. These were wonderful atmospheric pictures set in Sir Arthur Conan Doyle's times. In 1942, at another studio, the decision was made to update the series to the 1940s so the world's most famous detective could fight the Nazis. The first such film was *Sherlock Holmes and the Voice of Terror.*

The following celebrities' remains are contained in a locked vault in the basement of the mausoleum and are not available for viewing.

**Ann Sheridan,** 1915-1967. Known as the "Oomph Girl," she began her career in *The Great O'Malley* in 1937 and followed that with *Angels with Dirty Faces* in 1938. Known to have a fiery temper, she was often on suspension by the studio. Other films included *The*

*Man Who Came to Dinner* in 1941 and *I Was a Male War Bride* in 1949, with Cary Grant. Ann gave the best performance of her career starring with Ronald Reagan in *King's Row* in 1942. Married three times, Sheridan died of cancer.

**Edmund Gwenn,** 1875-1959. Gwenn is best known for winning an Oscar for his portrayal of Santa Claus in *Miracle on 34th Street* in 1947.

**Walter Huston,** 1884-1950. In 1948 he won a Best Supporting Actor Oscar for *The Treasure of the Sierra Madre.* His son John directed the picture and received two Oscars for screenplay and direction. Huston also starred on Broadway in the 1920s and was a powerful, compelling performer in motion pictures through the 1930s and 1940s. His dozens of film credits include *Abraham Lincoln* in 1930, *Dodsworth* in 1936, for which he received an Oscar nomination, and *Yankee Doodle Dandy* in 1942, for which he was again nominated for an Oscar. His ashes were given to his family, and their location is unknown. Huston's wife and his son John are buried at Hollywood Memorial.

**Raymond Massey,** 1896-1983. Though equipped with an English accent, veteran actor Massey was actually Canadian. His most memorable motion pictures were *Abe Lincoln in Illinois* in 1941; *Prisoner of Zenda* in 1937, in which he played the brother, Black Michael; *The Scarlet Pimpernel* in 1935; and *Pygmalion* in 1945, in which he played Henry Higgins. On TV he was the beloved Dr. Gillespie in *Dr. Kildare,* 1961-1966, taking over the role originally played by Lionel Barrymore. While he was cremated at Chapel of the Pines, his ashes are buried in New Canaan, Connecticut.

**Jay Silverheels,** 1922-1980. This popular Indian actor played Tonto on *The Lone Ranger* TV series from 1949 to 1957. He was born on the Six Nations Indian Reservation in Ontario, and after cremation his ashes were returned to Canada.

**Rachel Roberts,** 1927-1980. Roberts was an important and beautiful English actress/comedian who won three British Academy Awards for *Saturday Night and Sunday Morning* in 1960, *This Sporting Life* in 1963, and *Yanks* in 1980. She also appeared in *Murder on the Orient Express* in 1974. She was married to Rex Harrison for nine years. Her ashes were sent to Wales.

**Hal Ashby,** 1929–1988. Ashby began his motion picture career as a film cutter and won his first Oscar for *In the Heat of the Night* in 1967. He switched to directing and made *Harold and Maude* in 1971 and *Coming Home* in 1978, for which he received an Oscar nomination. He continued to make pictures, none particularly memorable, until his death at 59.

**Marilyn Maxwell,** 1921–1972. Maxwell was sort of a poor-man's Marilyn Monroe, who appeared in many films as a "come-on" blonde. She appeared many times with Bob Hope on his Christmas visits to GIs. Her ashes were scattered at sea.

John Barrymore — Early Hollywood elegance. Where did it go?

# 15

◆

## Calvary Cemetery

Calvary, a Catholic cemetery, is located on Whittier Boulevard in East Los Angeles, just across the road from its Jewish counterpart, Home of Peace. Calvary's 137 acres were consecrated in 1896. Throughout the cemetery, the fourteen Stations of the Cross, represented by plaster figures in glass boxes, have been strategically placed. On the grounds are many handsome monuments, including many angels. Most of the well-known people interred here are on the second floor of the main mausoleum. The main mausoleum has a cross on top and stained glass windows over the main entrance; it is set well back in the cemetery.

### The Barrymores

Initial plans called for **John Barrymore,** 1882–1942, to be buried here in a crypt near his brother and sister. His space in Block 352, F-3 was supposed to display an epitaph from Shakespeare, "Good night, Sweet Prince." Instead, John is buried in Philadelphia in a family plot. (For more details on John Barrymore's career and his bizarre wake, see the section "Fascinating Funerals and Wakes.")

**Lionel Barrymore,** 1878–1954. Located just above John Barrymore's empty crypt.

Lionel was widely known for his wildly inconsistent acting performances. He had previously tried everything possible to avoid being an actor but found himself consistently returning to the stage and screen as a source of income. Most contemporaries thought it was a foregone conclusion that the son of famous actors Maurice and Georgie Drew Barrymore would enter the family business. By 1904, Lionel was an established movie star and distinguished himself on the stage in the east, including his role in the hit play *The Copperhead* in 1918. Returning to Hollywood, Lionel won an Oscar for *Free Soul.* He then starred with John and Ethel in *Grand*

*Hotel, Arsene Lupin,* and *Dinner at Eight.* He injured his hip while filming *Saratoga* in 1937, and suffering from severe arthritis, Lionel ended up in a wheelchair. But this did not stop his film career. MGM wisely cast him as Dr. Gillespie in *Dr. Kildare* in 1938, the first of 15 films in the Kildare series. Director Frank Capra made two outstanding films with Lionel: *You Can't Take It with You* and, with Lionel as the mean Mr. Potter, *It's a Wonderful Life.* In 1948 John Huston used him well opposite Bogie and Bacall in *Key Largo.* Lionel lost his wife, Irene, in 1936 and never married again. He was also successful as a writer, turning out one novel and a family biography. A symphony and tone poem he wrote to honor his brother, John, was performed in both New York and Los Angeles.

**Ethel Barrymore,** 1879–1959. Block 60, Crypt 3F.

Ethel took to the New York stage and became a star in 1901 in *Captain Jinks of the Horse Marines.* Her other memorable stage roles included *School for Scandal* and *The Corn is Green.* In 1944, the elegant and aristocratic Ethel won an Academy Award for Best Supporting Actress in *None But the Lonely Heart.* Other nominations followed for *The Spiral Staircase, The Paradine Case,* and *Pinky.* Her last picture was *Johnny Trouble* in 1957. Though

The magnificent Barrymores — Royal, theatrical family.

Abbott and Costello — Frankenstein saved their careers.

not a particularly attractive woman, Ethel had many lovers. She was confined to bed the last two years of her life with arthritis and heart trouble.

**Lou Costello** (Louis Francis Cristillo), 1906–1959. Block 354, Crypt B-1, with his wife Anne, who died the same year.

Costello played the slow-witted, bumbling fat guy to Bud Abbott's lean, smart-mouth role in their comedy routines. As the team of Abbott and Costello, they first played vaudeville in the 1930s before moving on to Hollywood where their second movie, *Buck Privates,* was a big hit in 1941.

During the next five years they made ten movies, none of which was particularly successful, including the last one, *Here Come the Coeds* in 1945. Then in 1948 they made the wildly popular *Abbott and Costello Meet Frankenstein.* Four more "Meet" movies followed, with *Abbott and Costello Meet the Mummy* being the last. As their movie popularity waned, the duo turned to TV where they had success with *The Colgate Comedy Hour* from 1951 to 1954 and the *Abbott and Costello Show* from 1952 to 1954. The pair split up in 1956, and neither had any success as a single act. However, their popularity continues today and their fan clubs are active throughout the country.

**Mabel Normand**, 1895–1930. In a marble drawer in the main hallway.

Mabel Normand was an adorable silent film star who was brought to Hollywood from New York by Mack Sennett. She had been a highly successful model for magazine illustrators Gibson and Flagg. Just before her marriage to Sennett, she caught him with actress Mae Busch, who hit her with a vase. Either from the blow or from her $2,000-a-month cocaine habit, her behavior became erratic and unpredictable. This, along with the publicity from the murder of her lover, William Desmond Taylor, in which she was briefly a suspect, ended her movie career. (For more details of Taylor's murder and Normand's involvement, see the section "Death by Mysterious Circumstance" and the description in the "Hollywood Memorial Park" section.)

**John Hodiak,** 1914–1955. Next to Mabel Normand.

A somewhat wooden actor, Hodiak made his first three movies in 1943 for MGM: *Stranger in Town, Swing Shift Maisie* and *I Dood It.* His big hit was the lead in Hitchcock's *Lifeboat* in 1944. His other movies included the film noir *Somewhere in the Night* and *Battleground.* Hodiak's popularity began to wane in the 1950s, and he made several low-quality pictures. However, his Broadway appearance in *The Caine Mutiny* again brought him critical acclaim. He was once married to actress Anne Baxter.

**Pola Negri** (Apolonia Chalupec), 1899–1987. Block 56, Crypt E-19.

Pola was a sultry, exotic, erotic woman who was a man stalker, both on and off the screen, during the silent era. She supposedly had affairs with known woman chasers Charlie Chaplin and Howard Hughes. Her torrid romance with Rudolph Valentino, to whom she claimed she was engaged, ended with his death. Later she married a Polish count and much later a Georgian prince. Adolph Hitler supposedly watched Pola's *Mazurka,* a German-made movie, once a week.

**Ramon Novarro** (Ramon Samaniegos), 1899–1968. Died on Halloween. Buried under the grass at the front of the cemetery, Section C, Plot 584.

A friend of Rudolph Valentino, Novarro's first hit in silent movies was as Rupert in *The Prisoner of Zenda* in 1922. He followed this up with *Scaramouche,* with Rudolph Valentino, and then *Ben Hur.* Valentino gave Ramon a black Art Deco phallus with his name inscribed in silver to celebrate the very successful *Scaramouche.* The "Boy Wonder," Irving Thalberg of

MGM, personally took charge of Novarro's career and starred him in the successful *Mata Hari* with Garbo in 1931. Novarro's last three films for MGM were flops, and he retired from films in 1934. (For more information on Novarro see "Death by Mysterious Circumstance.")

Crystal Cathedral, from a drive-in to a magnificent cathedral.

# 16

◆

## Crystal Cathedral Memorial Gardens
## The "Westminster Abbey" of America

Ministering to his parishioners, both here and beyond, is one of the world's foremost and well-known dispensers of divinity, Dr. Robert Schuller.

He is in a class with world-renowned Billy Sunday, Norman Vincent Peale and Billy Graham. In the minds of many, he may even be on a par with the pope. The good and mighty preacher conducts Sunday sermons that are heard by millions around the world via television and satellite, as well as by thousands seated in his cathedral. The church was born in a drive-in theater and grew up in the surrounding orange groves to become the present magnificent glass cathedral located in Garden Grove, California.

How comforting it must be to those who anticipate being buried in the Crystal Cathedral Memorial Gardens to know that they will have a guide through eternity who is already pretty familiar with the territory and rules.

Soaring into the sky and visible for miles around is the shimmering, 236-foot Crean Tower. Inside are the Arvella Schuller Carillon and the Mary Hood Chapel. The base of the tower is the grand entry to the exclusive one-and-one-half-acre memorial garden that rests in the heart of the 30-acre Crystal Cathedral grounds.

The cemetery facilities include secure, serene and sacred resting places; "family gardens" in private settings; above-ground entombment; and an open-air mausoleum with individual, companion and family crypts for casket entombment. The Sanctuary of Praise offers exquisite stained glass niches, which are made up of brilliant colored glass blocks fashioned to form a cross; the cross is surrounded by a depiction of a field of beautiful flowers and shining stars. The Creation Mosaic niche wall depicts the beginning of life. A spring sunrise lights an infant hand as it grasps the thumb of a loving parent.

Dr. Schuller appointed Larry Davis to aid in the planning, development and construction of the cemetery, and all funerals held at or through Crystal Cathedral are under his direction. Mr. Davis has directed funerals as large as 4,000 people for three local policemen killed in the line of duty. He coordinated the funeral for Wolfman Jack, who was interred elsewhere. He also assisted the U. S. Department of Protocol in planning President Richard Nixon's funeral.

The gardens can accommodate 10,000 inhabitants. The nationally known pie lady, Marie Callender, is here. Talented pianist/composer Roger Williams, who frequently plays for Crystal Cathedral services, has reservations for his family. And of course, the Schuller family will rest here. Their reservation is in The Garden of Eternity.

This consecrated place has probably been in the plan of the universe for millennia, but when Dr. Schuller dreamed the miraculous dream for the cathedral and gardens, he made it work in only one lifetime.

# 17

♦

## Eden Memorial Park

Eden Memorial Park, a Jewish cemetery, is located in the Mission Hills area of Los Angeles at 11500 Sepulveda Boulevard, just above the Mission Hills Cemetery. Its most famous remains are those of Groucho Marx, whose ashes were stolen from the mausoleum in May 1982 and found the same day at Mount Sinai Memorial Park, a Jewish cemetery in the Hollywood Hills.

**Lenny Bruce** (Leonard Schneider), 1925-1966. Outside under a marker reading "Beloved Father—Devoted Son" and the line "Peace at Last."

Bruce was a lonely guy who, after he rigged a dishonorable discharge from the Navy, began hanging around Manhattan working in the burlesque scene as an emcee and comic. Lenny liked drugs and he liked jazz, which led him to his marriage to a stripper named Honey. They had a daughter named Kitty. After Kitty's birth, Honey got back on drugs, was arrested and received a sentence of two years in prison. Honey accused Lenny of being the informer and harassed him for it up to the time of his death. After he made several appearances on the Arthur Godfrey TV show, Bruce began to lose it, and once even appeared naked to emcee a burlesque show. His sick humor bought him an appearance on the *Steve Allen Show* and a feature in *Time* magazine. Heavily into drugs by the late 1950s, he was spending over $1,000 a week to support his cocaine habit, and he became increasingly out of touch with reality. His last days were spent in his Hollywood home, surrounded by Honey, his mother, and a variety of groupies and Strip drifters. He was found dead in his bathroom with a needle in his arm.

**Groucho Marx** (Julius), 1890-1977. In the Eden mausoleum.

The location of Marx Brothers **Harpo** (Adolph Arthur),

1888–1964, and **Chico** (Leonard), 1866–1961, is at Forest Lawn, Glendale. **Zeppo** (Herbert), 1901–1979, was cremated, and his ashes were scattered at sea. **Gummo,** 1893–1977, is in the Hall of Freedom Mausoleum, Sanctuary of Brothers at Forest Lawn, Glendale, with his wife, Helen.

Combining almost murderous slapstick with absurdist screen writing and total anarchy, the Marx Brothers were the craziest and most unique comedy team of the 1930s. Encouraged to enter show business by their mother, Minnie, the daughter of vaudevillian performers, Groucho, Harpo and Gummo, along with Janie O'Reilly, became a quartet of singers known as The Four Nightingales. Not very successful as singers, the brothers began to add chaos and slapstick humor to their routine as they developed their individual styles.

Groucho's style, the most recognizable of any comedian, was built around the grease paint mustache and eyebrows, glasses, a cigar and a stooped-over stride, along with fast-talking, wise-guy insults. Harpo, with his curls and long coat, became the woman-chasing mute, while Chico, with his Tyrolean hat, became the scam artist with the Italian accent. Zeppo and Gummo were the straight men.

In 1925 the Marx Brothers starred on Broadway in the hit show *Cocoanuts,* which they made into a film at Paramount four years later. At the same time, they were appearing on Broadway in *Animal Crackers,* which was also made into a film in 1930 and which produced the song that would become Groucho's signature, "Captain Spalding." After *Animal Crackers,* the brothers left for Hollywood, where they made what many critics think were their best films, *Monkey Business* in 1931, *Horse Feathers* in 1932, and the last, *Duck Soup,* the following year. *Duck Soup,* was a mish-mash of political satire, nonsense and sheer lunacy.

The brothers then moved to MGM where, under the guidance of Irving Thalberg, they filmed the madcap comedies *A Night at the Opera* in 1935 and *A Day at the Races* in 1937. Many of their movies featured Groucho as the despicable predatory stalker of rich widows, who were usually played by the wonderful character actress Margaret Dumont. All around them, Chico and Harpo turned the world into total, mindless chaos. During this period, Groucho's most famous line was immortalized:"One morning I shot an elephant in my pajamas. How he got in my pajamas, I don't know."

In the 1940s, after the death of Thalberg, the Marx Brothers made three forgettable films. Then in 1947, Groucho went on radio with what was to become a big hit show, *You Bet Your Life*. The show moved to television in 1950 where it ran for ten years. It was the perfect vehicle for the wisecracking, quick-witted, acid-tongued Groucho. As the emcee of this quirky quiz show, his signature line was "Say the magic word and you win 50 dollars," which was then delivered by a stuffed duck lowered into the scene from above. Groucho received a special Oscar from the Motion Picture Academy in 1973.

The Marx Brothers created comedy based on total anarchy.

# 18

### ◆

## Heaven Bound

He had lost a million dollars in his previously successful silver mine in Montana. For this reason 36-year-old Hubert Eaton found himself considering a job offer to manage a little run-down, near-bankruptcy cemetery on the outskirts of a Southern California town then called Tropico. In 1918 Tropico was annexed into the city of Glendale.

Originally a Missourian, Eaton was born in 1881 to a God-fearing Christian couple. His parents had a love of independence, a sense of adventure, fearlessness in the name of principle, and a strong conviction that, next to religion, the most important requirement in any life was education. A graduate of Tom William Newell College, one professor recalled Eaton was the best chemistry student he ever taught. Eaton followed a career in metallurgy and chemistry until his mining adventure.

Eaton first set eyes on Forest Lawn on a sunny, balmy, albeit winter New Year's Day in 1917. Ten miles away, floats in Pasadena's Tournament of Roses preceded the Oregon-Pennsylvania football classic that was to be played in Tournament Park. The Rose Bowl was not yet in existence. (Oregon won the game, 14 to 0.)

The year had begun in defeat and disaster for the Allies on the Western Front of World War I. Lloyd George was England's prime minister, the Russians were near collapse, and Woodrow Wilson was president. A young California had not yet found its business direction. Movies were in their infancy, but "America's Sweetheart," Mary Pickford, in the classic *Birth of a Nation,* called serious attention to the importance of films to the state's future. This industry and its participants would have considerable impact on the prospects of the little run-down cemetery in what was to become Glendale. Many industry personalities would, in time, become Forest Lawn inhabitants.

Amid the magnificence of sun-drenched, orange-scented, flowering Southern California, the cemetery was barren, untidy and weedy, with an unpainted shack centered amid some grim and ugly granite headstones. As author-reporter Adela Rogers St. Johns wrote in her tribute to Hubert Eaton, "A man couldn't get much spur or inspiration out of this.

"A cemetery. Like all cemeteries. Death at its drabbest, without hope or God. Everything that had to do with the passage from this life to another, everything connected with the services for the mortal clay just abandoned by the immortal soul was stark, ugly, shattering to those left behind." This little cemetery depressed him beyond words, and Hubert was convinced that the cemetery business was not for him.

"No, not for a mining engineer," he reasoned. "To go back home and begin again at the bottom as a geologist and chemist, that was the practical thing to do." But the thought persisted that there was something unfair and wrong that people should find their last resting place so damp, dismal and foreboding. No help for the living, no hope for the dead. Wasn't a Christian cemetery supposed to be part of the Christian doctrine in which the Resurrection had given proof of eternal life?

To live in hearts we leave behind is not to die. Friends and relatives could not possibly forget that they had left a loved one behind in this forsaken plot of ground. A wave of compassion washed over the man seated on the edge of the graveyard as he thought of the desolation of the dead. Every person born into the world must meet the moment symbolized by those tombstones. Sorrow, sadness, bitter grief, guilt, pain, loneliness—all of these were part of the loss brought by death. But there should be comfort and consolation, at least for the living. The decision Hubert Eaton made that day would change his life and the lives of millions of others. "A Memorial Park. A burial place dedicated not to death but to eternal life" became Forest Lawn's creed.

The original of today's five Forest Lawns is located in Glendale's metropolitan-residential area (one of dozens of Los Angeles suburbs "looking for a city" according to former Mayor Sam Yorty.) As you enter, you drive through the world's largest wrought-iron gates and are greeted by a magnificent panoramic view of acres of green grass, trees, statuary, fountains and ponds set in a background of grand mountains and unobstructed sky. A quiet, comforting peacefulness envelops you. There is no cadaverous stillness or macabre undertone. It is a park even children enjoy without fear of ominous presences.

Adela Rogers St. Johns, who wrote *First Step Up Toward Heaven,* the first book about Forest Lawn, describes what Hubert Eaton envisioned for his cemetery. It was to be a place where friends and relatives could visit their deceased in an atmosphere of comfort, consolation and hope. He would not accept the untidy, barren desolation that had greeted him years before. Forest Lawn is Eaton's dedication to eternal life, not to dismal death.

Forest Lawn's Glendale Gates — The gates at the end of the road.

# 19

## Forest Lawn, Glendale

Among the most famous of the famous buried in Glendale's Forest Lawn is **Walter Elias Disney,** 1901–1966, located in the garden to your left as you face the Freedom Mausoleum.

No one in the world has provided greater entertainment and more pleasurable hours than Walt. He is considered the most successful and influential producer in the history of moviemaking. Ever productive even as a youngster, he and his brother, Roy, had paper routes that they delivered at 5:00 A.M. Their financially unsuccessful father pocketed their money, so Walt secretly took a second paper route, as well as a job at a candy store during school recesses.

Stationed in France during World War I, Walt developed his artistic skills by decorating trucks and helmets for other soldiers. After the war, he began his career seriously by attending Kansas City Art Institute, later finding work as a commercial artist. With his boyhood pal Ub Iwerks, he worked at the Kansas City Film Ad Company. Walt produced commercials for local merchants that appeared in the city's theaters. Later Ub and Walt struck out on their own. Walt first created a series of fairy tale parodies. He found there was little money in fairy tales, and his penchant for perfection caused serious cash-flow problems. Broke but still ambitious, Walt set out for Hollywood, where he found his true niche.

Brother Roy soon joined him and became his lifelong business partner. Roy was the business element in their operation that made them and their studio multimillionaires, but they had some disappointments and disasters in between.

Walt's first cartoon animal was Oswald the Rabbit. Then came Mortimer (a.k.a. Mickey Mouse) in *Plane Crazy,* a silent. With the next cartoon, *Steamboat Willie* in 1928, he added a synchronized soundtrack. Both Walt and the mouse were instant sensations, making Mickey a big star and his boss a recognized genius. Then came Pluto, Goofy and Donald Duck to star with Mickey. Walt's perfection became corporate policy, and artists in the Disney organization were encouraged to constantly upgrade their work. Subsequently, an art school was established on the lot.

*Snow White and the Seven Dwarfs* was predicted to flop because it was the industry's first attempt at a full-length cartoon. It didn't flop. *Snow White* was a milestone, both artistically and financially. Music played a big part in its success, another first. *Pinocchio, Fantasia* and a host of other productions followed.

World War II caused an early setback in the studio's growth as Disney became active in training and morale-building films. Also, in 1941 a bitter strike disrupted the staff and the company. Still it wasn't long before *Dumbo, Bambi, The Reluctant Dragon,* the wartime tale *Victory Through Air Power, Der Fuhrer's Face, Good Neighbor Policy, Saludos Amigos* and *The Three Caballeros* were all in the can. In the late forties, TV productions became the next logical step, and film animation continued as well. Classics such as *Cinderella, Alice in Wonderland, Lady and the Tramp, Sleeping Beauty, One Hundred and One Dalmatians,* and *Mary Poppins* came later in Walt's career, topping everything he had done before.

Awards, which the Disney Studio and Walt won year after year, became *de rigueur,* and he became one of the most renowned figures in the entertainment world. Capping his career were the astonishing Disneyland parks, which almost bankrupted him but finally succeeded with Roy's help, and one must wonder what kind of world this would be without them.

Personal problems many times were devastating to this artist. In 1931, his driving ambition took its toll, along with his disappointment at not yet fathering a child. Later, in 1933, his daughter, Diane, was born. Once when the studio was deep in debt, he took an overdose of drugs but later recovered. His expression and attitude were usually dour and unyielding, which earned him no favor with his staff. Yet when he was asked about this by a reporter, he answered, "I don't have depressed moods and I don't want to have any. I'm happy, just very happy."

Walt was one of the early proponents of cryogenics (freezing bodies for returning to life in the future). He hoped to experience this phenomenon himself, but alas, it didn't happen. Today his ashes are in the family vault in Freedom Garden. His location faces the mausoleum and features a little girl sitting on a rock in front of a wall that lists his name and dates.

Walt didn't want to go at all. He wanted to stay around because he knew he had a lot more to give. However, he was taken with a cancerous left lung. Taken he was, but Walt Disney left behind many gifts and legends by which the world remembers him.

**Errol Flynn,** 1909–1959. In the Garden of Everlasting Peace, to the left of the George Washington statue.

Here, hopefully, Flynn has at last found peace. His grave is near the bronze statue of a woman with one hand around her waist and the other over her shoulder. Below it in the ground, his marker is inscribed "In memory of our father from his loving children." The marker was not placed on the grave until 1979, twenty years after his death.

Flynn was as swashbuckling in life as the characters he played in films. He was born in Tasmania and educated in Paris, London, Sydney and Ireland. He had worked in a myriad of jobs, including journalist, sailor, novelist, fighter and knockabout when he was discovered on his sailboat off New Guinea by a film crew. Some small film parts preceded his successful *Captain Blood* in 1935, in which he was a replacement for Robert Donat. That shot him to instant stardom. He was typecast as a hero-adventurer and with his lithesome body and handsome face, this ardent lover usually ended up stealing his admiring ladies from their kings, lovers and husbands.

Inheriting the dashing Douglas Fairbanks' crown, he effortlessly portrayed a legion of heroic characters. Men and women alike became his fans as he co-starred with many of Hollywood's legends, including Basil Rathbone, Nigel Bruce, and actress Olivia de Havilland, with whom he made eight films.

Adventurous, charming, sometimes rebellious and unpredictable, Flynn's wild escapades kept him in the news and kept him in hot water with the studios and his women. Not very discreet, he was notorious for his nonstop drinking and insatiable womanizing. In 1941, at the height of his popularity, he escorted Peggy Satterle, a dancer from the Florentine Gardens, to his yacht, the *Sirocca*.

She accused him of rape. A grand jury vindicated him, but the district attorney overruled the decision and prosecuted him. Jerry Geisler defended him and he was acquitted on all counts. In 1942 Betty Hanson charged him with statutory rape and again he was acquitted. His trials were attended with the same excitement as his films, but these episodes seemed to break his spirit. He began his decline in both his career and his personal life.

Flynn's wives were Lily Damita, Nora Eddington, and Patrice Wymore. Flynn volunteered for military service but was ruled 4-F because of a heart defect and recurring malaria. His son Sean, by Lily Damita, served as a military photographer, but at age 29 he disappeared and was presumed captured and dead. Flynn's decline accelerated after that.

His on-screen magic vanished, and his remaining films showed his deterioration. He was soon being cast in drunkard roles, such as in Hemingway's *The Sun Also Rises* and *Too Much, Too Soon,* in which he portrayed his old friend John Barrymore.

Flynn's final years afforded him some happiness aboard his beloved yacht, *Zaka.* During this time he worked on his autobiography, which was published posthumously. Accurately, it is titled *My Wicked, Wicked Ways.* (For another Errol Flynn anecdote, see the section "Fascinating Funerals" on John Barrymore.)

**Spencer Tracy,** 1900–1967. Just "Tracy" marks the wall of a private section, furnished with a marble bench surrounded by beautiful plantings. It is in the Garden of Peace to the right of the George Washington statue.

The "Actor's actor," as he was known, described his success with "Know your lines and don't bump into the furniture," but his talent was much more than that. He was praised by critics, admired by his peers and appreciated by the movie-going public. Dynamic, quiet and understated, he mesmerized audiences with simple gestures, expressions and body language, all making his characterizations believable.

A former Jesuit student, he initially intended to be a priest, but after Navy duty in World War I he was mustered out and enrolled in Northwestern Military Academy and Wisconsin's Ripon College. At Ripon he studied dramatics, which took him to New York's

Tracy — "Know your lines and don't bump into the furniture."

American Academy of Dramatic Arts, then into Broadway productions and some small films. He thought he had no future as an actor, but director John Ford saw him in *The Last Mile,* signed him with Fox and cast him in *Up the River* (which also featured his friend Humphrey Bogart). This role limited his assignments to tough guy and gangster parts, which disappointed him.

It was at this time that Tracy's heavy drinking first became noticeable. Undistinguished films finished his contract with Fox, and he was then "discovered" by MGM's production head, Irving Thalberg, who signed him to a long-term contract. He excelled in two films, with Myrna Loy in *Whipsaw* and Jean Harlow in *Riffraff.* He also appeared with Sylvia Sidney, Jeanette MacDonald and Freddie Bartholomew in Kipling's *Captains Courageous,* which won him his first Academy Award in 1937. His real-life hero role, portraying Father Flanagan in *Boys' Town,* won him his second Oscar in 1938.

Separated from his wife, Louise, his dalliances with actresses, especially (it is rumored) with Loretta Young, kept him busy. Tracy's greatest movie performances were with Katharine Hepburn. Their on-screen relationship developed into a very private, yet well-known, romantic interest between the two. The love affair lasted for 25 years until his death. A devout Catholic, Spencer and his wife never divorced, nor did Hepburn seek it. Hepburn was, and still is, totally devoted to him.

Tracy was not a naturally happy man. He had an explosive temper and drank too much, often disappearing on binges for days at a time. However, his relationship with Hepburn was calming and satisfying to him. He was deeply affected by his only son's deafness. Tracy and his wife devoted much time, money, facilities and service to the Tracy Clinic for the Deaf in an effort to help others with hearing disabilities.

In 1967, after a few years of seclusion, he accepted the lead role in *Guess Who's Coming to Dinner,* directed by Stanley Kramer. Unable to obtain insurance on Tracy due to his ill health, Kramer took on full responsibility for the risk, considerably shortened the star's work day and kept pressure off him. His performance was fine and convincing. For his portrayal he received a posthumous best actor Academy Award nomination, his ninth, which joined the two Academy Awards he won in 1937 and 1941. In a long, arduous speech in the film, Tracy spoke eloquently of the love he had for the woman in his life. Everyone knew he was expressing his caring for Hepburn, as, with tears in her eyes, did she.

Tracy, at the height of his illness, made a rare phone call to his friend, Garson Kanin, and happily said, "Did you hear? I finished the picture." Two weeks later, he was gone.

**Frank Borzage,** 1902–1962. In the middle section between the Freedom Mausoleum and the Statue of Immortality.

Frank Borzage was a sensitive, romantic and distinguished director, a favorite with audiences as well as his associates in the film industry. He directed many sentimental films and actors, but perhaps the most memorable, because it was his first, was the romantic *Seventh Heaven,* which starred Charles Farrell and Janet Gaynor. Borzage and Gaynor received the first of the Oscar awards, and the film was a box office sensation. The three of them made two more films, *Street Angel* and *Lucky Star,* before the advent of sound.

**Agness Underwood,** 1902–1984. Left of the George Washington monument facing the Freedom Mausoleum in the Sanctuary of Affection.

Aggie was the legendary female newspaper editor of the *Los Angeles Examiner* under William Randolph Hearst. Perfectly cast, she was small but mighty, tough and kind, feisty and demanding, and she produced a hell of a paper. Respected by all whom she worked for, Aggie became a legend in the world of journalism.

**Lilli Palmer-Thompson,** 1914–1986. Across Freedom Way at the opposite end of Freedom Court.

This delicate and beautiful actress, who seemed to know the secret of staying young, had endured the harrowing experiences of running from country to country to stay ahead of the Nazi threat to her German homeland. Her best Hollywood film was *The Four Poster,* which subsequently brought her international success and fame as she worked in Europe and the United States. Her humorous and witty 1975 autobiography, *Change Lobsters and Dance,* was a best seller.

From a personal point of view, Lilli Palmer is best remembered for courageously granting her husband, Rex Harrison, a divorce, even though she still loved him. She did it so he could marry Kay Kendall, the woman he loved and who was perilously near death from leukemia.

**Samuel Laird Cregar,** 1914–1944. Near Lilli Palmer-Thompson.

Cregar was the heavyset, creepy Jack the Ripper in *The Lodger*. The 300-pound actor lost 100 pounds and required a stomach operation because of physical complications. Then he died of a heart attack.

**Joan Blondell,** 1906–1979. Located in the open area between the Freedom Mausoleum and Court of Freedom in the private Garden of Honor.

Blondell was the actress everybody loved, but in films she never got her man. A Texas beauty contest winner, she landed in New York after touring the world with her vaudeville parents. She teamed with James Cagney in *Penny Arcade,* and they were both signed by Warner Brothers where they continued to work together.

This wide-eyed, saucy, sexy, brassy blonde appeared in more of that studio's films than any other actress during the 1940s. In real life, she did get her men. She was married to cameraman George Barnes, actor Dick Powell and producer Mike Todd.

In 1972, after a lengthy, successful career, she wrote her autobiographical novel, *Center Door Fancy.*

"A lifetime to go" reads the plaque of Spangler Arlington Brugh— **Robert Taylor.** His grave lies near Joan Blondell's to the side of a Greek statue of a woman holding flowers.

If only he did still have a lifetime to go. Too soon, Taylor died from lung cancer. As Barbara LaMarr was called "The girl who was too beautiful," so Taylor could have been labeled "The man who was too handsome." He had a perfect physique, black hair, and penetrating blue eyes.

Taylor was born in Nebraska in 1911 and died on June 8, 1969. He majored in music briefly before moving to California where he attended Pomona College. There he studied medicine but shortly took up acting. After a debut in a low-budget picture, *Handy Andy,* he was groomed for stardom. A popular leading man in romantic, collegiate, humorous and playful roles, he starred in at least four films a year.

During his World War II stint in the Navy, Taylor served as a flight instructor for the Air Transport Division, directing many training films and narrating documentaries. More mature when he left the service, he adapted his acting to tougher characters in hard-boiled westerns, suspense movies, some costume epics and Biblical spectacles, and some sinister roles. He appeared in the TV series *The Detective.* Taylor appeared with most of the beautiful and talented actresses of the era, often with Barbara Stanwyck, whom he married in 1939. They divorced in 1951, although her friends claim Barbara always loved him. He married Ursula Thiess, who was with him until he died of lung cancer attributed to smoking.

Taylor was eulogized at Forest Lawn's Church of the Recessional by an actor friend who was to later become president of the United States, Ronald Reagan.

**Jerry Wald,** 1911–1962. In the Columbarium of Honor.

A writer and producer, Wald was considered to be the original for Sammy Glick in *What Makes Sammy Run?* Bud Schulberg's novel of life in Hollywood.

**Clarence Brown**, 1890–1987. In the Columbarium of Honor.

He directed *National Velvet* and *The Yearling,* among other films. He was nominated by the Academy six times. He died of kidney failure at 97.

Nearby is **Clifford Odets,** 1906–1963.

Odets was a playwright who told his friends he would have rather been a composer. His best plays were *Waiting for Lefty, Awake and Sing, Golden Boy* and *The Country Girl.* He raised his two children alone and died at 57 of stomach ulcers and cancer. He despised his dying and in his final moments he raised himself from his deathbed and declared, "Clifford Odets, you have so much to do!

I want to fool you all and live so that I can redeem my last 16 wasted years." His son described his death as "A mountain blown to dust in two weeks."

Cary Grant and Zsa Zsa Gabor attended his funeral; Dinah Shore sent flowers. Danny Kaye, in his eulogy, praised Odets as a man with a completely humane faculty for sorrow and humor.

**Charlotte Shelby.** She was originally buried outside the Columbarium of Honor. However her daughter, Mary Miles Minter, had Charlotte and her Aunt Margaret removed and later scattered their remains, as she chose to have done with her ashes upon her own death.

Charlotte became famous as the mother of adorable 17-year-old, blonde and curly haired Mary, whose studio was fashioning her after Mary Pickford. But Charlotte's and Mary's involvement in the William Desmond Taylor murder ended Mary's movie career. Public opinion declared Charlotte guilty, but the case was never solved. (For more information on the Taylor murder, see the section "Death by Mysterious Circumstance.")

Perishing with her teammates in the Sabena Airlines crash in Brussels, Belgium, while on their way to compete in the World Figure Skating Championships, **Dona Lee Carrier,** 1940–1961, rests outside the Columbarium of Honor in Forest Lawn.

Her sentimental plaque shows the medal of the World Championships, 1961, with a flag and a skate blade through it. It explains that she was a gold medalist and member of the U.S. Figure Skating Team representing the United States in world competition to be held in Prague. Other quotes read, "Like a cup of gold on the ice." "Her grace and sweet spiritual fragrance touched many lives, Her loveliness glowed from within," which were probably newspaper comments, and from the Bible, "I will come again and receive you unto Myself. John 14:3." Dona Carrier, 21, died at the peak of her career.

**George Cukor,** 1899–1983. To the right of Carrier in an unmarked garden.

The discoverer of Katharine Hepburn, Cukor collaborated happily with her for nearly 50 years. While he was considered one of the finest of Hollywood's directors, he previously was a distinguished theatrical director on Broadway in the 1920s, working with Ethel Barrymore, among others.

Migrating to Hollywood, he worked as dialogue director on *All Quiet on the Western Front* and soon became a full director. Because he was a homosexual, male stars complained that his emphasis and favoritism was on the female stars, not on them. For this, he was dismissed from *Gone with the Wind* at Clark Gable's request.

He successfully directed *A Bill of Divorcement, David Copperfield, Dinner at Eight, Romeo and Juliet, Camille, The Women, The Philadelphia Story, Two-Faced Woman, Adam 's Rib, Pat and Mike, Born Yesterday, A Star is Born, My Fair Lady* and many other films before his death at 82. His wealth of talent helped make many stars successful including Greta Garbo, Robert Taylor, Cary Grant, Vivien Leigh, Spencer Tracy, Katharine Hepburn, the Judys (Holliday and Garland), Norma Shearer, Joan Crawford and dozens of others.

**Sam Cooke,** 1930–1964. Near George Cukor.

His plaque shows a couple in classic dress standing together looking toward a mountain, with the Bible verse from Song of Solomon 2:17, "Until the day breaks and the shadows flee away." (For more information, see "Death by Mysterious Circumstance.")

**Sammy Davis Jr.,** 1925–1990. In the Garden of Honors, buried near his grandmother, PeeWee, and his "Uncle" Will.

Sammy began tapping and singing as a child. However, his Hollywood and Broadway debuts came in 1956 with *Mr. Wonderful* on Broadway and *The Benny Goodman Show* on screen. Sammy then became a member of "The Rat Pack" with Frank Sinatra, Dean Martin, Peter Lawford and other Vegas-crazies. From then on, his screen persona was showbiz, gold-chain glitz, and he appeared with the "Pack" members in *Ocean's Eleven* and *Robin and the Seven Hoods* in the 1960s. Davis appeared in two more pictures with buddy Peter Lawford: in the 1968 thriller *Salt and Pepper* and again in 1969 with *One More Time,* a limper directed by Jerry Lewis.

In 1969 his show business style and genius for dancing and

singing made him a hit in *Sweet Charity* with other big talents including Shirley MacLaine, Chita Rivera and Ben Vereen. In 1989, in his final picture, *Tap,* with Gregory Hines, he turned in a wonderful performance of savvy and dignity as an over-the-hill song-and-dance man with a few tricks left in him. Sammy also appeared on TV in many musical specials, with stars like Liza Minnelli, and was famous for tapping and singing "Mr. Bojangles" and "I've Gotta Be Me."

His marriage to white actress May Britt and conversion to Judaism kept him alive in the newspapers. Davis wrote two autobiographies, including *Oh, God, Why Me?* and *Hollywood in a Suitcase.* A heavy smoker, he died of cancer. (For more on Sammy Davis Jr., see the section "Fascinating Funerals.")

**Charles Dillon Stengel,** 1890–1975. To the left of the Statue of Immortality on the back wall are the remains of "Casey" Stengel with his own quote, "There comes a time in every man's life, and I've had plenty of them." Above the quote appears a carved, painted cameo portrait over two crossed bats.

What a loss to baseball it would have been if Casey (named for Kansas City, his hometown) had become a dentist as was originally planned. But instead he turned to his real love. He did not do well academically in school; athletics was his best subject. He played fullback, captained the football team, and was the star of the city's champion basketball team. One of his teammates, William Powell, later became a famous actor.

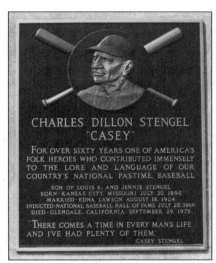

"Casey" Stengel—"There comes a time in every man's life, and I've had plenty of them."

Baseball was his first love, and he made a career of it. He was a scrappy, aggressive player who worked hard to please a crowd. He was also a troublemaker who fought at the drop of a baseball. He signed with the Brooklyn Dodgers organization and soon made the parent club. Eventually he played for the Pirates, Phillies, Giants and Braves. He became a goofy legend, playing jokes on his audiences and fellow ballplayers.

When he ended his spectacular playing career, he moved into management with the Brooklyn Dodgers. Later he managed the Giants, the Yankees, and the worst team in baseball history, the New York Mets. When he left the Yankees, he had won five pennants and two World Series. Casey's "Stengalese" became legend; it was his own language, unintelligible and rarely repeatable.

Casey's later years were tough. His wife, Edna, suffered a series of strokes that left her incapacitated. Casey was diagnosed with lymphatic cancer. While a patient in the hospital, he never missed listening to a game and always weakly managed to stand up for the national anthem. He died the day after the season ended. Surely he waited so he wouldn't spoil a baseball day for his friends, the teams and a nation of fans.

**Dan Dailey,** 1915–1978. Just outside Casey's wall, beyond the Court of Freedom.

Ever the song-and-dance man, Dailey was a most versatile actor. He was tall and solidly built, with fair hair and complexion, blue eyes and a mischievous grin. He was popular as a musical star and moved with exceeding style and grace. He first appeared at age four in a minstrel show and grew up to dance and sing in vaudeville, burlesque and stock. He then landed on Broadway in the original production of *Babes in Arms*. MGM found him and put him in a variety of roles. He appeared in *The Mortal Storm, Ziegfield Girl, Lady Be Good* and *Panama Hattie*. He and Betty Grable were teamed in *Mother Wore Tights*. Because they complemented and liked each other, they became a popular team. When musicals became less popular, Dailey went back to stage and nightclubs as well as appearing in several TV series. A pleasant-mannered ladies' man, he was married and divorced three times.

**Johnny Mack Brown,** 1904–1974. Beyond Stengal's wall in the open mausoleum.

Brown was a renowned athlete, an All American halfback from the University of Alabama who, after catching two touchdown passes in the 1926 Rose Bowl game, turned down offers to play professional football in favor of a movie career. He made his mark that same year starring with Joan Crawford in *Our Dancing Daughters.* It was the film that made Joan a star. Brown appeared with Greta Garbo in both *The Divine Woman* and *A Woman of Affairs* and with Norma Shearer in *Lady of Chance.*

His fate was sealed when King Vidor cast him in the title role of *Billy the Kid,* playing a romantic western leading man. He was happy becoming a Western series star and made over 200 movies riding with his horse, Reno. Called "The best punch in pictures" by stuntmen, he also thrilled audiences with his expert gun twirling.

In the adjoining section behind the Statue of David in the private Garden of Memory is the *Mystery of Life* work of art. It features an angel and eighteen exquisite marble dancing-girl figures. It is the burial place of **Earl Carroll,** who died in 1948.

Carroll was a competitor of Florenz Ziegfeld in featuring beautiful girls, dancers and theatrical extravaganzas. The motto of his theater, which still stands on Sunset Boulevard across from the Palladium Ballroom and is used for television filming and special shows, was "Through these portals pass the most beautiful girls in the world." Carroll was killed in a fiery plane crash. With him at the time was his beautiful companion Beryl Wallace, who had been featured in many of his shows. Her ashes are buried with him.

His probated will directed that the marble monument for himself and his "closest friend" be erected over his grave, and he provided $50,000 for it. Eaton's board wasn't pleased. Misinterpreting, the *Los Angeles Examiner* reported "Showman Earl Carroll wanted nude dancing girls (symbolizing the beauty he glorified) etched in on his marble tomb" and even suggested that Beryl would be nude, or worse, in a bathtub.

Eaton saw nothing wrong or irreligious in Carroll's desire. He said, "Other men list their achievements in driving engines, riding horses as Cavalry generals, trying cases at law, and a lot of other things. Why shouldn't a man of the theater record his measure and medium of success in his chosen field?" Eaton was on the side of truth and obligation to fulfill Carroll's last will and testament if it could be done within the bounds of good taste and without offense to anyone.

The will fight dragged on until 1951, when Superior Court Judge John Clark approved Carroll's request. To the *Examiner's* chagrin, the "nude girl" turned out to be an exquisite nude angel, a work of art purchased by the cemetery in 1916, long before Carroll's death in 1948.

In the same garden, up the steps and on the right, is a plain plaque against the wall in memory of **Atwater Kent,** 1873–1949.

Kent was a great and wealthy influence in Los Angeles, particularly in the development of the west Los Angeles suburb of Bel Air. While still a teenager in Vermont, he made the first outboard motor, as well as a portable meter to test dry-cell batteries. He revolutionized the automobile industry with a one-spark ignition and then began manufacturing radios. He then took on the entertaining side of radio as the sponsor of the *Atwater Kent Hour,* a Sunday night program of classical music.

Moving westerly, toward the Columbarium in the Sunlight Garden, we find **Harvey S. Mudd,** 1888–1955. A mining engineer and president of Cyprus Mines Corporation, he is best known for his contributions to education. One of the Claremont group of colleges (America's answer to England's Oxford) is named for him. He was a trustee of the California Institute of Technology and a founder of the Southern California Symphony Association.

In the center of a garden, surrounded by individual walled-in plots, outdoor mausoleums and verdant plants, is **Kathryn Kuhlman**, who died in 1976.

Kuhlman was a phenomenon. She toured the country for over 20 years holding prayer and healing services, most notably at the Shrine Auditorium in Los Angeles, which accommodates many thousands. Kuhlman would psychically select members of the audience and, along with her many volunteers, name and describe their ailment, then pray with them and touch and heal.

Like her predecessor, Aimee Semple McPherson, she would throw away their wheelchairs and crutches. Those touched would faint dead away into the arms of attendants, then wake up and scream in astonishment that they were well. Reputable physicians were always on stage to attest to the healing of lameness, cancer, arthritis, and miscellaneous pains. Hundreds at every service would witness her power. This writer saw her on several occasions and can attest that her healings seemed very real. Kuhlman died while recuperating from open-heart surgery. Unfortunately, like many other psychics and physicians, she couldn't heal herself.

**Abe Lyman,** 1899–1957. In the same area, near Kuhlman.

Here rests the well-known band leader of The Californians and songwriter who is remembered for his hit compositions "I Cried for You," and "What Can I Say, Dear, After I've Said I'm Sorry?" In addition to playing across the country, he was a fixture in the early days of the famous Cocoanut Grove in Los Angeles. He gave his audiences great pleasure, as did his brother, whose Mike Lyman's restaurant was well known in Los Angeles. Unknown to many, however, it was also a popular dining place for the criminal elements of the city.

Still moving westerly, through the Mystery of Life and before the Court of Christus, to the right of Abe Lyman, is actor **Warner Baxter,** 1893–1951.

He was best known for his role as the *Cisco Kid,* for which he won an Oscar in 1929. He was also the guy who, in *42nd Street,* encouraged the understudy to "Go out on stage a kid, and come back a star." Unfortunately, he endured a lobotomy (which at that time was believed to be a cure for many things) to relieve the pain of his arthritis. It relieved it, all right. Three weeks later, he was dead.

Behind Baxter rests **S.Z. "Chubby" Sakall**, 1883–1955.

Chubby's name on any movie roster assured the viewer it would be fun. One of his last roles was as the roly-poly waiter in *Casablanca*.

Beside Chubby lies **Charlie Ruggles,** 1886–1971.

With his impeccable comic timing and matchless dialogue delivery, he was a natural for sophisticated comedies. He appeared in more than 100 movies as well as theater, radio and television. His director brother, Wesley, lies next to him. Wesley was one of the original Keystone Kops.

**Humphrey Bogart,** 1899–1957. In the last columbarium on the left, on the right wall beneath the statue of a woman rests this consummate and talented actor.

Born the son of a Manhattan doctor father and a Park Avenue mother, Bogart grew up in a well-to-do social atmosphere. He attended Phillips Academy in Andover, Massachusetts. After being expelled from this fashionable school for failing five subjects and committing many infractions, he enlisted in the Navy. When he mustered out, he got caught up in the drama of Broadway and subsequently landed in Hollywood.

Bogie was not a leading-man type. Slight of stature, weather-beaten, and with a perpetual scowl, he was at the right place at the right time—Warner Brothers. At the end of the war, tough guys were the popular genre. His trademark lisp made him even more sinister. Regarding the lisp, one explanation is it that his snarl and lisp were the result of an ammunition blast aboard ship while he was in the Navy, where he sustained facial wounds and paralysis. Another theory suggests that when he was transporting a seaman to Portsmouth Naval Prison in New Hampshire, the prisoner smashed Bogart across the mouth with his handcuffs in an effort to run free. Bogart shot and wounded him but was left with a permanent scar on the right side of his upper lip and a lisp. Both theories sound plausible, so it's your choice.

Four times married, Bogart's first wife was an actress ten years older than he. That marriage lasted a year. Marriage number two, to actress Mary Philips, could not survive their separate careers. Wife number three was Mayo Methot, a tough lady with whom he fought physically, emotionally and constantly. The pair was always in the news, throwing Thanksgiving turkeys and kitchen knives at each other; battling in, and being thrown out of, nightclubs; and

Bogie?  The Gerber baby food baby?

drinking and brawling in public. This union lasted for a harrowing seven years.

Meanwhile, and surprisingly, Bogart's career was in high gear. His role in *The Petrified Forest,* on both Broadway and in the film, was successful and won for him a contract with Warner Brothers. He played gangsters, killers, ruffians and even a zombie. He said he owed his stardom to George Raft, who turned down several of the movie roles that made Bogart a star. During the filming of *To Have and Have Not* in 1944, he met and married Lauren Bacall, who was 25 years his junior. They had an uncanny chemistry that appealed to the public, and they appeared in four films together. Though never gaining superstardom during his lifetime, Bogart is today considered the most popular male star of Hollywood's Golden Age.

Theorists suggest that Bogie's morose and sometimes sulking manner was the result of his early humiliation because his illustrator mother submitted his photo to become the beautiful child for a Gerber baby food ad. Bogie got the job. As you see in the photograph, he is holding the portrait of his "pretty baby self." He was cute.

Liquor and cigarettes took Bogie out. In 1956 his esophagus and the cancer encircling it were cut away. He spent that final year at home, with his adoring and attentive Lauren, holding court with his friends. Daily he grew weaker and more skeleton-like, until one morning he slipped into a coma and was gone. While a brief memorial service was in progress at All Saints Episcopal Church, he was being cremated at Forest Lawn.

The famous gold whistle that Bacall presented to Bogie to commemorate her line from *To Have and Have Not* ("If you want me, just whistle. You know how to whistle, don't you, Steve? You just put your lips together and blow.") went with him. It has been over 40 years since Bogie's departure. Bacall has moved on with her life, still slim and beautiful, working in the theater and enjoying their children. Occasionally you can still recognize Bacall's husky voice on TV voice-overs.

**Victor McLaglen,** 1886–1959. On the other side of Bogart.

Described aptly as a British-born Wallace Beery, McLaglen was a supporting player and character lead. His gruff charm had a winning quality. A clergyman's son, he was a wheat farmer, gold prospector, pearl diver, professional boxer, and then an Army captain in World War I. In his various characterizations, he could always be counted on for a credible job. In 1935, he won the Best Actor Oscar for *The Informer*. As he became increasingly ill in his 70s he retired, then died of a heart attack two years later. His son Andrew, an assistant director, worked with his father on *The Quiet Man,* for which he won a Best Supporting Actor Oscar nomination, and later directed him in *The Abductors*.

**Judy Canova,** 1913–1983, and **Leon "Zeke" Canova**, 1898–1980. Near McLaglen.

Hollywood's hottest hillbilly, Judy as a child was part of her parents' vaudeville act. Later she became a well-known singing hillbilly and comic performer. The broad, toothy grin and shrieking yodel were her trademarks. A very likable lady, she is still fondly remembered. Her plaque reads "Love and Laughter" and her husband Leon's, who is buried with her, reads "One Who Loved." Their daughter, Diana Canova, is also an actress.

**Buddy Adler,** 1908–1960, and **Anita Louise Adler Berger**, 1915–1970. In the corner garden.

Ranking high on lists of Hollywood's most beautiful women, Anita Louise was cast in many films, usually typed as a wide-eyed innocent and/or the virginal younger sister. With these kinds of similar roles, she never could become a top-ranking star. She starred in the *My Friend Flicka* series in the 1950s and in *The Stepford Wives* in the 1970s. Her plaque reads "Love Surrounds her Beauty." She was married to Buddy Adler, the head of 20th Century Fox production, when he died at 51 of lung cancer. His most renowned film was *From Here to Eternity,* which won nine Academy Awards.

**Mary Pickford Rogers,** 1893–1979. Garden of Memory.

In a scant 26 years Mary acted, wrote, directed and produced some of the most impactful, progressive, moral, spiritual, humorous and entertaining motion pictures. One must conclude that with her tiny hands, she was a major factor in the sculpting of the new and developing industry.

When she was five, she started acting to help support the family following her father's death. She appeared in early films, a curly haired doll of a child who became a giant voice behind and in front of the camera. A capable dramatic actress and an astute businesswoman, she produced many of her own pictures. She negotiated some of the toughest starring contracts in silent film history, was one of the founders of United Artists, and was a founder of the Motion Picture Relief Fund.

She then became the leader of Hollywood society as the owner, with her husband, Douglas Fairbanks, of fabulous Pickfair, where royalty, heads of state and other important people were feted. She grew as an actress as did her fortune and circle of fans. One might say that the latter was part of her undoing. She was so adored as the golden-haired minx and as "America's Sweetheart," her fans could never accept her growing up to play mature roles. Mary, it would seem, respected this and retired early so she could be held in the memory of her friends and her fans as they wished to picture her.

Mary had three husbands, including Owen Moore and Douglas Fairbanks. But none was so enduring, loving and adoring as the handsome, talented and wonderful fellow in Hollywood who loved her for years before they married. Charles "Buddy" Rogers appeared with Mary in *My Best Girl* in 1927, and they married in 1936.

Mary was born Gladys Marie Smith on April 9, 1893, in Toronto, Canada, and died on May 29, 1979, in Santa Monica. She and Buddy were married for over 40 years. Today Buddy still lives on the Pickfair property in a new home with his beautiful second wife, Beverly. Still as handsome as the original "America's Boyfriend," he and Beverly attend many social and charitable functions in their town. He spends much of his time aiding, financially and with personal appearances, the many charities he and Mary supported. His fans are pleased that he now has someone to care for him with the same devotion and love he has given. And oh yes, he plays a lot of golf!

Mary is at peace in a garden that bears her name. The large marble monument shows a classically dressed group of three women and four small children. One woman is leaning on a horn of plenty, another is blowing on a goat's horn, while the third has her ear cupped as if trying to hear the sound. The babies appear to be happily clambering about this scene of plenty, while two doves are in flight above. Buried with Mary, is her mother, Charlotte; her sister, Lottie; and her brother, Jack. Mary, thanks for the memories.

**Terry Allen Kath**, 1946–1978. In the private garden to the left.

Kath was the lead singer and guitarist for the rock group Chicago. His marker reads "The memories of love he left on earth, all the world has shared." Rare and gifted, he was a gentle man whose riches were a symphony of songs for young and old because he cared." His marker, naturally, is decorated with musical notes.

On the day of his death he was enjoying himself at the home of a friend. As he was about to leave, he pulled an automatic pistol out of his pocket and began playing with it, twirling it around his finger. His host asked him to stop, and he answered "Don't worry, it's not loaded. See?" He mischievously put the gun to his temple, pulled the trigger, and killed himself. End of song.

Merle Oberon with David Niven — The good life on the Riviera.

**Merle Oberon Wolders,** 1917–1979 (born in Tasmania as Estelle O'Brien Merle Thompson).

Her slim figure, raven hair and exotically beautiful face marked her for stardom simultaneously on two continents during the 1930s. She was discovered by Alexander Korda, who groomed her for leads in *The Private Life of Henry VIII, The Scarlet Pimpernel,* and *The Private Life of Don Juan,* playing opposite Charles Laughton, Leslie Howard and Douglas Fairbanks, Sr.

Korda sold "shares" in Oberon's contract halfway around the world to Hollywood producer Sam Goldwyn, who immediately starred her in *The Dark Angel,* for which she was Oscar-nominated. She starred for several years in productions in Hollywood and London, always appearing in prestige performances for both employers. She and Korda were married in 1939 but divorced in 1945. She then married Lucien Ballard and continued in starring roles.

Alexander Korda's nephew Michael, who is a book publisher, fictionalized Merle's life and revealed the dark secret that she was "half-caste," in his novel *Queenie.* She later married younger Rob Wolders who, in his devotion, cared for her for the rest of her life.

**Mitchell Ayers,** 1909–1969. Left of the Court of Christus.

A renowned band leader and composer, Ayers' career ended when he was run down by a car while crossing a street in Las Vegas. With him was his friend Betty Phillips, who was seriously injured. He is missed, especially by Connie Stevens and Perry Como, for whom he worked as music director.

In Ascension Garden lies **Ted Knight,** 1923–1986. Using his given name, Theodore C. Konopka, his marker bears the masks of comedy and tragedy.

Ted Knight — "Bye, Guy."

On the bottom is the inscription "Bye, Guy," which was the trademark quote from his successful role as the pompous announcer on the *Mary Tyler Moore Show.* Not only was he an Emmy-winning performer, he also won five bronze stars in World War II. Surgery to remove a urinary tract growth was the cause of his death.

**Robert Alda,** 1914–1986. Farther down the lawn in the Ascension Garden.

He was born Alphonso Giuseppe Giovanni Roberto D'Abruzzo. A handsome vaudevillian and screen actor, Alda debuted as composer George Gershwin in *Rhapsody in Blue* in 1945. He was the son of an immigrant barber and a typical, elegant Italian. On Broadway in *Guys and Dolls,* he starred as Sky Masterson, the smooth-talking gambler and lover. He won most of the drama awards in 1950, including the Tony, Drama Critics Circle, and Donaldson. Living in Rome in the 1960s, he appeared in many European co-productions.

Another of his claims to fame is having a successful son, Alan Alda, who has starred in many movies and in the award-winning TV series *M\*A\*S\*H\*.* His daughter-in-law, Arlene, is a successful author and photographer.

**Ralph M. Byrd,** 1909–1952. In the Eventide section.

Byrd is best known for his film role as Dick Tracy in 1938.

**Suzan Ball Long,** 1933–1955. In the same area as Byrd.

Her epitaph reads "Love attends you on your new adventure." Her fans worried with her when it was revealed that a knee injury during a dance rehearsal caused a malignancy in her right leg, which resulted in amputation. Valiant and courageous, three months later she married her love, actor Richard Long, appeared in a TV drama, and made the film *Chief Crazy Horse.* Despite treatment, the cancer spread to her lungs and she passed away at age 22.

**Ethel Waters,** 1896–1977. In the Ascension Garden.

Waters is buried under a marker with the epitaph "His eye is on the Sparrow," the song that she made famous because of her sensitivity and exquisite interpretation. She was born into poverty and stole food to keep alive until she found work as a Philadelphia hotel chambermaid. Encouraged to appear in an amateur show, she was wildly received and began her career as a blues singer, known as "Sweet Mama Stringbean."

She retrieved her original name of Ethel Waters in the 1920s and starred in Harlem nightclubs and black and tan shows on Broadway. Her most famous role was as the warm, maternal cook in *The Member of the Wedding*. Fighting diabetes, she saw her weight balloon to 300 pounds. Ill and tired in her later years, she chose to stop singing. However, she sang for the Billy Graham crusades and in the White House for Richard Nixon.

> I sing because I'm happy,
> I sing because I'm free.
> His eye is on the sparrow,
> And I know he watches me.

**Adela Rogers St. Johns,** 1898–1988. In the Great Mausoleum, Columbarium of Memory, #19873.

The world's first woman reporter and certainly the most colorful, she was a soft yet tough sob sister, a hard news journalist who wrote for the Hearst Newspapers for decades. William Randolph Hearst hired her when she was still a teenager. She was a story advisor to L.B. Mayer; published short stories and several books, many of which were converted to motion pictures; was a member of the Washington press corps covering several presidents; acted as "Mother Confessor" to Hollywood in her 20s; and was a star reporter covering national and international events, crimes, trials and romances.

She scooped the Lindbergh kidnapping trial decision; was the first to interview the abdicated King of England and his Wally when they moved to the Bahamas; was the first national reporter to arrive at the scene in Honolulu after the Japanese invasion; was the first woman sportswriter and first movie magazine editor; and was influential in creating laws for women's suffrage, juvenile and prison reform, hospital regulations and the 18th Amendment. She had her own television show; taught university classes; printed the first eyewitness report on Hitler's Secret Air Force (which she

Author Margaret Burk with Adela Rogers St. Johns, the world's first and best woman reporter, on the steps of Hearst Castle.

uncovered while teaching Russian journalists to play poker) and won the Medal of Freedom Award, the highest Presidential honor given to a civilian by the United States government. And she did all this while bearing children, and raising and supporting a family as a single mother. Closely associated with Richard Nixon (he was her grocery delivery boy when she lived in Whittier), she wrote many of his speeches.

Adela had frustrating memories of her beloved grandfather's funeral. She chose a new dress that he had never seen "to cheer him up." She walked downstairs to the parlor where his wake was being held to tell him goodbye and for him to see how prettily she had dressed for him. Death was not hard for the little girl to accept as her preacher grandfather had taught her that it is just a transition, that you go to a better place. She knew he would be waiting "on the shore" for her when it was her turn to go. Immediately upon reaching the bottom stair, she was scooped up by several nervous hands and was hustled back upstairs to "dress properly."

Brokenhearted, she didn't understand that in the days of deep mourning, heavy black clothes, veils and buckets of tears, even little girls couldn't wear red!

For her own funeral, Adela wanted the ceremony to be a celebration of her life and especially requested for her granddaughters to wear, of course, red.

Books written by Adela include *Final Verdict; Honeycomb; Tell No Man; Love, Laughter and Tears; No Goodbyes; Some are Born Great;* and *First Step Up Toward Heaven* (the story of Hubert Eaton and Forest Lawn). She also wrote hundreds of short stories, profiles and newspaper specials.

Her father was the esteemed attorney Earl Rogers. She is survived by her children, Elaine St. Johns and Richard St. Johns, and several grandchildren and great-grandchildren.

In 1977, along with co-founders Margaret Burk and Marylin Hudson, Adela created Round Table West, the largest book and author club in the United States, which is still active and encouraging the reading and writing of books.

**Ed Wynn,** 1886–1966 (Isaiah Edwin Leopold). In the Columbarium of the Dawn, on the right wall, marked with a plaque reading "Dear God, Thanks. Ed Wynn."

It might be easy to imagine Ed wearing one of his comic hats, even in his resting place. His first routine as a child was clowning around with his father's hats from his millinery business. This carried over to his vaudeville days billed as "The boy with the funny hats." At the height of his career he owned 800 hats along with 300 matching coats, which he wore to portray his characters.

He performed in the Ziegfeld follies in 1914, subsequently writing, producing, directing and composing music for many of his Broadway successes. He was billed as "The Perfect Fool." He pioneered radio comedy as the popular "Texaco Fire Chief." He was not as successful in films because his character was too buffoonish. Television was a better medium for him until, at his son Keenan's insistence, he proved he could be a very serious dramatic actor. He appeared in many films, on a few occasions with Keenan. He was thrilled to be nominated for an Academy Award for his role as the dentist in *The Diary of Anne Frank.*

Twenty years later **Francis Xavier Aloysius James Jeremiah Keenan Wynn,** 1916–1986, was laid in the crypt above his father, Ed. Following in the footsteps of both his father, Ed, and his grandfather, Frank Keenan, Keenan worked in stock and on radio before signing a long-term contract with MGM. A versatile and successful actor, he could play every kind of supporting role. Later he moved to New York, where he worked almost exclusively in television, and at this time he and his father worked together in the drama *Requiem for a Heavyweight.* He published his autobiography, *Ed Wynn's Son,* in 1959, and Keenan's son Ned wrote a revealing book about growing up in their difficult show-business family called *We Will Always Live in Beverly Hills* in 1990. Continuing the family show-business tradition, another son, Tracy, is a Hollywood screenwriter.

**John Anson Ford,** 1883–1983. In the corridor near the Wynns. Dedicated to his commitment as a Los Angeles County Supervisor,

Ford developed county parks and cultural facilities and helped keep Los Angeles politics clean. His epitaph is "Public service, humanitarian."

As it is with so many clowns, **W. C. Fields'** (William Claude Dukenfield), 1880–1946, comic genius stemmed from a childhood of sadness, physical abuse and poverty. He escaped from this life at eleven and took to the streets. Juggling was his act in vaudeville; then he was signed for motion pictures (silents). He was not too successful until talkies featuring his snarling voice, bulbous nose and grouchy patter made him seem and sound funnier. He made many films that became classics, until his health gave out from his excessive drinking.

Still able to do radio work, he teamed with ventriloquist Edgar Bergen and his wooden dummy Charlie McCarthy and was immediately successful. Again tackling films, his popularity rose to greater heights, as did his drinking. Estranged from his wife and son, his later mistress, Carlotta Monti, said he was "Crotchety, larcenous, suspicious, shifty, erratic and mercenary," which was the character he played as well. He identified with Dickens' Oliver Twist's childhood and hardships and used many of his comic names based on Dickens' characters.

W.C. Fields — "All things considered, I'd rather be in Philadelphia."

Born on January 29, 1880, he died in 1946, Scrooge-like, on Christmas Day. Interred in an outside corridor to the left of the Hall of Aspirations, the marker bears only his name, but he is remembered for his voiced epitaph "All things considered, I'd rather be in Philadelphia."

**Charles W. Nash,** 1864–1948. In the Sanctuary of Courage, beneath a statue of a youth coaxing a bird to come to him. Nash was a pioneer in the

United States automobile industry. He became president of the Buick Motor Company in 1910, reorganized the company, and made it financially successful. He was elected president of General Motors Company (now Corporation) in 1912 when it was near bankruptcy. It also prospered under Nash's leadership.

Nash resigned from General Motors in 1916. He then bought an automobile firm from which he formed Nash Motors Company. He was president of the company until 1932 and board chairman until he died. The Nash firm merged with Hudson Motors in 1954 and became American Motors.

**Hermione Gingold,** 1893–1987. In the Sanctuary of the Holy Spirit. Her vault simply states her name and the inscription "Actress."

Noel Coward recognized and employed her talents as a child. Not overly beautiful, she was an excellent, serious English actress and had great screen charisma with comedic leanings. This was particularly evident in Meredith Wilson's *The Music Man,* in which she played the role of the mayor's wife. She was unforgettable as the courtesan grandmother in *Gigi,* singing the duet "I'm Glad I'm Not Young Anymore" with Maurice Chevalier. A very forthright and witty lady, when a television talk show host asked if her latest husband was dead, she answered, "That's a matter of opinion."

**Paramahansa Yogananda,** 1893–1952. The Sanctuary of Golden Slumber seems a fitting resting place for a man whose life was devoted to spirituality, meditation and yoga.

Born in Calcutta, he arrived in California in 1920 and attracted several hundred thousands of devotees to his Self-Realization Fellowship philosophy. His places of worship still remain, one in Los Angeles and others in Malibu and San Diego. He wrote *Autobiography of a Yogi,* which sold millions of copies and is still in print. It has been recorded that he had the power to slow his pulse in one wrist but not the other, suggesting that he could subordinate his body to his mind. An embalmer declared the guru's body was so devoid of impurities that it showed no signs of decay for three weeks.

**William Boyd,** 1895-1972. In the Sanctuary of Sacred Promise in a large marble drawer rests Hopalong Cassidy.

The "Hoppy" roles he played called for Western law and order, old morality and getting the girl. He was a true favorite, especially of young people. Years later, he would not appear in public for fear of disappointing his fans because he was not the strong, dashing figure they remembered.

Of the same generation and in the alcove above "Hoppy" rests **Gene Austin,** 1900-1972, whose signature was the song "My Blue Heaven," whose theme is reflected in his inscription:

> There's a new blue heaven in the sky,
> Where loving friends will never die.

More musicians seem to take center stage here. The list continues with prolific composer **Max Steiner,** 1888-1971, across the way from Austin. He is renowned for his film scores, which include *Gone With the Wind, Casablanca* and *The Big Sleep,* and for his three Academy Awards: *The Informer, Now Voyager,* and *Since You Went Away.*

**Isham Jones,** 1894-1956. Inside the Sanctuary of Twilight.

It is interesting that this former mule driver in the coal mines would become a most sensitive "Inspired bandleader and composer," as his inscription reads. "'I'll See You in my Dreams' was his song and he will always remain in the dreams of those who love him," the inscription adds. He is also remembered for "It Had to be You," "Indiana Moon," "Swinging Down the Lane" and "I Can 't Believe It's True."

**Josef Hofmann,** 1876-1957. Also in the Sanctuary of Twilight.

Born in Poland, he was a musical genius and child prodigy. He was recognized publicly at age six and made his New York debut at 11. Because of the close watch by the Society for the Prevention of Cruelty of Children, Hofmann was not allowed to play again until the age of 18. Then he once again fascinated, charmed, illuminated and delighted audiences with his exquisite playing. Because he was a short man with small hands, his talent was all the more exciting and amazing. He designed a piano with the keys slightly shaved so as to better accommodate his hands.

**Alfred Newman,** 1901–1970, Sanctuary of Eternal Prayer.

Newman composed scores for more than 250 films, winning Academy Awards for seven of them including *Alexander's Ragtime Band, With a Song in my Heart* and *Love is a Many Splendored Thing.* His epitaph reads:

"Musician in heaven"
He will take him in his arms,
He will lift him up on high,
He will show him all the charms
Of his mansions in the sky.
He will let him hear the songs
That the angel voices sing.
He will be where he belongs
In the chorus of the King.

Opposite the door to the Sanctuary of Harmony is a beautiful stained-glass window dedicated to **Marian Lemerett**. It shows a woman in her study with an open book, a globe nearby, and the Biblical injunction "Wisdom is the principle thing. Get wisdom, and with all thy getting, get understanding."

In the Corridor of Mercy is the original Tonto, **Chief Thundercloud,** a.k.a. Victor Daniels (1899–1955).

On the landing downstairs is the sarcophagus of the famous comedian **Joe Penner,** 1904–1941. He died of a heart attack in his sleep at age 37 but will always be remembered for his question, "Wanna buy a duck?"

Nearby is **Grant Withers,** 1905–1959, Loretta Young's first husband whom she married when she was 17. They made one film together, after which they were soon divorced. He died of a sleeping pill overdose.

"Auntie Em" in *The Wizard of Oz,* **Clara Blandick,** 1881–1962, rests nearby in the Columbarium of Security. Suffering from arthritis, she dressed up in a beautiful gown, made up her face, and then lay down and pulled a plastic bag over her head. She was dead at 81.

As in his movie *Life,* **Lon Chaney Sr.,** 1883–1930, lurks in an unmarked vault behind a vase. He was the son of deaf-mute parents and attributed his unique portrayals to them as he grew up trying to entertain them.

His career began as a singer/dancer, but his true calling was in playing grotesque roles in such films as *The Phantom of the Opera, The Hunchback of Notre Dame* and *The Road to Mandalay.* In *Tell It to the Marines,* he invented a way of throwing his shoulder out of joint to make him look even more bizarre. This left him permanently lame. Finishing with his swan song *The Unholy Three* he used five different voices as well as his disguises. Severely anemic, he contracted pneumonia and it was discovered that he had lung cancer. He hemorrhaged unexpectedly and died at 46.

Stepping outside of the Great Mausoleum is a beautiful monument to **Jean Hersholt,** 1886–1956. The sculpture shows a boy riding a goat and waving a dead bird over his head (inspired by the Hans Christian Andersen tale of the boy who went forth into the world to win a princess and a kingdom). Hersholt's eulogy honors him as "Actor, Cultural Leader, Humanitarian."

Considered one of the great silent film character actors, he gained recognition in the talkies as *The Country Doctor,* in which he played the Dionne quintuplet's physician. He created the role of Dr. Christian in a series of films. He received many awards, tributes and honorary degrees for his many philosophical endeavors. In 1948 the King of Denmark knighted him. Annually, a Jean Hersholt award is presented to an outstanding actor on the Academy Awards program.

Back inside is the *Last Supper Window,* which honors seven notable people. It is one of Forest Lawn's best known and most beautiful works of art copied from the original painting by

Leonardo da Vinci in Milan. A dramatic narrative about the window is given at scheduled intervals.

Easily recognized is **Gutzon Borglum,** 1867–1941.

Depicted in bronze on his plaque are the sculptures of his creations, Presidents Washington, Lincoln, Jefferson and Theodore Roosevelt on Mount Rushmore. The work was begun in 1927 when Borglum was 60 and was nearly finished when he died of a heart attack after gallbladder surgery. He was a student of Auguste Rodin and created the statue of Lincoln in the rotunda of the Capitol in Washington, D.C.

Prior to the Mount Rushmore creation, he was working on a mammoth sculpture at Stone Mountain, Georgia, showing the faces of Robert E. Lee, Jefferson Davis, Stonewall Jackson, and 1,200 other Confederate figures. Conflicts developed between the committee that had ordered the work and Borglum, causing him to be fired. He destroyed the models of the memorial and was indicted for larceny and malicious mischief. The charges were withdrawn when he completed the memorial.

"I Love You Truly," one of the best known songs ever written, was composed by **Carrie Jacobs Bond,** 1862–1946, along with 175 other compositions. The money she made from this hit was invested in an estate called *The End of the Road.* Her marker shows a piano and a concert hall.

**Rudolf Friml,** 1879–1972, has a piano on his marker also. He is sitting behind it.

Friml composed many great operettas, including *The Firefly* and *The Vagabond Kings.* He also wrote "The Indian Love Call," which Nelson Eddy sang to Jeanette MacDonald in one of their many films together. He attributed his longevity to his love of music and his physical ability to stand on his head for ten minutes, at the end of which time his wife would walk barefoot up and down his back. He said, "I'm so full of music that if I don't sit down and let some of it flow, I would burst from the pressure. Music is a gift of God. It brings so much happiness and so much peace to everyone."

Also, under the *Last Supper Window* are scientist **Robert Andrews Millikan,** 1868–1953, who won the Nobel Prize in physics for his work on electrons; California educator **Rufus B. Von Kleinsmid** and Forest Lawn Artist **Jan Styka.**

The seventh and last notable figure under the *Last Supper Window* is Forest Lawn's founder, **Hubert Eaton,** 1881–1966, who is honored by a bronze cameo. He and his family are buried in the private room on the right, which reads "Eaton" over the door. It was he who took over the small cemetery in 1913 that grew to be the unique and comprehensive cemetery park Forest Lawn. Read Forest Lawn's and Eaton's history in the chapter titled "Heaven Bound."

**Clark Gable,** 1901–1960, and **Carole Lombard,** 1908–1942. Together again, they are interred side by side in the Sanctuary of Trust.

Their simple, white marble wall crypts have brass plates bearing only their names and dates. On the other side of Carole is her mother, Elizabeth Peters, who died in a plane crash with Carole.

Masculine and rugged Gable always seemed to need mothering.

Clark Gable leaving Carole Lombard's funeral.

Having lost his own mother at ten months, he married two women many years his senior who were also helpful to his career. Josephine Dillon, his acting coach, taught him Shakespeare and acting techniques; socialite Ria Langham taught him the social graces.

Gable was rugged enough to be a man's man and women were wild for him, particularly after he portrayed Rhett Butler in *Gone With The Wind,* a role he reluctantly accepted in order to earn enough money to divorce Ria and marry Carole Lombard.

Gable with Lombard.

Born into a transient family (his father was a wildcat oil driller), Gable dropped out of school and worked with his dad in the Oklahoma oil fields for several years. Later he joined a touring stock company to learn the acting business. Under Dillon's tutelage he worked diligently and did land a few silent film roles. His role in *The Last Mile* on Broadway and as a villain in *The Painted Desert* won him attention and a contract at Warner Brothers. He starred in films with actresses Joan Crawford, Norma Shearer, Greta Garbo, Jean Harlow and Claudette Colbert, Loretta Young, Myrna Loy, Marilyn Monroe and Carole Lombard, whom he eventually married. With Vivien Leigh as Scarlett O'Hara, he played his greatest and most memorable role as Rhett Butler.

Gable began seeing Lombard after her divorce from William Powell, fell madly in love and married her. He called her Ma to his Pa. The perfect companion for him, Carole was the sportswoman he needed. She hunted, fished and farmed with him and shared zany jokes that they played on each other.

Carole first appeared on screen as a child of 13 in the silent film *A Perfect Crime.* Melodramas, Westerns, and Mack Sennett comedies followed as she evolved into the saucy, fast-talking blonde who appeared in many successful, tailor-made-for-her vehicles. She became Hollywood's top comedy actress of the 1930s. Sexy, funny and freewheeling, she could also play convincing dramatic roles.

A true star, never to be closely replicated, Carole's memorable films include *Hands Across the Table, Love Before Breakfast, My Man Godfrey* (opposite her real-life ex-husband, William Powell), *Nothing Sacred, True Confession* (cast with her frequent and highly compatible co-star Fred MacMurray), *Made for Each Other, Mr. and Mrs. Smith* and her last film, *To Be or Not to Be,* which was released after her death.

Serving the government on a war bond drive during World War II, Carole cancelled her train ticket back from Indiana to California and took a TWA DC-3 instead to get home to Clark faster. Carole's mother, a practitioner of astrology and numerology, predicted disaster and at first declined to accompany her. She did, however, reluctantly board the plane with Carole. Her premonition came true as the plane crashed into a mountain, killing all on board. Gable was on the scene almost immediately, having to watch his wife's charred body brought down from the snow-capped mountains on a stretcher pulled by mules.

In her will, written two years earlier, Carole requested that she be buried at Forest Lawn and in her "best color," white. Both requests were granted. Although burned almost beyond recognition, her gown was pure white, created by her friend and designer, Irene.

Clark was totally devastated and did everything he could to forget his sorrow. In 1942 he joined the Air Force. He served with distinction, participating in several bombing raids over Nazi Germany, achieving the rank of major and ultimately receiving the Distinguished Flying Cross. He returned to Hollywood, still very despondent. Adela Rogers St. Johns, an old friend of his, and L.B. Mayer were asked to keep him company and to find suitable films for him. He made several lackluster films until his successful *Command Decision,* then *Mogambo* with Ava Gardner (a remake of *Red Dust* that he had made with Harlow 21 years before). Both films confirmed that he was still as macho and desirable to women as ever.

After Carole's death, Gable married and divorced two women whom friends thought bore physical resemblances to Carole. The first was Sylvia Ashley (a sales girl elevated to the title of Lady upon her previous marriage to Lord Ashley), who was also married and widowed by Douglas Fairbanks. The second was Kay Spreckels, formerly married to the Spreckels sugar heir. Gable at last seemed content with Kay. He was very fond of Kay's two children, but as with Carole, he still yearned for a child of his own.

The Arthur Miller film *The Misfits,* directed by John Huston, was to be Gable's last film. On location with Montgomery Clift and Marilyn Monroe (who was married to Miller at the time), Gable performed most of his own arduous stunts. His patience on the set, waiting through Marilyn's interminable delays and absences, was considered extraordinary. The picture was a great success, but Gable wasn't around to enjoy it. He died of a heart attack at the Hollywood Presbyterian Hospital on November 16, 1960. Sadly, he never saw his son, whose birth he had so happily anticipated. John Clark Gable was born a few weeks after his father died. Clark would be proud. Like him, John Clark is an actor and rancher.

**David O. Selznick,** 1902–1965. In the Sanctuary of Trust, near Gable.

A true son of Hollywood and the film business, Selznick followed in his producer father's footsteps, producing even bigger and better pictures. He worked with top stars Gregory Peck, Katharine Hepburn, Cary Grant and Joseph Cotten, to name a few. Vivien Leigh, with Clark Gable, made one of the all-time favorites, *Gone With The Wind*, for Selznick. His other films included *A Star is Born, Intermezzo, Rebecca, Duel in the Sun* and *Tender is the Night*. One of his discoveries, more important to his personal life than his career, was the lovely star Jennifer Jones, whom he married and was still married to at the time of his death.

One of filmdom's saddest tragedies was the accidental death of **Russ Columbo,** 1908–1934, whose resting place is in the Sanctuary of Vespers.

Originally a violinist with Paul Whiteman and other orchestras that played the Cocoanut Grove in the Ambassador Hotel, he got an extra break when Whiteman put a microphone in front of him and told him to *sing*. Columbo had a crooner style not unlike Bing Crosby, who had been dismissed by Whiteman because of his uncontrolled drinking. Crosby and Columbo became competitive, and it was a toss-up as to whom the public favored. A romantic, Valentino look-alike, Columbo wrote his own signature song, "Prisoner of Love," and his career was on the upswing.

Columbo was about to become engaged to one of the screen's most popular stars, Carole Lombard. They had a spat just prior to a weekend they had planned to spend together. Carole went to Lake Arrowhead alone, and Columbo visited his best friend, Lansing Brown, who had a photography studio across from the Ambassador Hotel. As they were admiring Brown's antique gun collection, which he kept locked up in his home, Brown showed a dueling pistol to Columbo. It fired a slug that shattered Columbo's left eye, piercing his skull. He lost consciousness and died two hours later. A bereaved Carole mourned her lover and compassionately wrote postcards to his mother, who was ill, signed them "from Russ" and had them mailed from all over the world so she would think he was on tour. Russ's mother never knew that he had predeceased her.

Identical twins **Yansci "Jenny" Dolly**, 1892–1941, and **Roszika "Rosie" Dolly**, 1892–1970, rest beneath a marble statue nearby in the main hall.

Petite and beautiful with sparkling personalities, they starred in the Ziegfeld Follies and many Broadway and London musical productions, becoming international stars. Retiring at age 35, they lived on the French Riviera, returning to America years later. Jenny Dolly was frightfully disfigured in a 1933 automobile accident and, hating her fate, hung herself from a cord attached to a curtain rod. Rosie carried on, married three times, and enjoyed being feted and remembered by her many fans. Twenty-nine years later, she died from a heart attack and joined Jenny.

Showman **Sid Grauman**, 1874–1950, is a relative unknown, but his creation is known worldwide. He is found in the Sanctuary of Benediction.

One of Hollywood's greatest attractions is the forecourt of Grauman's Chinese Theater (now Mann's Chinese Theater) where a visitor must-see is crowded from morning until night. Stars from 1927 to the present have imprinted their hands, feet and even Joe E. Brown's mouth and Betty Grable's leg in the cement for posterity. Allegedly the custom began when Norma Talmadge accidentally stepped into freshly laid cement. Several hundred signatures now appear in the courtyard. To name just a few, Elizabeth Taylor, Jean Harlow, Jimmy Stewart, Dean Martin, Ginger Rogers, Gloria Swanson, George Burns, Jack Benny, Clark Gable, John Wayne, Gene Kelly, Bing Crosby, Joan Crawford, and Rhonda Fleming, who is now Mrs. Ted Mann, all autographed their imprints.

A bachelor, and a sentimental one at that, Grauman lived at the Ambassador Hotel in Los Angeles, where he also kept a suite for his mother. When she died, he retained her rooms for many months with instructions that they not be disturbed.

**Jean Harlow**, 1911–1937. Platinum blonde Jean became a sensation and star. She stood out because she had a sexy persona different from most other actresses of her era.

She was discovered by Howard Hughes and co-starred with

many of Hollywood's leading men, Gable, Cagney and Tracy, among others. Affectionately called "Baby" by cast and crew, she was a Hollywood favorite. Her romances were torrid, and her second marriage was to studio executive Paul Bern, who came to an ignominious end. Soon afterward, she died of ailments that could have been avoided if she had had proper medical treatment, which her Christian Science mother denied her. (For more information on Harlow and Bern, see the section "Death by Mysterious Circumstance.")

**Irving Thalberg,** 1899–1936. Befitting the importance and prestige of Thalberg, his private mausoleum cost $50,000 in 1936.

The "boy wonder" of the industry, he became production chief at Universal at 20 after his start as personal secretary to legendary studio founder Carl Laemmle in his New York office.

Though sickly since childhood, his genius was legendary, and at 24 he was the creative director of MGM. His rise to power was immortalized by writer F. Scott Fitzgerald in the book and film

Norma Shearer and Irving Thalberg on their wedding day.

*The Last Tycoon.* The guiding force behind the studio's top films, Thalberg demanded the highest quality in every facet of his films, while shortening time and labor with his assembly line applications. Some of his successes were *The Merry Widow, The Big Parade, Mutiny on the Bounty,* and *Romeo and Juliet.* He died at 37 during the production of *A Day at the Races.* The Academy of Motion Picture Arts and Sciences annually presents the Irving G. Thalberg Memorial Award to a producer whose work exhibits "the most consistent high level of production achievement."

**Norma Shearer,** 1900–1983. Thalberg's widow outlived him by 46 years and joined him in his crypt (as Norma Arrouge).

She became one of MGM's major stars, and although she was a fine actress, upon winning important roles and productions she incited jealousy among other female stars, even if they were not suitable for her roles. Unmistakably, however, she did receive preferential treatment as her husband lovingly groomed her for stardom. He saw that she got the best makeup, the smartest gowns and the ablest cinematographers possible. She was beautiful, but her eyes were oddly focused and she had to be photographed from just the right angle.

She was more than a capable actress, confirming Thalberg's faith in her ability. Oscar-nominated for *Their Own Desire,* she won an Oscar for her starring performance in *The Divorcee.* Other nominations she won were for her roles in *A Free Soul* (co-starring with Clark Gable), *The Barrets of Wimpole Street,* and *Romeo and Juliet* (with Leslie Howard). Yet another nomination resulted from her role in *Idiot's Delight* (again opposite Gable). She retired from the screen in 1942, living comfortably on what she and Thalberg had earned.

Shearer was remarried happily to a ski instructor, Marty Arrouge. Janet Leigh is still grateful for her influence. Upon seeing Leigh's photo at a ski resort, Shearer arranged a screen test and the rest is Cinderella-like history. Still movie-minded, she spotted handsome clothing executive Robert Evans at a swimming pool, thought he bore a strong resemblance to her late husband, and suggested him to play Thalberg in the Lon Chaney film *Man of a Thousand Faces.* Her brother, Douglas Shearer, was MGM's sound department head for decades, winning 12 Oscars for achievement on individual pictures and developing many technical innovations still being used today.

At the end of what seems like "Movie Star Hall," in a small niche, is **Jack Carson,** 1910–1963.

A Canadian import, Carson had few equals, if any, in playing the roles in which he excelled. The big, friendly, sometimes slow-witted, sometimes cynical comical actor enjoyed both semi-star and star status. He was the type who never got the girl, except in real life.

He was once married to beautiful actress Lola Albright. He died of stomach cancer on the same day as his close friend, Dick Powell.

**Theda Bara** (Theodosia Goodman), 1890–1955. Studio hype made her the daughter of an eastern ruler, one of Hollywood's first "manufactured" stars. Her movie name was an anagram for "Arab Death." Actually, she was the daughter of a tailor and got her start working as an extra in films. She was considered a sex symbol because of her exotic features and ample figure and became a hot property when she mouthed her famous line, "Kiss me, you fool!" in the silent film *A Fool There Was* in 1915. She played famous vamps such as Cleopatra, Salome, Carmen and Madame Du Barry. When her characterizations became outdated and audiences snickered, she quit the screen cold.

**Laverne Andrews,** 1913–1967. Laverne's death broke up the greatest girls' singing trio ever known.

During World War II the Andrews Sisters traveled wherever the troops were to entertain them and to bring them a bit of home. Laverne was the eldest; Maxine was born in 1916 and Patty in 1918.

Bing with the Andrews Sisters.

Patty is the only one surviving today. Maxine was still entertaining and teaching in colleges when she died in 1995. Their special songs included "Bie Mir Bist Du Schion," "Rum and Coca Cola," "I'll Be With You in Apple Blossom Time" and "The White Cliffs of Dover. "They were also featured in many films, including *In the Navy, Buck Privates, Follow the Boys, Hollywood Canteen, Road to Rio* and *Her Lucky Night.* Their big voices, big hearts and big shows will remain with American GIs forever.

In the Freedom Mausoleum, at the rear of the cemetery close to Arlington Road, rest many of Hollywood's favorites.

From the entrance and on the left is Heritage Hall. A large (almost life-size) bronze bust of **Alan Ladd,** 1913–1964, created by sculptor Lia DiLeo, is inscribed with the Edgar Guest poem:

Success

I hold no dream of fortune vast,

Nor seek undying fame.

I do not ask when life is past that many know my name.

I may not own the skill to rise to glory's topmost height,

Nor win a place among the wise,

But I can keep the right.

And I can live my life on earth

Contented to the end,

If but a few shall know my worth

And proudly call me friend.

His autograph is on his vault, and the inscription reads "Beloved Husband and Father." In the Hollywood world of six-footers, including Wayne, Gable, Cotten, Taylor and others, many doubted that five-foot, five-inch Ladd could cut it. But cut it he did, and big. His handsome, expressionless face, his deep voice and cool manner, brought a different type of hero to moviegoing audiences. Ladd's greatest champion was his agent, Sue Carol, who also became his wife.

His first studio experience was as a grip at Warner Brothers. He began acting in local theatrical productions, radio shows and small film roles. With films such as *A Gun for Sale, Paper Bullets,* and

*Captain Caution,* he rose to the top ranks, appearing in westerns, war dramas and crime films. Two of his best roles were in *Shane* and in Harold Robbins' *The Carpetbaggers.* Son David became an actor and son Alan Ladd Jr. is a successful movie producer and studio executive.

Ladd lived the last years of his life in Palm Springs. He had opened a fashionable gift and hardware store there in the 1950s, and it still bears his name. Responding to the friendliness of that small village, Ladd could often be seen in his front yard waving to his friends passing by. Successful career, good life, devoted family—one can only wish that his death, caused by an overdose of alcohol and sedatives at 51, was accidental. With him in the vault, of course, is Sue.

**Clara Bow,** better known as the "It Girl," 1905–1965, has the lower vault (under the Ladds) with her husband, **Rex Bell,** 1903–1962.

A kid from the poor side of Brooklyn, born of an abusive father and off-balance mother, she longed to escape. She did when she won a *Movie Magazine* talent contest, which brought her to Hollywood and a film contract. Clara's high spirits and exuberance were a tonic for an America just pulling out of a depression, to say nothing of her lack of pretense and undisguised sexual openness. Not an act, this was the real Clara. Some of her films were *Mantrap, Kid Boots, Fascinating Youth, Children of Divorce, Get Your Man* and *Red Hair.* She ended 1927, her peak year, in the first Oscar-winning Best Picture, *Wings.* This is where she met a "bit player," Gary Cooper, who became her beau. Her footloose behavior resulted in several scandals and caused the studios no little problem. Her torrid romances with many lovers, including director Victor Fleming and Gary Cooper, whom she had stupefied, were legion.

In 1927 she starred in the film *It,* which dramatized author Elinor Glyn's theory that some women possessed a certain indefinable, irresistible magic, called "It," a quality that Bow had in spades. The consummate Jazz Baby, her bobbed red hair, bee-stung lips, loose lingerie and tiny, curvaceous body inspired women everywhere to mimic her style. Thus, the Roaring Twenties were born.

Clara Bow — The "It" Girl.

Her extremely public private life kept her in the headlines, but rumors that she had entertained the entire USC football team one night were wildly exaggerated. She did party with them in her home, but the fact was that these young men had great affection for Clara. One late night, after she had too much to drink, a taxi driver dropped her off at a hotel. The manager had, once again, put her to bed in a suite. The USC team was celebrating a victory at the same hotel, and when they learned she was there, they took turns sitting outside her room making sure that no one bothered her. This story was later told by a team member, Marion Michael Morrison, a.k.a. John Wayne.

Clara's meteoric success in silent films didn't continue with the arrival of the talkies because she was ill at ease about her Brooklyn accent, and it showed. Her career also suffered disastrous results when it was discovered that her secretary had been sharing her bank account as well as her clothes and boyfriends. Clara fired her, and the secretary, Daisy DeVoe, retaliated by publicly discussing Clara's foibles and sexual exploits. Clara became extremely depressed, put on weight and lost the effervescence that was her trademark. She and Paramount parted.

Clara married the very handsome and respectable cowboy actor Rex Bell. The couple moved to his Nevada ranch, where she enjoyed her life and raised two sons. In 1932, she lost weight, moved to the Fox lot and gave great performances in *Call Her Savage* and *Hoopla* (both in sound). However, the Roaring Twenties became a whisper, and filmgoers moved on to new fads and fancies and passed her by.

Clara lived out her life in Hollywood. She was a severe insomniac, and late nighters could often hear her calling in to radio stations to visit with talk-show program hosts and announcers. Marilyn Monroe was a great fan of Clara's and called on her often for advice regarding her own sexy roles.

Husband Rex Bell, long in love with Clara, stood by her and gave her the only stability she ever had. He was elected lieutenant governor of Nevada and in 1962, while campaigning for the governorship of that state, collapsed and died of a heart attack. Clara lived three years longer.

Also in the Freedom Mausoleum is **Nat "King" Cole,** 1919–1965.

A preacher's son, he was born in Montgomery, Alabama, and moved to Chicago with his family when he was four. He became a citizen of the world by virtue of his talent and died in a hospital in Santa Monica of lung cancer. A natural at the piano, he played "Yes, We Have No Bananas" when he was a tot, and immediately his parents provided lessons. He started his training with classic music such as Bach, Beethoven, and Rachmaninoff. As a teenager, he learned from radio and records, then created his own style, which has been widely copied.

At 17, he had finished high school, married and formed his King Cole Trio, pioneering chamber jazz. During the 1940s, he recorded his own hits, "Sweet Lorraine," "Nature Boy," and, based on his father's sermons, "Straighten Up and Fly Right," all of which have become classics and lasted through the years. It was in a little cafe on Vine Street in Hollywood where Nat's trio was playing that his singer did not show up. The club manager said his audience expected to hear some vocals, so Nat sang what he thought wasn't too good, but was his best. History was made that night. He became renowned for his voice and has since sold millions of records and albums including the hits "Unforgettable," "When You Fall in Love" and "They Tried to Tell Us We're Too Young."

He was married for the second time to Maria Hawkins, a young singer with the Duke Ellington Band. She was from a wealthy and social family who helped to manage Nat's career and put his affairs in order.

The couple moved into Hancock Park, a staid, wealthy and fashionable neighborhood in Los Angeles. At that time, Nat was welcome in all of the finest hotels and clubs in the world. However, it is said that a committee was formed to tell Nat that they did not want any "undesirables" living in their community. His answer? "If any move in, I'll let you know."

When his daughter, Natalie, was 11 years old, she sang with her father and Barbara McNair in the play "I'm With You" at the Greek Theater. She later built a successful singing career with her hit records *Dangerous, Inseparable,* and *Thankful.* She has won Grammy Awards, American Music Awards and Soul Train Awards.

Natalie watched her father die from smoking-related diseases. She was a smoker herself and always said she wanted to quit. Perhaps by now, she has.

As musicians and performers live on by virtue of their work, so Nat has an even greater popularity in posterity. Natalie, through some magical and technical genius, used the tracks of Nat singing his hit, "Up" and mixed her voice with his to produce a duet. She did it again with "Unforgettable," which became another big hit, and Nat King Cole lives on, not only with his own body of work but also with this tribute from his daughter.

Natalie said, "My father was as natural a man as you could ever meet. If God gives me success, I hope I can handle it with as much grace and humility as he did."

Still in the Freedom Mausoleum, between Nat "King" Cole and the Burnses, we find the exquisite **Jeanette MacDonald, 1901–1965.**

With her operatic voice, she made movie operettas popular, along with her co-star, Nelson Eddy. Together they starred in *Naughty Marietta, Rose Marie, Maytime, The Girl of the Golden West, Sweethearts, New Moon, Bitter Sweet* and *I Married an Angel.* All were costume epics that made the pair heroic to their international fan clubs, clubs that still exist and celebrate their lives and films.

She was first a Broadway chorus girl—until her voice was heard! Her first film was with the French singing sensation, Maurice Chevalier, in *The Love Parade.* She then made several other films (before she teamed up with Eddy) that made her one of the most popular stars of the early talkie era. She also co-starred with Clark Gable and Spencer Tracy in *San Francisco,* a hugely successful 1936 drama in which she sang the title that became the Bay City's unofficial theme song.

Easing up on film-making, Jeanette sang frequently on stage and in concert for years but eventually had to stop because of a heart ailment that contributed to her passing. Although she was often mistakenly thought to be married to her co-star Eddy, Jeanette was married for 28 years to Gene Raymond. Eddy and Raymond bore a strong resemblance to each other. One of her last public appearances was to sing "Ah, Sweet Mystery of Life" at her mentor, Louis B. Mayer's, funeral in 1957. Mayer was known to have had a romantic interest in Jeanette.

**George Burns and Gracie Allen.** "Make that Gracie Allen and George Burns," George told a camera crew at Gracie's tomb a few days before his death.

He visited every month to be with his "Googie." He always said he was going to change the name of their act and give Gracie top billing when he died. Gracie, 1906–1964, and George (Nathan Birnbaum), 1896–1996, share a crypt in the Freedom Mausoleum. He reached the venerable age of 100, and little did he know he would be joining her soon. George's devoted fans expected him to live forever, and but for an unexpected fall, he might have.

George grew up on the Lower East Side of New York City. By the age of seven, he knew that singing, soft-shoe dancing and telling jokes was what he wanted to do with his life. He dropped out of school in the fourth grade and at the age of 13, he bombed with his first vaudeville act. At 16, George took up cigar smoking as part

George Burns — "Say Goodnight Gracie." Goodnight George.

of his act, and it became his trademark. At 17 he married his partner, Hannah Siegel, because her parents wouldn't let their single daughter go on the road unmarried. They quickly divorced when the gig ended and then a jobless 17-year-old dramatic artist entered George's life. She was Gracie Allen.

In their first routine, Burns had Gracie feed him straight lines so he could tell the jokes, but nobody laughed. Instead, they broke up over Gracie's straight lines. From that first day on, George became the straight man, Gracie did the jokes and got the laughs. It went this way:

George: "Did the nurse ever drop you on your head when you were a baby?"

Gracie: "Oh, we couldn't afford a nurse. My mother had to do it."

George and Gracie married in 1926 and began a love affair that continued beyond her death in 1964 and no doubt continues beyond his. Their careers included vaudeville, radio and films, and they became more popular each year. In 1950, they had their big TV series hit, *The Burns and Allen Show,* which ran through 1957. In 1958, Gracie retired to spend time raising their two adopted children, Ronnie and Sandra. George tried two more TV series alone, but neither had the magic of working with Gracie. Then he settled down to being himself, enchanting his audiences with a combination of one-liners, a little soft-shoe and his way with a wealth of old songs.

In 1975, he played in the movie *The Sunshine Boys* (replacing Jack Benny, who had died), and this won him a Best Supporting Actor Oscar. He followed this up with more films, including the highly successful *Oh God!* series.

"I got the hook a lot. But I'd rather be a flop in a business I love than a success in felt hats," he said. "All I ever wanted was to be with Gracie and in show business," which he still was at 100.

**Dorothy Jean Dandridge,** 1922–1965, in the Columbarium of Victory.

This beautiful actress and singer was vibrant, talented and ultimately, tragic. A former child performer, she was the first black woman to sing at the Waldorf-Astoria's Empire Room, first to appear on the cover of *Life* magazine and first to be nominated for an

Academy Award for Best Actress. *Carmen Jones, Island in the Sun* and *Porgy and Bess* were three of her great roles. At the time of her death, she was negotiating for two films and was arranging for singing engagements in several countries. Hers was a seemingly successful career, but her personal life was troubled. Her death was a mystery. Perhaps answers can be found in her autobiography, *Everything and Nothing.*

**Clara Ward**, 1924–1973, and **Gertrude M. Ward**, 1901–1981, in the Sanctuary of Commandments.

This seems a fitting place for Clara, who first sang with her sister, Willa, and her mother, evangelist Gertrude, in black churches. Their first commercial appearance was in 1957 at the Newport Jazz Festival. Concerts and TV followed.

**Joe E. Brown**, 1891–1973, Outside the Great Mausoleum.

The family monument shows a classically dressed man and woman with their three small children, the smallest resting on

the father's shoulders. It was originally built as a memorial to Brown's son, Captain Don Evan Brown, Commander of the First Squadron, Sixth Ferrying Group, Air Transport Command, Army Air Force, Long Beach. His plaque reads, "Killed in line of duty, October 8, 1942, Palm Springs CA."

Greatly respected in the film industry, Joe E.'s marker reads, "Beloved husband, understanding father, cherished friend. His courage in the face of trouble, his modesty in the rewards of triumph won the love and esteem of people all over the world. His personal integrity

Joe E. Brown — "Nobody's perfect."

and devotion to all people

reflected the love of the Saviour into whose hands his life was given."

The death of his beloved son almost 30 years before his own created the pain the popular comedian lived with the rest of his life. A former circus clown, vaudevillian and stage star, who also played and had a passion for semi-pro baseball, he made his first film in 1928. Continuing his movie career, he became a star with *Sally, On With the Show, The Tenderfoot, You Said a Mouthful, Elmer the Great* and *Alibi Ike.* In his fey way he was successful as Flute in Warner's all-star production of Shakespeare's *A Midsummer Night's Dream.* He was the perfect Captain Andy in the stage and screen versions of *Showboat,* and he was ideally cast in *Around the World in 80 Days* and *It's a Mad, Mad, Mad, Mad World.*

He alternately played soft-spoken Milquetoasts, loudmouthed egotistical rubes and the forgotten man and was known for his loud bellow, slow double take and breathtaking pratfalls. He was an original.

Moviegoers will never forget his role in *Some Like It Hot,* 1959, with Marilyn Monroe, Tony Curtis and Jack Lemmon. Lemmon, posing as a girl musician hiding out from gangsters, romanced Brown, the indulged millionaire, who fell for him/her. Racing across water in a fast speedboat at the end of the movie, he told Lemmon he wanted to marry "her" and would take her to meet "MaMa." Lemmon, having some misgivings said, "She won't like me."

"Oh yes, she will."

"But I smoke and drink."

"It's all right, she'll like you."

Unable to convince Brown, Lemmon shouted, "But I'm a boy!"

To which Brown answered, "Nobody's perfect."

Brown wrote his autobiography in 1959, titled (as was his philosophy) *Laughter is a Wonderful Thing.*

**Aimee Semple McPherson,** 1890–1944, in front of the Great Mausoleum.

Guarded, as she was in life, Aimee's monument has a heavy chain supported by four steel posts. Two kneeling angels bow their heads in respect for the woman who was considered "God's Little Child."

As a young girl she marched with the Salvation Army, but as a teenager she chose to follow a theatrical career instead. Even though this choice didn't stay open to her for long due to her youthful marriage to Pentecostal preacher Robert Semple, the combination created the adult Aimee, as the public and her devoted fans knew her. Robert took her to China where they served as missionaries until he contracted malaria and died. Aimee, pregnant with her first child, Roberta, left there after her daughter's birth.

Living with her mother in New York, Aimee became restless and soon married Harry McPherson. Son Rolf was born, and she decided she again wanted to be an evangelist. Not being of the tent and gospel persuasion, McPherson took off. Aimee, mother Minnie, and the two children wended their way to California, adventurously preaching along the trail, in an Oldsmobile with gold letters that asked, "Where will you spend Eternity?" Aimee had found her calling.

Six weeks after her arrival in Los Angeles, she was winning an enthralled audience in tents. She then moved into Philharmonic Hall, which accommodated thousands, and she filled it. Minnie was the financial strategist. Her astute money management soon allowed the building of Angelus Temple in 1923. It had a prize, a massive 30-foot golden organ, and it seated 5,300. Known as the Four Square Gospel Church, it is still in operation.

Aimee wowed her audiences. People from all states in the Union were flocking to golden California and were ripe for the small-time gospel that Aimee fervently expounded. She preached an

Aimee Semple McPherson — "Give your life to Jesus, and your money to me."

old-fashioned combination of hellfire, brimstone and salvation that was irresistible. On her "call" to "Give your life to Jesus," people would overflow the aisles, coming to the altar to be saved. They came particularly to receive her healings, when they would throw away their wheelchairs and crutches. Proof of these miracles was in an upper room at the temple, open to the public, which housed hundreds of castoff physical aids.

She broadcast daily from her in-house radio station, KFSG ("Kalling Four Square Gospel"). For her Sunday sermons, blonde Aimee, in formal glorious white (as in "bride"), would walk down the aisle. She descended the ramp toward the altar on the arms of two very attractive young men, to the tumultuous applause and standing ovation of the audience. At the end of her rousing sermon, which dramatically featured angels, disciples, sinners, and even Jesus, she would request, "Get your offerings ready. I only want folding money. I don't want to hear the rattle of coins."

They obeyed and the church and Aimee prospered. With it all, Aimee did great good for a people just coming out of a national emotional and monetary depression. She raised their spirits and hopes. She had become one of America's icons. She was widely accepted by the kind of enthusiasm later accorded such stars as Presley and Sinatra. But this wasn't enough for Aimee.

With the appetites of a tempestuous, spirited and sexual woman (by then long divorced from McPherson) she entered into an affair with her radio engineer, Ken Ormiston. Escaping her mother's eye and wrath, they took a holiday in Europe, returning only when newspapers reported her unlicensed sojourn. She didn't stay home for long. A few weeks later Aimee "disappeared."

The world was searching for her, and a few claimed to have spotted her in other states and in a local hotel. Thousands held forth on the beaches of Southern California (particularly at Ocean Beach) praying for her or her body to return. Only her mother was suspicious and enraged. Aimee reappeared in Agua Prieta, Arizona, with her unbelievable (except by her devotees) tale of the kidnapping. She was not distraught; not a hair was out of place, and apparently there had been no struggle. Aimee and mother Minnie were indicted for perjury, suggesting the whole escapade was bogus. Radio and newspapers had a field day. They were never convicted because too much public opinion was in favor of the"high priestess."

Aimee's explosive and frustrated personality caused her to break with mother Minnie and later with daughter Roberta. She maintained a relationship with son Rolf.

Either this world was too much for Aimee or the other way around. In her early 50s, she took an overdose of seconal, hopefully accidental, and the lights went out on this colorful figure.

**Frank Baum,** 1856–1919, and his wife, **Maud Gage Baum,** 1861–1953, in Section G.

Baum's fourteenth book about the fictional country of Oz, became the world-renowned and beloved *The Wonderful Wizard of Oz.* With its success, Baum moved his family to Hollywood, built a retreat he named "Ozzott," and enjoyed his aviary, which housed several hundred birds. His epitaph was, "Now we can cross the shifting sands." Could it be he was referring to his beloved Oz?

Builders of Southern California can be found in Forest Lawn. In the Iona section is **Eli Clark**, 1847–1931, his wife **Luci,** 1851–1942, and her brother, **General Moses A. Sherman,** 1853–1932. Their monument shows a kneeling woman looking heavenward with two children praying.

Sherman and Clark built a number of railways, which became part of the Southern Pacific rail system, on various parcels of land they owned. They were instrumental in creating industry and housing at the turn of the century.

**The Duncan Sisters—Rosetta,** 1901–1959, in Whispering Pines; and **Vivian,** d. 1986, in Cathedral Slope.

They were the world famous "Topsy and Eva." Touring America and Europe with their *Uncle Tom's Cabin,* they became international delights. Their theme song, "Rememb'ring," appears on Rosetta's tombstone. The inscription continues, "One of the world-famed Duncan sisters of musical comedy success 'Topsy and Eva.' One blessed with a great talent to evoke laughter and pathos. The immortal compositions with her sister Vivian will long be remembered. Established forever in our hearts." Rosetta was Topsy, the one in blackface, and Vivian played the pretty little white girl. The sisters continued with films and club appearances until Rosetta was fatally injured in an automobile accident. They were separated in death when Vivian died in 1986 and was buried in the Cathedral Slope section.

Nearby is **Jane Darwell,** 1879–1967, who was frequently seen as a motherly type character actress. Her last role was as the Bird Woman in *Mary Poppins.*

**Susan Peters,** 1921–1952. Her life was cut short when, hunting with her husband, actor Richard Quine, her rifle discharged accidentally. It lodged a bullet in her spine. She continued her career from a wheelchair in roles such as Amanda in *The Glass Menagerie* and Elizabeth Barrett in *The Barretts of Wimpole Street.* Plucky though she was, her struggle was too difficult. Her doctor said she lost the will to live.

Jack Oakie — He had a million friends.

**Jack Oakie** (Lewis Delany Offield), 1903–1978, on the hill.

The actor Oakie, in movies as in real life, was the best friend, the guy next door who takes the blame and never gets the girl, all the while smiling, wisecracking and having a party. Everybody liked Jack and he had a million friends. He was one of the screen's most expert second bananas and a genuine scene stealer. Contracted at various times to most of the major studios, Jack also turned in some credible starring roles, including *The Fleet's In, College Humor,*

*Hit the Deck, Once in a Lifetime, That Girl from Paris, Last of the Buccaneers* and several musicals with Lucille Ball and Betty Grable. Increasing deafness finally forced him out of the business. His widow, Victoria Horne, published his memoirs, *Jack Oakie's Double Takes.* A most devoted wife and widow, Victoria keeps Jack's memory alive by celebrating every birthday and holiday and by inviting people frequently to retrospectives of his films. His epitaph reads:

In a simple double take
Thou hast more than voice e'er spake.
When you hear laughter, that wonderful sound,
You know that Jack Oakie's around.

**Lawrence Tibbett,** 1896–1960, down the hill to ground marker 794.

His marker reads "Beloved in life, in memory." This opera star went from a life of utter despair as a child to the highest pinnacles of success as an adult. It has been said of him that because his great-aunt and uncle planted the first navel orange tree in California, his family was "firmly rooted in the state" long before his birth.

His youth was shaken when he was only seven. His father, a deputy sheriff in Bakersfield, was shot and killed while pursuing the notorious Wild Jim McKinney. He later moved to Los Angeles where he studied voice and music.

In 1922 he moved to New York where he auditioned for the Met. He was not an immediate success, but when he played the part of Ford in Verde's *Falstaff,* his second act monologue brought down the house in one of the wildest and longest displays of audience approval in Metropolitan history. The audience gave him a standing ovation for 15 minutes. He became a favorite of the Met and of other audiences. Tibbett had over 70 roles in his repertoire and introduced many new operas that stayed in the Met's schedule on the basis of Tibbett's great performances.

Greatly respected for his immense vocal range and beautiful baritone voice, he studied seriously and brought originality and character to his roles. Hollywood beckoned him and he received an Academy Award nomination for *The Rogue Song* and starred in *New Moon,* both in the film and on the Broadway stage. He was unique in the world of opera for his forays into less operatic music. One of his specialties was "On the Road to Mandalay." He also pioneered operas to be sung in English, proving that this could draw a wider audience to opera.

A strong advocate of labor unions, he helped to form the American Guild of Musical Artists and the American Federation of Radio Artists. His final performance was replacing Pinza in *Fanny* in 1956. Retired for four years, he died two days after undergoing surgery for an old head injury.

**Gus Kahn,** 1888–1941, near Tibbett. Lyricist Kahn wrote many popular songs:"My Blue Heaven,""Mammy," and "Whoopee," to name a few.

Russian actress **Madame Alla Nazimova,** 1879–1945, while making American films, was the head of a lesbian cult "endeavoring to promote religion, peace and prosperity."

On a lower floor, in the Sanctuary of Gratitude, is **Francis X. Bushman**, 1883–1966. The "handsomest man in the world" was considered King of the Movies, and indeed he was, as he made over 400 films.

Together as brothers and entertainers, the **Marx Brothers** were somewhat separated in death. Chico, Harpo and Gummo rest in Forest Lawn; Groucho is in Eden Memorial Park. Zeppo was not interred; he was cremated and his ashes were scattered at sea.

**Elizabeth Louise Young,** 1910–1994. Graceland #3, Lot 5905.

Father did know best when, after an eight-year courtship, Robert Young married his Betty. Sweethearts in high school, they remained affectionate friends while he continued his education at the Pasadena Playhouse and she studied at the University of Southern California. Betty became a professional singer, playing many of the leads in college plays.

Meanwhile "Bobbie," as she always called him, was discovered for his acting ability. He appeared in more than 100 films but

Betty Young with Bob, her love for 70 years.

became unforgettable starring in both *Father Knows Best* and *Marcus Welby, M.D.* Four lovely daughters came from this union. Betty was known for her charm, warm friendship, enthusiasm, love of life, and love of Bob.

In days when leading men were more attractive if single, Bob and Betty eloped and were married in nearby Santa Ana by a Justice of the Peace. Having no witnesses, the judge produced two men who agreed to stand up for them at the ceremony. They spent their one honeymoon evening dancing at the Cocoanut Grove, where they were greeted with headlines in the *Herald Examiner* announcing their marriage. The two helpful witnesses were reporters! Bob was sure his career had ended on the spot. Not so, however. His career and their wedded bliss lasted more than 62 years.

When she was still a new bride, a salesman talked Betty into buying six cemetery lots in Forest Lawn on the installment plan. She always insisted that she was a brilliant real estate investor because the value of the property increased astronomically over the decades.

People often asked if she missed her singing career. She always answered, "No, I simply gave up one career for another." Her career was Bob and their girls.

**Also at Forest Lawn, Glendale:**

**Minta Durfee Arbuckle,** 1889–1975, who never stopped believing in her husband Fatty's innocence.

**Bob Burns,** 1893–1956, the actor who achieved fame by inventing an instrument, the bazooka, which made a flatulent sound. The famous army antitank weapon was named after it.

**Michael Curtiz,** 1888–1962, director of *Life with Father, White Christmas,* and *Casablanca,* which brought him an Oscar.

**George G. "Buddy" DeSylva,** 1896-1950, the lyricist who gave the world "April Showers," "Varsity Dog," "Look for the Silver Lining" and "You're the Cream in my Coffee."

**Lloyd C. Douglas,** 1877-1951, physician and author of the best-selling novels *The Robe, Magnificent Obsession* and *The Big Fisherman,* which were all made into films.

**Sydney Greenstreet,** 1879-1954, stage and character actor, best known for roles in *The Maltese Falcon* and *Casablanca.*

Others include **Marlin Hurt,** 1906-1946, the white male who played Beulah, the black maid on *Fibber McGee and Molly.* **Bert Kalmar,** 1884-1947, lyricist who wrote "Three Little Words" and "Who's Sorry Now?" **Marie MacDonald,** 1923-1965, model turned actress, nicknamed "The Body." **Fifi D'orsay,** 1904-1983, Canadian leading lady during the 1930s. **Franklin Pangborn,** 1889-1958, most frequently typecast as the disconcerted hotel clerk. **Dimitri Tiomkin,** 1899-1979, the Russian composer who garnered Oscars for his scores for *High Noon, The High and the Mighty* and *The Old Man and the Sea.* **Richard Whiting,** 1891-1938, the composer of *'Til We Meet Again* and *Beyond the Blue Horizon* and father of songstress Margaret Whiting. **William Wyler,** 1902-1981, the director who helped form the Un-American Activities Committee investigations; he won Academy Awards for *Mrs. Miniver* and *The Best Years of Our Lives.* **Joe Yule,** 1894-1950, a vaudevillian and also Mickey Rooney's father.

## Artwork at Forest Lawn, Glendale

*Baptism of Jesus*—bas relief in the Triumphant Faith Terraces.

*The Christmas Window*—stained glass located in the Holy Terrace in the mausoleum's grand staircase.

*Christus*—located in the Court of Christus. A recreation of Bertel Thorvaldsen's original.

*Church of the Recessional*—inspired by Rudyard Kipling's church of St. Margaret in Rottingdean, England.

*The Crucifixion*\*—by Polish artist Jan Styka, located in the Hall of Crucifixion-Resurrection.

*David*—full-size Carrara marble recreation, located in The Court of David.

*Duck Baby*—Forest Lawn's first statue.

*Durer Window*—Medieval stained glass dating back to the 13th century, created by Albrecht Durer.

*The Finding of Moses*—statue and pool.

*Jesus, Mary and John*—mosaics in the Triumphant Faith Terraces. Reproduction of Raphael's original.

*La Pieta*—replica of Michelangelo's original, carved from pure white Carrara marble, located in the Great Mausoleum.

*Last Supper Window**—in the Memorial Court of Honor in the Great Mausoleum. Recreation of Leonardo daVinci's work.

*Little Church of the Flowers*—counterpart of the little English church at Stoke Poges.

*Madonna of Burges*—exact recreation of Michelangelo's original. Located in the Great Mausoleum.

*Medici Madonna and Child*—located in the Great Mausoleum.

*Mystery of Life*—located next to the Court of David. A statuary group, it is an original work by Ernesto Gazzeri, depicting the meaning of life.

*The Resurrection**—located in the Hall of Crucifixion-Resurrection. Painting by Robert Clark.

*The Signing of the Declaration of Independence*—mosaic located in the Court of Freedom.

*Temple of Santa Sabina*—created in the fifth century; original site was in Rome, Italy.

*Transfiguration*—mosaic in the Triumphant Faith Terraces. Reproduction of Raphael's.

*Twilight* and *Day and Night*—featured in the Memorial Court of Honor in the Great Mausoleum, a recreation of Michelangelo's work.

*George Washington* and *The Republic*—statues located in the Court of Freedom.

*Wee Kirk O' The Heather*—Annie Laurie's love story is told in the stained-glass windows of this reproduction of her church in Scotland. Mementos of Maxwelton, her home, are also here.

In the Forest Lawn museum there are dozens of finely crafted bronze and marble statues. The Freedom Mausoleum reflects our great American heritage in rare marble, statuary and stained glass.

*The Crucifixion, Resurrection* and *Last Supper Window* complete *The Sacred Trilogy.*

Author Margaret Burk and her husband Harry on their wedding day at the Ring of Aldryth in the Church of the Recessional, Forest Lawn, Glendale.

# 20

## From the Cradle to the Grave

It can be a comforting thought to know that in a lifetime, a myriad of comforting and celebratory arrangements can be adroitly accommodated at Forest Lawn with simply a phone call.

Beginning as a place to respectfully say farewell to a loved one, a place for family and friends to celebrate a life, or a place for the living to find solace within the beauty of its spacious gardens appear to be Forest Lawn's goals.

Babies are featured in much of Forest Lawn's statuary, and newborns are welcomed here for christenings. Charming and beautiful locations are available to celebrate the beginning of earthly life, and provisions are made for spiritual beginnings as well.

Weddings in a cemetery?

One day in 1922, a couple strolled about the park, enjoying the gardens, the swans and the Duck Baby's pond. They were engaged to be married, and the Little Church of the Flowers (Forest Lawn's first church) seemed to invite them inside. Cora Willis said to her fiancée, Archie Howes, "I want to be married here."

They went to a man in charge who called Dr. Eaton, knowing full well that a wedding in a cemetery wasn't a good idea. "This is a cemetery," he insisted to the couple. But instead of declining their request, Dr. Eaton let out a whoop. This was the innovation that he had been waiting for—the realization that Forest Lawn lifted people's spirits and was a happy place.

The Little Church of the Flowers set the pattern for the other four churches that were subsequently built. They are replicas of some of the most cherished of churches, with warm woods, colorful stained-glass windows, beautiful flowers and singing birds inside. They provide a setting to feed the senses and to make a bride feel happy and look beautiful.

So from this beginning, Forest Lawn became the first of all

wedding sites to hire a wedding consultant. They were in the business, and slowly the business grew. One wedding was performed in 1922, two or three more in 1923, five or six in 1924, and twenty or thirty in 1926. By 1927, the originality had worn off, the newspapers ceased to cover the events and a new tradition had been born. To date, over 70,000 people have been married at Forest Lawn.

Before long, Forest Lawn could offer weddings in their three beautiful churches: the Little Church of the Flowers, Wee Kirk of the Heather and the largest, The Church of the Recessional. Presently, eight nondenominational churches are available in the five locations. The sacrament of marriage in beautiful and loving surroundings offers an emotional and fulfilling experience and a serenity that's unexplainable. One of your authors knows; she was married there.

# 21

◆

## Forest Lawn, Hollywood Hills

Eaton was gratified by the success and acceptance of the original Forest Lawn Cemetery in Glendale. The idea of providing funerals and related services and places of rest to other Los Angeles neighborhoods seemed to be the logical next step for Hubert Eaton's company. So it was that the beautiful Hollywood Hills Park came into being.

The emphasis here is on American history, and within its acres one can experience the rich traditions of the North American continent dating back to 1200 B.C. A Toltec warrior introduces the Plaza of Mexican Heritage, which contains 18 replicas of artifacts from early Mexico. The Museum of Mexican History includes data, photos, sculpture and costumes from our continent's earliest civilizations.

Without going near Philadelphia you can experience *The Spirit of '76*, one of 25 historic scenes from the *Birth of Liberty* mosaic. Without visiting Italy, you'll be able to see *Moses,* Michelangelo's reproduced masterpiece. Thomas Jefferson is here, as is Abraham Lincoln. You can quietly pray in the Church of the Hills, a duplicate of the church where poet Henry Wadsworth Longfellow worshiped. You can even visit his study!

As you'd expect in a Hollywood cemetery, many Hollywood celebrities rest here, including **Lucille Ball,** 1911–1989, in the Columbarium of Radiant Dawn.

Few people are aware, but Ball spent 20 years slaving in the trenches making "B" movies, doing bit parts, and appearing with actors such as Eddie Cantor, the Three Stooges and the Marx Brothers. After a diet of musicals, comedies and a few dramas, she and her Cuban-born husband, Desi Arnaz, formed a television production company, Desilu, to produce the sitcom series *I Love Lucy.* The rest is history. The public quickly recognized Lucy's comedic gifts. She was a physical as well as a quick-witted comedienne.

Lucille Ball — We all loved Lucy.

While her series was building a huge audience, Desilu also became one of the major suppliers of programming to the networks. Desi himself provided many innovative ideas to the medium. Desilu bought the old RKO studios, and when Ball and Arnaz divorced in 1960, she continued to run the studio herself, as well as continuing the *Lucy* sitcom for another 12 years. In total, Lucy received four Emmy awards for *I Love Lucy.*

In the 1960s, she made a few not too successful films, including *The Facts of Life* with Bob Hope. Her last picture, *Mame,* was released in 1974. Lucy is a treasure, an icon, certainly the most beloved comedienne of her time. *Lucy* continues to be shown around the world in syndication. Lucy's children, Lucie and Desi Jr., got their start in her sitcoms. Today both still maintain successful careers in show business, Lucie in Broadway musical hits and Desi Jr. as a rock star and actor.

**Joseph Frank "Buster" Keaton,** 1895–1966. On the outside lawn along the right wall.

He received his nickname at age six months, when he crawled on stage during his parents' vaudeville act, received great applause and fell down a flight of stairs. His dramatic entry into show business was witnessed by the great Harry Houdini, who was touring with the Keatons. Houdini rushed to pick up the baby, who was laughing! Allegedly Houdini remarked, "That was some buster your baby took." And the name stuck.

The "Great Stoneface" comedian's persona was the same offstage as on. Performing with his parents from age four, he was a human football, kicked and hurled around the stage like a somber rag doll while maintaining the straight, non-expressive countenance that became his trademark. His adroitness and acrobatic skills taught him how to avoid injury, until the violence of the act grew real as his father sank into alcoholism. As a youth, Buster met popular comedian Fatty Arbuckle, who hired him for a role in his next two-reeler.

Films were Buster's milieu, as there was much room for improvisation. He became popular as a result of his performance in films like *The Boat, Sherlock Jr., The Navigator* and *The General,* which are considered classics today. His popularity extended all the way to Paris where his brilliant mime at the Cirque Medrano was the toast of the town. He is especially remembered for his work with Chaplin in *Limelight,* and he starred, always with a stone face and porkpie hat, in Samuel Beckett's *Film* in 1964.

His domestic life, however, was not as successful as his movie career. With Natalie (of the three beautiful Talmadge sisters) he produced two sons. Eventually their parting was said to be because he needed emotional support and was an active, involved man, while she preferred home and hearth. Friends thought the Talmadge family played a part in the breakup too, interfering with the couple's lives by suggesting they have no more children. Natalie moved into a bedroom of her own and Buster, after their parting, began drinking excessively. He became obsessed with bridge and other women and soon faced bankruptcy.

After a short second marriage, Buster married 21-year-old Eleanor Norris, who organized his life, budgeted his money and gave him the love he longed for. Twenty-five years later, with his marriage and career still solid, he was diagnosed as having lung cancer. He refused new work and attempted to rest, but to no avail. Three months after the diagnosis, one of the world's greatest comedians was gone at 70.

But what goes around comes around. Buster and Fatty Arbuckle remained good friends, and when Fatty was involved in his grievous scandal with Virginia Rappe, Buster stood by him and saw that he continued to work, even though his days as a star were over.

**Bette Davis** (Ruth Elizabeth Davis), 1908–1989, in the Court of Remembrance.

Most aspiring actresses would have given up after hearing Universal Pictures president Carl Laemmle's evaluation. After seeing Davis's picture debut in the 1930 film *Bad Sister,* he described her as "having about as much sex appeal as Slim Summerville." However, Davis was as tough as she was bright. Even in high school she worked hard at being an actress, appearing in student productions as well as regional theater, chasing the dream that someday she would become a recognized star. And despite studio critics, her struggles to succeed in pictures, while enduring a disastrous personal life, did not stop this brilliant, feisty unique woman

Bette Davis with Ginger Rogers —
"Fasten your seatbelts, it's going to be
a bumpy ride."

from achieving a star status far above that of any other Hollywood actress.

"You've got to care," Davis asserted, "Everything has to be done right. If it's worth doing at all, it's worth doing right." And when asked about her movie magic that captured audiences, she said, "My eyes are basically my face, and, of course, that's very important with the camera because the camera very seldom lets you lie, you know. You can see the truth.

"The skeleton of your acting is in your head, your brain, and that comes out in your eyes. What comes out of your eyes is caring, but it's also being the person you're trying to be. You'd better be thinking every minute about something. Lots and lots of actors aren't thinking every minute. They're waiting for their cues. I've always tried to show some reason why this person became like that, because nobody's all bad—or all good. Nothing is all black and nothing is all white. There are grays. But, there have to be reasons."

Davis's Oscars include *Dangerous* in 1935 and *Jezebel* in 1938. Her eight other Oscar nominations were for performances in *All About Eve, Dark Victory, The Leper, The Little Foxes, Now Voyager, Mr. Skeffington, The Star,* and *What Ever Happened to Baby Jane?* Her other outstanding performances included *Of Human Bondage, The Private Lives of Elizabeth and Essex, The Man Who Came to Dinner* and *Pocketful of Miracles*. On television, Davis won an Emmy for 1979's *Stranger—A Story of a Mother and Daughter.*

Born in Lowell, Massachusetts, Davis came to Hollywood at the age of 21. "They sent a man to meet my train," she said, "and he went back to the studio alone. He said he hadn't seen anyone at the station who could possibly be a star."

However, Bette was encouraged by George Arliss, who told the studio brass, "I don't care what she looks like, this girl has the makings of a great actress."

Bette made four disastrous trips to the altar, marrying Harmon "Ham" Nelson, Art Farnsworth, William Sherry, and Gary Merrill, which prompted her to say, "Sex is God's joke on human beings." With Sherry, an ex-Marine and aspiring artist who physically abused her, she had one daughter in 1947, Barbara Davis Sherry, known as B.D. In 1985, B.D. wrote a tell-all book, *My Mother's Keeper.* Davis herself wrote two autobiographies, *The Lonely Life* in 1962 and *Mother Goddamn* in 1973.

Interestingly, Merrill, who never quite made it as a leading man in pictures, played his best role as Davis's paramour in *All About Eve.* This brilliant, sophisticated and cynical look at life in the theater was written and directed by Joseph Mankiewicz and went on to win six Oscars, while giving Davis her most famous line as aging theatrical star Marge Channing: "Fasten your seat belts, it's going to be a bumpy night." And bumpy it continued to be when Merrill married Davis, seven years his senior, in 1950. The two stayed together for ten years, adopting two children: Margo, who was severely retarded, and Michael. The marriage finally fell apart due to Merrill's heavy drinking and fights with Davis.

In 1977, Davis became the first female to receive The American Film Institute's Lifetime Achievement Award.

Up several stairs, two walls past the George Washington statue, you will see the plaque of **Stan Laurel,** 1890–1965, which reads, "Master of Comedy. His genius in the art of humor brought gladness to the world he loved."

Sentimentally, his wife, Ida K. Laurel, is below him in the ground. Her inscription reads simply "Beloved Wife." She was his eighth marriage but his fifth wife; he married Virginia Rogers three times.

Raised in English music halls, Stan made his first trip to America as part of a musical-comedy troupe that also included Charlie Chaplin. Hal Roach hired him but felt his "dead eyes" (blue) were a problem because they did not photograph well. Laurel worked on and off for Roach, primarily as a gag writer and director.

Laurel's soon-to-be partner, Oliver Hardy, began his career as a boy soprano and ran a movie theater in Georgia. His girth made him a natural in silent comedies, and he too landed at the Hal Roach studio. How the two comedians came together no one seems to remember, but within the time they made their first two-reeler, they were off and running. The public loved them and their zany antics, and their films remain classics today.

The 1932 three-reeler, *The Music Box,* in which they tried to deliver a piano up an enormous flight of stairs, won an Academy Award. The film was "Perfection itself," according to Leonard Maltin, one of America's foremost movie critics. Laurel and Hardy worked together in harmony, going their separate ways when not filming. Oliver played golf and partied. Stan loved to explain that people knew his hobby. "I married them all," he said.

Laurel retired from the screen after Hardy's death in 1949. He suffered a diabetic stroke in 1955 while living in Santa Monica. His funeral was attended by nearly 500 friends, including Buster Keaton and the rest of filmdom's "clowns." (For more details on Laurel and Hardy, see Hardy's entry in the "Valhalla Memorial Park" section.)

**Ray Bidwell Collins,** 1889–1965. To the left of Stan Laurel.

His marker reminds the world that he was Lieutenant Tragg on *Perry Mason.*

**William Talman,** 1915–1968. Also to the left of Stan Laurel.

His marker does not mention that he played the District Attorney Hamilton Berger on the same show. And he lost every case to Perry! Talman's career was demolished when he was busted in a drug raid at a Hollywood party. He successfully beat the "possession" charges with the defense that he was naked at the time of his arrest. This earned him the nickname "Nudey" Talman in the trades.

**Borden Chase,** 1900–1968. His is the other marble plaque on the wall with Stan Laurel. It reads, "Writer-Patriot. You have to help people when they need help. His philosophy of life and work."

**Rex Ingram,** 1895–1969. On the other side, in the last row of markers by the garden wall. His marker refers to his most famous role, in *Green Pastures:* "DeLawd—Remembered always."

**Marty Feldman,** 1934–1982. In the second garden, near the wall.

Feldman died unexpectedly of a heart attack at 48. He had a strange, unique look, composed of a red mop of curls, prominent nose and chin, and especially protruding walleyes, which he seemed to be able to stick out further on demand. He is best remembered for Mel Brooks' *Young Frankenstein* and *The Adventures of Frankenstein,* ("No, Frankensteen"). His epitaph, written by his wife, reads "He made us laugh, he took my pain away."

**Benjamin Sherman "Scatman" Crothers,** 1910–1986. Garden of Heritage.

Primarily a musical performer, his scat singing gave him the nickname. He taught himself to play drums and guitar and formed a band that traveled the Midwest, ultimately landing in Hollywood. He was in great demand in both TV and films. His bald pate, wrinkled face and superb talent made him a favorite with movie fans and especially with Jack Nicholson, with whom he worked in *The Fortune, One Flew Over the Cuckoo's Nest* and *The Shining.* Crothers also appeared in the TV series *Chico and the Man.*

**Bruce Wayne,** 1933–1986. Garden of Heritage.

Known as the "Dean of America's Traffic Reporters," Wayne was the first traffic reporter to use a helicopter.

**Charles Laughton,** 1899–1962, and **Elsa Lanchester,** 1902–1986. Courts of Remembrance on Ascension Road, up the steps to the first right.

A great English actor, Laughton was gassed during World War I. Years later he died from cancer of the spine. He gave a perfect, believable characterization of any role he played. He was *Nero, Captain Bligh* and *King Lear.* In 1933 he won a well-deserved Academy Award for his lusty portrayal of the king in *The Private Life of Henry VIII.*

Elsa Lanchester (Mrs. Charles Laughton) died more than 20 years after her husband and was buried at sea. Trained as a dancer by Isadora Duncan, Elsa made her way into acting immortality with impish, put-on characterizations that were unique to her. She is especially remembered as *The Bride of Frankenstein* (with her four-foot hairdo), in *Witness for the Prosecution* and in many supporting roles to Laughton. Married in 1929, their marriage was compatible although their union was said to be an unconventional one. (Our description today might be more candid.) Elsa was a good wife, a great actress and an Academy Award nominee for *Come to the Stable,* in which she played a dotty artist.

**Clyde Beatty,** 1909–1965. Against the back wall, three positions over.

He was the greatest wild-animal trainer in the world, the forerunner of all similar acts that have copied him. Working with lions and tigers, he could make them leap to their perches and sometimes keep them there. He was mauled over 100 times and had scars and claw tracks across his face and body to prove it. He wrote about these experiences in his many books. He died quietly of natural causes at 56, unlike his noted French counterpart, Jean Pezon, who became "lionized in his pet Brutus' stomach." Beatty is commemorated by a bronze plate with his signature and a seated lion on the top. It is inscribed, "Forever enshrined in our hearts."

**Albert Hay Malotte,** 1895–1964. On the left side of this area, opposite Beatty, Marker 341, against the wall. Malotte wrote *The Lord's Prayer* and the score to Disney's *Lady and the Tramp.*

**Ernest Loring "Red" Nichols,** 1905–1965. On the left in the Columbarium of Remembrances is cornetist and leader of the jazz group Red Nichols and His Five Pennies, a popular dance quintet.

**Marie Wilson** (Katherine Elizabeth White), 1916–1972. On the side wall, Vault 61274.

She was a forerunner to the voluptuous, curvaceous, beautiful, not intellectual Marilyn Monroe-type blonde. Marie played the role of *My Friend Irma,* which was successful on radio, at the movies and on TV. But probably even more memorable was her long-running role at the Vine Street Theater in Hollywood, co-starring with Ken Murray in *Blackouts.* During the war years, it was the hottest show in town, the number one attraction for both visitors and locals who saw it many times. When Marie left for the New York stage, Ken had difficulty finding another actress with her personality and measurements.

**Marty Melcher,** 1914–1968. Back wall in a plain vault bearing only his name.

He was an agent, business manager, and promoter, mostly for his wife, Doris Day. He died from congestive heart failure and complications of a stroke at 54. He had just finished co-producing *With Six You Get Egg Roll.* His devotion to the Christian Science religion prevented him from seeking the medical treatment some say could have saved his life. Rumors persist that his bad management left Doris almost bankrupt, but she recovered a substantial amount of money by suing Marty's estate and his lawyer after his death.

**Art Kassel,** 1896–1965. Opposite Melcher in Crypt 60987.

*Kassels in the Air* was the theme song that always announced Art and his band. Sweet dance music and great arrangements were his forte. In the center of his crypt is a small stylized castle commemorating his band.

**Wladziu Valentino Liberace, "Liberace,"** 1917–1987. On the right in the Courts of Remembrance.

Too soon at rest is one of the most dynamic and creative performers of our time. Liberace was the surviving brother of twins. His brother was born skeletal and "under the veil" (suffocated by a film of the placenta), while he weighed a robust 13 pounds. From his loving mother and musical father, "Lee," as his friends called him, inherited great warmth and even greater talent. He was not only a brilliant musician, he also had the flair for glamour and enthusiasm that made his audiences love him.

He played piano at age four and later showed enough musicianship to receive a scholarship to the Wisconsin College of Music. Realizing that his classically trained musician father had trouble finding jobs, he opted to play in beer halls and burlesque shows to earn a living. He created his own audience-pleasing versions of "Three Little Fishes," an elegant Chopinesque selection, "Chopsticks," "Claire de Lune" and "Beer Barrel Polka" for starters. He

Liberace — The glamour boy.

parodied himself by wearing outrageous,flamboyant clothes, including sequined hot pants, gargantuan robes of fur and feathers.

Audiences adored him. Reluctant husbands and boyfriends tried to stay away, but they too became enchanted with his humor, smile and showmanship. He played all the stellar night spots in the world, for presidents and VIPs, and appeared in many movies, along with his lavish pianos and gold candelabra. One memorable night he played Madison Square Garden for a crowd of 15,000, for which he received the largest check the Garden had ever paid, $138,000. The piano motif was his trademark, seen in his swimming pool, furniture, jewelry, and accessories. Whenever possible, the piano was there.

Liberace's warmth, charm and generosity apparently were his undoing. His obvious sexual preference did not come to light until after his death, and it is suggested that he may not have even known he had contracted AIDS. His good friend, Phyllis Diller, suspected it because of his sallow look and loss of weight. AIDS was not reported by his doctors as the cause of death. Liberace passed away at his home in Palm Springs.

At the insistence of Riverside County Coroner Raymond Carillo, Liberace's body was retrieved from Forest Lawn after his burial and autopsied. The results of that autopsy are still not known.

Liberace's family is as close in death as they were in life. Their large white sarcophagus has atop it a classical statue of a woman holding flowers and looking into the distance. Below her is Frances (1891-1980), "Our Beloved Mom," brother George (1911-1983), who with his violin appeared professionally with Liberace; and Liberace. In the center of the sarcophagus is a wrought-iron piano candelabrum with Liberace's signature, which was created by the pianist himself.

**T. Marvin Hatley,** 1905-1986, and **Haven Gillespie,** 1888-1975. To the right of Liberace.

Both were composers. Hatley is remembered for composing the Laurel and Hardy theme song. Gillespie wrote over 600 songs, including "That Lucky Old Sun" (which Frankie Laine made famous), "Breezing Along With the Breeze" and the very special "Santa Claus Is Coming to Town," which appears on his tombstone.

**George Raft,** 1895–1980. Behind the Liberace Mortuary in the Sanctuary of Light, near a statue of a woman with a toddler.

Hollywood's man-about-town, Raft had a penchant for beautiful women and the charm to interest them. Betty Grable was one of his favorites. Raft began his career as a prizefighter, then a dancer on Broadway in Prohibition nightclubs, where he became friends with some of America's biggest racketeers. Finally he made it to the movies. He was the ideal type for the gangster roles he played, with his aloof manner, slick hair and impeccable tailoring.

In *Scarface, Quick Millions* and *Hush Money* he performed with great reality. He co-starred with Alice Faye and Carole Lombard in lighter, but no less menacing, fare. He had the reputation for not being a very good actor and turning down good roles, such as *The Maltese Falcon,* which made Humphrey Bogart a major star. He married a woman who wouldn't divorce him, in spite of his dalliances with other women. His story was made into a film in 1961 with Ray Danton playing Raft.

Known for his rakish dress, elevator shoes, purple shirts with yellow ties, and white ties on black shirts, he played in over 60 films. His Hell's Kitchen gangster pals included Bugsy Siegel. At 73 he was broke and being dunned by the IRS for $75,000 in back taxes. He explained, "When I was going good I had three servants, a publicity man, an agent, lawyers and 9 million parasites. I don't know where it all went. That's showbiz!" He died at 85 from emphysema and ulcers.

**Freddie Prinze,** 1954–1977. To the left of George Raft, close to the wall.

A tragic, still young, attractive and charismatic actor, his epitaph reads, "We love you. Psalm 23." Though somehow expected, Prinze's suicide was still shocking. His fans and viewers seemed to be aware of his off-screen frustrations. Too young perhaps, succeeding too quickly, he went from an unknown stand-up comedian to a host of the *Tonight Show* and the star of *Chico and the Man.* It was too much to handle. Cocaine, Quaaludes, the reassurance of his friends, a devoted wife and new baby couldn't sustain him. His suicide note said, "I must end it. There's no hope left. I'll be at peace. No one had anything to do with this. My decision totally, Freddie Prinze." (See also the section "Death by Mysterious Circumstance.")

**Wanda Hendrix,** 1928–1981. Vault 4349, facing George Raft's tomb.

Her marker reads, "To know her is to love her." A petite and charming film star, she was married to James L. Stack and to war hero Audie Murphy. She died of pneumonia.

**Reginald Gardner,** 1923–1980. In the Sanctuary of Reflection.

His marker bears the masks of Comedy and Tragedy with the inscription, "The angels of Avalon shall be with you evermore." A British actor, Gardner played humorous roles in *The Man Who Came to Dinner* and *Mr. Hobbs Takes a Vacation*. *My Fair Lady* was his biggest role. He began with Beatrice Lillie revues, doing an imitation of a lighthouse, train and wastebasket—a versatile entertainer!

**Nudie,** 1902–1984, on the wall, Vault 2301-2.

Anyone living in Hollywood would recognize Nudie's enormous Cadillac convertible with the huge moose horns in front and western designs covering the chassis. Nudie designed colorful, sequined and decorated suits for country and western stars and similar suits for wannabes. A well-known character, his marker shows a cowboy roping his label, *Nudie's Rodeo Tailors*. His shop was in the San Fernando Valley.

**Forrest Tucker,** 1919–1986. Six positions from the end and eight up, in the Sanctuary of Reflection.

Beginning his acting career on a lark, he was coaxed into trying out for films while vacationing in California in 1940. He made his debut in William Wyler's *The Westerner,* supporting Gary Cooper and Walter Brennan. He was handsome and huge with wavy blonde hair and blue eyes. He played heavies, soldiers and comedic characterizations. One of his more memorable roles was opposite Rosalind Russell in *Auntie Mame.*

**Tony Fontaine,** 1927–1974. On the front of the outside wall is a white marble bench that is dedicated to, "America's beloved gospel singer."

Starting as a pop singer with "Cold, Cold Heart" and "Syncopated Clock," he found the Lord after a near-fatal traffic accident. His film biography, *The Tony Fontaine Story,* was translated into 19 languages and shown around the world. He died of cancer.

**Andy Gibb,** 1957-1988. Diagonally across the mausoleum wall in Vault 3442.

Following the careers of his older brothers, the Bee Gees, Andy Gibb began performing solo in his native Australia. A successful, handsome young man, his number one singles were "I Just Want to Be Your Everything" in 1977 and "Shadow Dancing" in 1978. His private life was plagued with cocaine problems, which he unfairly blamed on his breakup with actress Victoria Principal. In 1983, because of his drug problems, he was dismissed from the stage cast of *Joseph and the Amazing Technicolor Dreamcoat,* in which he was perfectly cast. He entered the Betty Ford Clinic for treatment two years later. He was 30 when he died in a hospital in Oxfordshire, England, after complaining of stomach pains. The cause of his death is unknown.

**Harry F. Mills,** 1913-1982. On the back outdoor wall, Vault 3442.

Harry was the spokesman for the famous, fabulous Mills Brothers, who entertained the public for 50 years. A fixture on the American musical scene, their harmonies and suave style influenced many black singing groups. Among their biggest hits were "Paper Doll" and "Glow Worm." Harry's marker reads, "Your love will remain in our hearts forever."

**Johnny Eager-Tanner,** 1924-1963. On Vesper Drive, Vault 3235.

Johnny was an English actor. His inscription requests, "If you need me, Precious, whistle." (If it were only so easy!)

**Ruth St. Denis,** 1879–1968. Farther down the wall, in Vault 3116. The renowned dancer's epitaph reads:

> The gods have meant that I should dance,
> And in some mystic hour
> I shall move to unheard rhythms
> Of the cosmic orchestra of heaven.
> You will know the language of my wordless poems
> And will come to me
> For that is why I dance.

On the right is an Art Nouveau image of Ruth with a large aureole and the inscription "Ruth St. Denis, Pioneer and Prophet." "Miss Ruth," who felt herself karmically linked to Isis, the Egyptian goddess of fertility and consolation, began her career creating dances in the Egyptian genre. She settled in Los Angeles, where she opened the Denishawn School of Dance. There she attracted such pupils as Martha Graham and Dorothy and Lillian Gish. Ruth was a spectacular artist and dancer.

**Ernie Kovacs,** 1919–1962. Farther down on the lawn, nearly across from the water tower.

His theatrical talents and innovative, madcap theater were without peer. Early in his career he suffered poverty and from an illness that put him in a hospital terminal ward for a year and a half. He found work in Trenton, New Jersey, at a local radio station. Ten years later, in 1951, he went on TV for the first time. There he not only performed, he developed many new techniques that expanded the creative use of the TV camera. Shortly after his TV debut, Ernie hired a nearsighted, gorgeous singer, Edie Adams, whose chief function was to sing while Ernie thought up new routines. Ernie and Edie married and moved to New York, where he wrote skits for other performers. His TV talent first gained national attention when he did a half-hour filler for NBC in 1957. His subsequent hit, *The Ernie Kovacs Show*, ran in 1956 and 1957. His success was ironic because, for the first time, Ernie was silent. His routine consisted of mime, incorporating a surrealistic world that he used as a foil for his humor.

A smash hit, he was besieged with offers from Hollywood and was on his way. He made several films, and his TV specials were popular and attracted large audiences. An avid poker player, his trademarks were his large moustache and even larger cigar.

After a long, hard day's work he attended a christening party, after which he told Edie he would drive himself to PJ's in Hollywood for a nightcap. While driving, he attempted to light his cigar, lost control of his car on the wet road and smashed into some telephone poles. He died almost instantly, a victim of his customary cigar. His marker reads, "Nothing in Moderation" and "We all loved him."

To Kovac's left is his daughter **Mia Kovacs,** 1959–1982. "Daddy's Girl. We all loved her too."

Twenty years after her father's death, Mia also ran her car off the road and crashed. She was thrown through the sunroof and died two hours later. Edie was left with great debts to settle while she continued to raise Ernie's other daughters. In 1962 she launched her own TV show, *Here's Edie.* Later she bought and worked on a ranch. The indomitable Edie was successful, later writing her autobiography, *Sing a Pretty Song.*

**Amanda Randolph,** 1896–1967, and **Lillian Randolph,** 1914–1980. In the Gentleness section.

These two were sisters and actresses. Amanda was the cantankerous mother-in-law on *Amos 'n Andy* and the maid on *The Danny Thomas Show.* She died of a stroke. Her marker is inscribed "An inspiration to the young actors and actresses, hers was a life of giving."

**Jack Soo,** 1917–1979. Gentleness section, Plot 3980.

Born Goro Suzuki in Oakland, California, Soo's acting career came to a quick halt when he was interned during World War II because of his Japanese ancestry. Upon his release, he starred in both the stage and screen versions of *Flower Drum Song.* His most famous role was as Sergeant Nick Yemana on *Barney Miller,* where he played a slow-moving detective who couldn't make a good pot of coffee.

**Diane Linkletter,** 1948–1969. Enduring Faith section.

Diane's marker bears the inscription, "Darling, we loved you so much." How devastating for the Linkletters to lose their daughter in such a tragic manner. She was a sad casualty of the 1960s drug culture and Timothy Leary's influence. A bad LSD trip caused her to feel she was losing her mind. One day as she discussed her plight with a friend in her sixth floor apartment, she moved to the kitchen window and leaped out. Her startled friend tried to stop her but could catch only her belt loops. At 21, she was gone. Twenty-seven years later, in 1996, Linkletter and Leary inadvertently attended the same social function but didn't speak to one another. It was only a few weeks before Leary's death, and Linkletter seemed somewhat appeased to see his wasted condition. Afterward Leary cried over and over, "He wouldn't look at me. He wouldn't look at me." (More on Leary in "The Out-of-Towners.")

**Sabu Dastigar,** 1924–1963.

He was known only by his first name, Sabu, in films. He was the son of an elephant driver in India when he was picked from his perch by Robert Flaherty to play in *Elephant Boy.* He starred in *The Jungle Book, Song of India* and *Hello, Elephant.* Sabu died of a heart attack at 39. Sabu's brother, stunt man **Sheik Dastigar,** 1913–1960, is one row back. Their markers show a couple side by side, gazing toward the mountains. Both plaques are inscribed "Til the day breaks and the shadows flee away."

**Roy Disney,** 1893–1971, and **Edna Frances Disney,** 1890–1984. Across Evergreen Drive in Sheltering Hills.

Roy was Walt's brother and right-hand man. His marker reads "A greatly humble man, he left the world a better place." Roy was considered a conservative counterweight to Walt's fantastic ideas and dreams. It was his financial genius that held the studio firmly in place. He was cautious, but his business ability parlayed Disney Studios into a multi-million-dollar empire. After Walt's death in 1966, Roy oversaw the creation of his brother's dream, Epcot Center in Florida.

**Lester (Smiley) Burnette,** 1911-1967. Farther up the hill in Plot 266.

Gene Autry's sidekick in 81 movies, Smiley was also the cheerful engineer on *Petticoat Junction.* He played a hundred different musical instruments and wrote a cookbook. His dedication asserts he was "A dedicated entertainer who brought joy to others."

**Helen C. Travolta,** 1912-1978. To the right of Smiley.

Helen was John Travolta's mother. Her marker has masks of Comedy and Tragedy with a rose floral design. Her family has dedicated her marker to her as their "Dearly beloved wife, mother and actress."

**Jack Webb,** 1920-1982. In Plot 1999.

Known by millions for his Joe Friday role in *Dragnet,* his series was probably the forerunner of today's realistic cops-and-robbers shows. The slate marker says simply, "Jack Webb."

**Robert Weiss,** 1928-1992, and **Jackie Dashiel Weiss,** 1930-1992. Both were interred on April 11, 1992, niche 64626 in the Columbarium of Valor.

Husband and wife both died mysteriously within three months of each other. (For details see the section "Death by Mysterious Circumstance.")

**Horace M. Heidt,** 1901-1986. Memorial Drive at the Murmuring Trees section.

Tall, blonde and handsome, Heidt was the epitome of band leaders. He also directed talent shows that were responsible for bringing attention to Art Carney, Al Hirt, Gordon MacRae and the King Sisters, among others. *Family Night with Horace Heidt* featured the Musical Knights from his dance band. The large classical marble statue that is his memorial shows a family, all dressed in togas and with downcast eyes. The mother's head is lifted and rests against her husband's head. The base bears Horace's creed, "Tis better to build boys than mend men." Horace Jr. followed in his father's footsteps and also had a band.

**Godfrey M. Cambridge,** 1933–1976. To the right of Heidt and up the hill.

Cambridge was described in his obituary as "sometimes fat, sometimes thin, sometimes jolly, sometimes bitter." His large frame carried 300 pounds. He was in good spirits when he collapsed of a heart attack while working on a movie set in Burbank. He was playing the role of Idi Amin in the TV movie *Rescue at Antibbe.* A West Indian, Cambridge attended school in Nova Scotia and later enrolled in Hofstra University and City College of New York. He worked as a judo instructor and airplane wing cleaner, among other odd jobs, while waiting for his break into films. He was featured in *Take a Giant Step, Watermelon Man* and *Cotton Comes to Harlem.* He was active in civil rights causes.

**Oswald G. Nelson,** 1906–1975. Opposite the Murmuring Trees, across Evergreen Drive

Uneasy lies "Ozzie," architect of the *Ozzie and Harriet Show,* which was a 22-year attraction on both radio and television. The Nelsons were perfect, the ideal family next door, but with warts and all. As youngsters, both of their sons appeared on the show with Ozzie and Harriet, giving the boys experience and jobs in show business. From outside appearances, their personal life was ideal, unlike the lives of many showbiz families.

Tragically Rick, idolized as a rock star by a generation of young people, was killed in a plane crash after his father's death. Rick and his band were on their way to Dallas to perform in a New Year's Eve show when the plane went down. Today his blonde, long-haired twin sons continue to entertain.

Ozzie had a charmed youth. At 13, he was the youngest Eagle Scout in the United States, which earned him a trip to a Boy Scout Jamboree in London. Ambitious, he went out for football and lacrosse, was on the swim team at Rutgers University in New Jersey, and earned his law degree in 1930. Copying the popular Rudy Vallee, he bought a megaphone, formed a band and toured the country. His star vocalist was the beautiful Harriet Hilliard, whom he married. She was featured in their *Ozzie and Harriet Show* and also made several movies. She followed him in death in 1995.

Ozzie was furious when he learned at 65 that he had liver cancer. Never a smoker or drinker, he had led a morally clean and healthful life. "Why me?" he asked.

**William Conrad,** 1920–1994.

Conrad was a heavy, rumbling-voiced actor who is best remembered as the private eye he played on TV's Cannon from 1971 to 1976. He starred in two other TV shows, *Nero Wolf* and *Jake and the Fat Man.* His film work from 1947 to 1977 included *The Naked Jungle* in 1954.

**Telly Savalas,** 1925–1994.

Savalas was a bald, tough character actor, best remembered as the lollipop-addicted detective on the hit TV series *Kojak* from 1973–1978. He was in his mid-30s before he turned to acting and made dozens of pictures during his career, including *The Dirty Dozen* and *Kelly's Heroes.* His best-remembered line, "Who loves ya baby?" came from the TV movie *The Marcus Nelson Murders.*

**Jeffrey Lynn,** 1909–1995.

Lynn came to Hollywood in the 1930s, where he made a series of motion pictures at Warner Brothers, including *Letter to Three Wives* with Humphrey Bogart. After a tour of duty in the Air Force in World War II, he acted on stage in plays such as *Dial M for Murder.* In 1965 he began a five-year stint on the soap opera *Secret Storm.* He turned to real estate for a career in 1968, while continuing to act in cameo roles on TV in series such as *Murder, She Wrote.* In the 1980s, he became involved in the Center Theater in Los Angeles as an actor and producer. He died at 86.

**Bert Convy,** 1935–1991, Court of Liberty to left of walk

This tall, dark and handsome game show host was one of the earliest. He won Emmys in 1976–1977 for Best Host for *Tattle Tales* on CBS. He died of cancer and a brain tumor.

The police honor their own.

# 22

◆

## Forest Lawn, Covina

Forest Lawn's Covina Hills Cemetery, located at 21300 Via Verde Drive, Covina, California, is the fourth Forest Lawn, established in 1965. It offers everything in one place, including funeral services, interment, mortuary, church and flowers. This allows for easy arrangements without a procession over crowded streets and freeways.

As with the other cemeteries, the public is invited as guests to view the art and historical artifacts at any time. Featured is the world's largest religious mosaic, *The Life of Christ*, measuring 172 feet long and 35 feet high, showing 26 scenes from the life of Jesus. There are mosaic recreations of the greatest scenes from Michelangelo's immortal Sistine Chapel ceiling paintings and an identical reproduction of Old St. Georges Church in Fredericksburg, Virginia, where patriots George Washington, James Monroe and John Paul Jones once worshiped. Rare marble, colorful stained glass, bronzes, paintings and mosaics are displayed in the scenic park situated on a hill overlooking the San Gabriel and Pomona valleys. In the background is a spectacular view of Mount Baldy.

On a spring day in 1996, a procession of 1,000 uniformed police officers on their motorcycles, headlights on, with several hundred squad cars following, entered the cemetery. Most impressive, traffic was stopped on the freeway and on all roads leading to the park as the police department honored one of their own. They were there to honor fellow officer Daniel Fraembs, 37, who had been fatally shot, the first officer killed in the line of duty in Pomona's 108-year history. Fraemb's name will be added to the black memorial marble wall at the Los Angeles County Sheriffs Training Center.

Angels watch over us.

# 23

⬥

## Forest Lawn, Cypress

The Cypress facility is located at 4471 Lincoln Avenue, Cypress, California. If it hadn't been for Hubert Eaton with his love of God, country and history, many millions of people would not have the opportunity to see and appreciate the original art and replicas of the finest statuary, mosaics, paintings and other major works, which have been presented in all of the Forest Lawns.

Surrounded by the beautiful lawns, trees and gardens of Cypress Cemetery is the exact bronze replica of Michelangelo's *David. The Ascension* is also recreated here, comprising over a million pieces of Venetian glass tile in 3,000 different shades and colors. Stained glass and bronze and marble statuary greet you at every turn. You may even transport yourself to the old Saint John's Church in Richmond, Virginia, where Patrick Henry delivered his never-to-be-forgotten "Give me liberty or give me death" speech. A perfect replica of Saint John's is located on the Cypress grounds.

The Cypress experience is similar to visiting several museums, but at no cost. You'll enjoy the peaceful surroundings while contemplating your own existence or that of a loved one who may be resting there.

Among other priceless works found here is *Christ in the Garden*, an original marble sculpture. The Church of Our Fathers features historical mementos from the colonial period. The *Window of the Healing Cross,* depicting the healing miracles of Christ, is located in the Church of Our Fathers.

Buried in Cypress is **Karen Carpenter,** 1950–1983. Karen died of cardiac arrest caused by severe anorexia. Just when everybody thought she had conquered her eating disorder, her weakened physical condition caused the heart attack. A beautiful and popular singer, she and her composer-pianist brother enjoyed great success as The Carpenters. Their careers took off when they couldn't get a major record company interested in their music. They produced their own recording and peddled it to radio stations, where it became a huge hit, "We've Only Just Begun." Karen shares a crypt with her father, Harold, in a mausoleum at Cypress.

# 24

## Forest Lawn, Long Beach

This cemetery, located at 1500 East San Antonio Drive in Long Beach, California, became Forest Lawn's fifth facility in 1985.

Small and exquisite, here one can enjoy extraordinary examples of Spanish Renaissance architecture. You'll view a reproduction of Raphael's classic *Paradise* fresco. You'll believe you are in a little Spanish town when you step inside the Spanish Colonial Chapel, featuring stained glass windows that spell out the story of California's early history. And you'll especially enjoy the Cathedral Tower, part of the Sunnyside Mausoleum. Originally constructed in 1925, it has long been a favorite Long Beach landmark.

Check your watch for accuracy with the renowned Foucault pendulum, which keeps precise time while making one complete revolution every 42 hours and 48 minutes.

A reproduction of Raphael's classic *Paradise* fresco.

Al Jolson — "Mammy . . ."

# 25

## Hillside Memorial Park

Hillside is located at 6001 Centinela Avenue near Culver City, California. The most striking landmark of Hillside Memorial Park is entertainer Al Jolson's monument, which can even be seen from the nearby San Diego Freeway. The monument, with its six towering marble pillars and a dome, was designed by famous architect Paul Williams.

On the ceiling of the dome is a mosaic of Moses holding the Ten Commandments, surrounded by clouds. Under the dome is Jolson's tomb, with a nearly full-sized statue of him nearby in his famous singing pose, down on one knee with his arms open wide. In front of the monument, supposedly honoring Jolson's request to be buried near a waterfall, water cascades down the hill from step to step for 120 feet.

**Al Jolson** (Asa Joelson), 1886–1950, is located in a tomb underneath the dome of his monument.

Known as Jolie to his friends, Jolson used blackface and white

chalk on his lips to accent his famous rolling eyes. Jolson became famous as a jazz singer and immortalized many tunes such as "Mammy," "Rock-a-bye Your Baby with a Dixie Melody" and his theme song, "You Ain't Heard Nothin' Yet." His father was a stern, humorless rabbi named Moshe Joelson, who had little use for his son. His mother, Naomi, died when Al was only eight. By the age of 12, Jolson was in vaudeville, singing and telling jokes, with little initial success for nearly eight years, until he came up with his famous blackface trademark. Always a nervous performer, for some reason being in blackface relaxed Jolson, allowing him to tell his jokes and sing songs in his famous rock 'em style.

He soon caught the attention of the Schubert brothers, who began featuring him in their Broadway shows, where he starred on the New York stage from 1911 to 1937. *The Jazz Singer,* released in 1927, was the first talkie and an instant success for Jolson. He quickly followed it up with *The Singing Fool* in 1928, *Say It with Songs* in 1929, *Big Boy* in 1930, and *Hallelujah, I'm a Bum* in 1933. Jolson, who never was much of an actor, saw his career begin to decline in 1937. He was given parts in *Rose of Washington Square* in 1939 and *Rhapsody in Blue* in 1945. But when it came time to make *The Jolson Story* in 1945, the producer hired young actor Larry Parks to play Jolson and lip sync to his songs. At home, Jolson was less of a star, divorcing three wives, including the young, great, popular performer Ruby Keeler. Their marriage lasted from 1928 to 1939 before she sued him for divorce. Ruby died in 1993 and is buried at Holy Sepulcher Cemetery in Orange, California. She had retired to the desert where she played championship golf until a stroke derailed her.

The Hillside Mausoleum at Hillside Memorial Park is just behind Jolson's monument. Lots of windows give it a sunny atmosphere, and there is an atrium in the center that allows part of the mausoleum to be outdoors.

**David Janssen** (David Harold Mayer), 1930–1980. Halfway down the garden in a crypt.

His inscription reads, "My love is with you always." Janssen is best known as Dr. Richard Kimball from the hugely successful TV series *The Fugitive,* which ran from 1963 to 1967. His other TV series were *Richard Diamond, Private Detective,* which ran from 1957 through 1959; *O'Hara, U.S. Treasury,* 1971 and 1972; and *Harry O,* 1974 through 1976.

Janssen was less successful in motion pictures. He had parts in *Bonzo Goes to College* in 1953 and later in *From Here to Eternity, The Green Berets,* and *Inchon.* (Additional information on Janssen's funeral can be found in the chapter "Fascinating Funerals.")

**George A. Jessel,** 1898–1981. Three drawers above Janssen in the mausoleum garden.

He was often called "America's Toastmaster General." Jessel was best known for the dozens of eulogies he delivered at celebrity funerals, including one for his friend Al Jolson. In addition to funerals, Jessel also earned his Toastmaster credentials at roasts, dinners, inaugurations and tours for the USO. He starred in the stage version of *The Jazz Singer* in 1925 and went on to become a producer of Fox musicals.

Married several times, he was once heard to say, "She was my third wife, but I can't remember her name." Her name was Norma Talmadge, who is buried with her family and sisters at Hollywood Memorial.

**Dick Shawn** (Richard Schulefand), 1929–1988. On the same wall as Janssen in the mausoleum garden.

Shawn was a very popular comedian and actor whose best known films were *It's a Mad, Mad, Mad, Mad World* and *What Did You Do in the War, Daddy?*

**Jack Benny** (Benjamin Kubelsky), 1894–1974. At the end of the Hall of Graciousness in a black sarcophagus with his wife, Mary Livingston Benny, 1906–1983.

His inscription reads, "Beloved Husband, Father, And Grandfather, A Gentle Man." Benny grew up in Waukegan, Illinois, where he learned to play the violin as a child. He quit school at the age of 12 and became a violinist in vaudeville theaters. He then played in a duo with a pianist before becoming a solo act doing comedy bits between his violin numbers. At various times he changed his name, becoming Ben K. Benny, and finally, Jack Benny.

Benny courted and finally married a May Company department store salesgirl named Sadye Marks in 1927. Sadye changed her name to Mary and joined Jack on the vaudeville circuit.

During the early years, Benny made two movies: *The Hollywood Review of 1929* and *Medicine Man*. His big break came in 1933, when Canada Dry sponsored him in a radio show and he was voted the Most Popular Comedian on the air. He continued in radio and by the 1940s had put together the cast that would be with him in all his shows on radio and TV: Mary Livingston, Phil Harris, Don Wilson, "Rochester," and Frank Nelson. The shows revolved around Jack's reputation for being stingy, his underground money vault and his ancient Maxwell automobile. The show was called *The Jack Benny Show*, and it ran on TV from 1950 to 1965.

In addition to radio and TV, Benny also made more motion pictures, including *The Broadway Melody of 1936*, where he met Eddie "Rochester" Anderson and Phil Harris. Other pictures included *Buck Benny Rides Again* in 1940 and the picture he loved to kid about as nearly sinking his career, *The Horn Blows at Midnight*, released in 1945.

Jack loved comedy and loved to be entertained. His favorite "stingy" joke was one he did on radio:

Benny is walking home one night when he is confronted by a crook. The holdup man presses a gun in his side and barks, "Your money or your life." After a long pause, the holdup man snarls, "Come on, hurry up." "I'm thinking, I'm thinking," Benny says. The audience's laughter was timed at over two minutes.

And then there was the following (true) classified ad that ran in a Sacramento newspaper: "Two women about Jack Benny's age would like small, unfurnished house. Would like to pay what Benny would like to pay."

**Eddie Cantor** (Edward Israel Iskowitz), 1892–1964. Eddie and his wife, Ida (1892–1962) are in the second row up to the left of Benny, opposite the stairs.

Cantor, a singer famous for his rolling eyes, first made several silly love story movies, usually playing opposite the striking Goldwyn Girls, one of whom was Lucille Ball. His first movie was

*Kid Boots* in 1927. This was followed by *Whoopee* in 1930 and *Ali Baba Goes to Town* in 1937. In all, he would make over a dozen movies in the 1930s, all with the same plots. Only the casts, characters, and locations changed.

Most people remember Cantor for his popular radio show, which ran throughout the 1930s and featured his wife, Ida; the theme song "Ida, Sweet as Apple Cida"; and his five daughters. He received a special Oscar in 1956 for his numerous humanitarian efforts. Over the years, Cantor also wrote four volumes of memoirs, the last being *As I Remember Them* in 1962. Eddie is quoted as saying, while composing his own epitaph:

> Here in nature's arm I nestle,
> Free at last from Georgie Jessel.

**Jeff Chandler** (Ira Grossel), 1918–1961. Upstairs in the second section.

Chandler was a rugged, virile leading man of the 1950s. Blood poisoning, brought on by complications during a back operation, took his life at the age of 42. His first movie role was in *Johnny O'Clock* in 1947. Following that movie Chandler played only Indian roles, including Cochise, for several years. In the 1950s, Chandler was cast mainly as an adventurer in movies such as *Away All Boats* and his last film, *Merrill's Marauders*, released in 1962.

**Arthur Freed** (Arthur Grossman), 1894–1973. Outside, in a small garden.

Freed, a songwriter-producer, wrote many popular songs, including "All I Do Is Dream of You," and "Singin' in the Rain." As a producer of musicals, he won Oscars for *An American in Paris* in 1951 and *Gigi* in 1958.

**Percy Faith,** 1908–1976. In the same row as Freed.

Faith was a songwriter-producer-arranger with more than 45 albums to his credit. In 1955 he received an Oscar nomination for his song "Love Me or Leave Me."

**Vic Morrow,** 1932–1982. Outside, Block 5, in the Mt. Olive section.

Morrow first appeared as an actor in *The Blackboard Jungle* in 1955. Other films quickly followed, including *God's Little Acre* and *Portrait of a Mobster,* in which he played the role of Dutch Schultz. From 1962 to 1967, he played the tough Sergeant Chip Sanders in the TV series *Combat!* In the 1970s and early 1980s, Morrow continued to appear in movies, TV movies, a series and a miniseries while doing some writing, producing and directing. He was killed while filming a pyrotechnically complex stunt for the *Twilight Zone* movie. The stunt involved explosives and a helicopter, which was blown out of control, killing Morrow and the two little Vietnamese girls he was holding in his arms. Morrow's daughter is actress Jennifer Jason Leigh.

**Meyer Harris "Mickey" Cohen,** 1931–1976.

Cohen was a tough, flashy racketeer, rumored to be the mob's enforcer on the west coast, and controlled activities such as prostitution and bookmaking. An ex-prize fighter, five feet, five inches tall, Mickey had a temper and enjoyed using his fists. He loved gambling and flashy clothes, which he tossed away rather than having them cleaned. At different times he ran glitzy restaurants and a men's clothing store on the Sunset Strip.

Several attempts were made to "hit" Mickey, including one at his home on Moreno Avenue in Brentwood, where 30 sticks of dynamite left a crater 20 feet wide and 6 feet deep where his bed had been. After this incident, it was rumored that he had disposed of some of his enemies himself.

Convicted of income tax evasion twice, Cohen spent the years 1952–1955 and 1961–1972 in prison. He survived being shot at twice, once when Jimmy "The Weasel" Fratiano and two other gunmen shot up Cohen's haberdashery and missed him entirely. The other time was in front of Sherry's, a Sunset strip nightclub, when Cohen and three associates, including Lana Turner's boyfriend, Johnny Stompanato, were hit by shotgun fire, killing one man and slightly wounding Cohen. Cohen later suffered from a severe beating with a metal pipe in prison, from which he never fully recovered, although he died from natural causes.

# 26

## Hollywood Memorial Park

Hollywood Memorial, called "The Queen of Cemeteries," is one of Southern California's earliest and is located in the heart of the movie kingdom. More stars than there are in the sky are planted within her walls and grounds.

Burial here in the 1920s and 1930s was tantamount to playing the Palace, as stars and studios tried to outdo each other with burial glamour and attendance, somewhat like vaudevillians each endeavoring to be flashier than the act before. People didn't enjoy the life span they do today because medicine hadn't yet lengthened lives, and the fast life that surrounded the world of theater and film often hastened the stars' demise. Glamorous and well-attended funerals continued to be as competitive as had movie roles and careers.

But even today there is still space to be had and interesting neighbors to be laid next to. In fact, more than 400 internationally known motion picture artists, industrialists, newspaper publishers and philanthropists are enshrined at Hollywood Memorial, virtually all the early "builders" of Los Angeles and Hollywood.

**I. N. Van Nuys** and his father-in-law, **Colonel Isaac Lankershim,** bought 100 Hollywood acres in 1899 and started digging Hollywood Memorial. With the magnificent Forest Lawn arriving in the 1920s, the cemetery lost some of its attraction and business. Neighboring Paramount Motion Picture Studios needed and acquired 40 of its acres.

A Cupid and Psyche monument awaits your arrival just beyond the front gate. Soon you reach Maple Drive (not the Beverly Hills Maple Drive) and the Grounds section, where you should find the flat marker of **Carl "Alfalfa" Switzer,** 1927–1959, or so we were advised, but we never could find it. The marker features two Masonic symbols and a side view of Petey, the *Our Gang* dog.

The Otis family, founders of the *Los Angeles Times* newspaper.

Switzer was the freckle-faced Little Rascal in the movie shorts of the same name. As Alfalfa, he wore suits and crooned an off-key "I'm in the Mood for Love." When kid comedies became unfashionable, so did he. He worked as a bartender and hunting guide but developed an anger that was to be his undoing. During an argument over a valuable hunting dog, Switzer broke a glass clock over Bud Stiltz's head. He then pulled out his knife. Stiltz pointed his pistol and shot the 51-year-old "Little Rascal." A justifiable homicide verdict freed Stiltz of any blame. Next to Alfalfa rests his father, G. Fred Switzer, whose marker resembles a gas pump.

The film industry blossomed along with the orange trees in warm and sunny Hollywood. Both the little village and her big sister, Los Angeles, were fast growing and prospering, developing businesses, properties and tycoons as new arrivals sought their share of California's "good life." The Chamber of Commerce was having a field day. Hollywood Memorial soon became known as the best and most central location for these good citizens of the city to lay down their heads for their final rest.

Across from "Alfalfa" are the impressive *Los Angeles Times* dynasty family's farewell statements. **General Harrison Gray Otis,** 1837–1917, and his wife **Eliza Otis,** 1833–1904, are memorialized with a tall sphere that can be seen from any place in the park.

A Civil War hero, Otis came to Los Angeles and became the editor and publisher of the *Times.* Revering his time in the military, he built his offices to resemble barracks, called his employees the "phalanx" and his mansion on Wilshire Boulevard the "Bivouac." Furthering the image, he wore his chest full of medals for photographs. He prospered with his wise investments and bought substantial Southern California acreage, especially in the San Fernando Valley. There his Los Angeles Suburban Homes Syndicate, which included Henry E. Huntington and railroad magnate E.H. Harriman, was located. The syndicate purchased huge tracts made available through editorials in his newspaper favoring bond issues, the vehicle that brought water to the valley.

The labor unions were Otis's nemesis. He fired strikers and cut his printers' salaries, and when they protested, he brought in scabs from the Midwest. He fought the International Typographers Union, which resulted in an explosion at the *Times* building on October 1, 1910, killing 20 men. Perhaps Ironworkers Union member James McNamara was not aware when he set a suitcase full of explosives against the building shortly after midnight that a crew was inside working on the morning edition. This was the culmination of 20 years of bitter labor union disputes at the *Times.* The McNamara brothers were responsible for the tragedy. John earlier had blown up the Llewellyn Iron Works in Pennsylvania on Christmas Eve. The brothers were illegally seized and brought to Los Angeles. In their historic trial, they were defended by renowned defense lawyer Clarence Darrow, who allowed them to plead guilty so they could avoid the death penalty.

To commemorate the tragedy, Otis dedicated an impressive monument to the victims. It shows an eagle looking down from on high to a cloaked figure mounted on a separate pedestal. The epitaph is a beautiful tribute to "Our Martyred Men." The general died at 80 of heart disease. One morning, after finishing breakfast, he said simply, "Take away my tray; I am gone." And so he was.

Centered between the Otis and employees monuments is a monument decorated with patriotic eagles. It commemorates

"Our Martyred Men" — Memorial to the 20 *Los Angeles Times* employees killed by a bomb in 1910 during a labor dispute.

**Harry Chandler,**1864-1944, and his wife, **Marion Otis Chandler,** 1866-1952. Chandler, Otis's son-in-law, evidenced the same qualities as Otis. He amassed a fortune in real estate, fought the unions, and ran the *Times* in the same dedicated way. A workaholic, Harry died at the same age as Otis did, and of the same cause.

Well regarded and respected, Harry's son Norman Chandler took over the business and, in a gentler manner, developed the paper to even greater heights. Upon Norman's death, his son Otis took over the helm. Otis had learned the newspaper's operations from the ground up by training in all departments, and he was ready. The *Times* continued to grow under Otis's reign. The less popular *Herald Examiner* eventually went under, leaving Los Angeles with only one major newspaper. Otis purchased additional newspapers, TV facilities and corporations throughout the country. Again, the *Times* prospered. A youthful semi-retired Otis still officiates but has time for his leisure and hobbies, which include his vast collection of antique cars. While in college at Stanford, Otis was a contender in the Olympics.

Mrs. Norman (Buffy) Chandler, Otis's mother, the daughter of wealthy Buffums department store owners, also was active in an official capacity with the *Times.* She now lives in retirement in a Hancock Park mansion. Mrs. Chandler will be long remembered for her many successful causes on behalf of the city of Los Angeles, particularly the phenomenal Music Center, whose restaurant is known as "Buffy's Tavern."

**Paul Muni,** 1895-1967. Grounds section, Grave 57, Row 00, Section 14.

The son of actors, Paul Muni came to the United States in 1902 and later took up his own career in the Yiddish theater. He then landed on Broadway in *We Americans* and was seen and signed by Fox. His starring performance in *The Valiant* was based on a vaudeville play about a death row convict with a self-sacrificing streak of nobility. His performance earned him an Oscar nomination in 1929. He was the kind of actor who worked best when he totally absorbed a character in his roles. In *Seven Faces* he showed his versatility by playing seven different characters. In *Chain Gang,* his portrayal of the unwitting criminal accomplice won for him his second Oscar nomination. The Oscar finally came for his role in *The Story of Louis Pasteur.* When he returned to the stage, he won a Tony for his role in *Inherit the Wind.*

**Nelson Riddle,** 1921–1985. In T-Building, N702, T7, Corridor T-1.

He was a composer and musician born in Hackensack, New Jersey. Riddle's music was heard on many film scores, musicals, television series, and the stage. He worked with Burt Reynolds, the Carpenters and Mickey Spillane, directed the AFI Salute to Frank Capra and the all-star party for Lucille Ball, and was awarded an Oscar in 1974 for his musical direction on *The Great Gatsby.*

A marble rocket ship rises in the air just beyond the Chandler enclave. The inscription reads, "The Atlas Pioneer in space here symbolizes the lifetime activities of **Carl Morgan Bigsby**."

Bigsby was a pioneer in the graphic arts, he was an afficionado of space. His monument is a replica of the Pioneer Atlas as it orbited the earth on December 18, 1958. It reads that Carl Bigsby was

No, this isn't a memorial to Buck Rogers.

"Retired by God." His wife, Constance, must have enjoyed her life with him. Her inscription says, "Too bad . . . we had fun."

On Woodland Avenue rests **J. Dabney Day**, 1872–1929, with a large open Bible, followed by **George Townsend Cole**, 1874–1937, in three-quarter profile, wearing a carelessly tied necktie.

George was the youngest son of Senator Cornelius Cole, one of Lincoln's confidants. He was a landscape and portrait painter, using new techniques in his artwork. He died of acute indigestion in his studio, in the arms of his companion, actor Jimmy Wolfe.

Following George Cole, philanthropist, is **Frederick W. Blanchard**, 1864–1928. His monument shows a mournful young woman, her face nearly covered with her very long hair.

### Colonel Griffith J. Griffith, 1850–1918.

Across from Blanchard in the Highland area is Colonel Griffith J. Griffith, the man who presented the very beautiful Griffith Park to the city of Los Angeles—but not before its accursed and diabolical history had affected its succession of owners. Unbelievable misfortunes, floods, fires, tragedies and even ghosts controlled its destiny.

*Wickiup* (tent) housing for the native Gabrielino Indians originally occupied the property. The land had been presented as the Los Feliz land grant to Jose Vicente Feliz in exchange for belated pay while in the service of the Spanish before the colonization of California. Feliz then served as corporal in charge of the founding of the Pueblo de Los Angeles and was its first city manager from 1895 to 1900. He became known as "Little Father" because of his courage and dedication in protecting the pueblo.

Jose was murdered, after which the property passed to Feliz's nephew, Juan Jose Feliz y Valenzuela, and then upon his death to Juan's son, bachelor Jose Antonio Feliz. Jose Antonio had intended for his niece, Petranilla, to inherit it. However, she was duped out of the land by a crafty crook who held the hand of the dying man and made his mark on an instrument assigning it to "Mr. Crook." Petranilla took umbrage at his duplicity and put a hex on him and the entire Los Feliz grant, which lasted through many successive owners. Feliz and his descendants lived on the property for 68 years, and during that time four flags flew over it: Spain, Mexico, The Republic of California and the United States.

"Mr. Crook," Don Antonio Coronel, conveyed the entire property to his lawyer, who in turn sold it to a wealthy and elegant American, Leon Baldwin. Mr. Baldwin spared no expense in improving the ranch and dairy. He fenced the property and remodeled the old

Feliz house into the perfection of elegant comfort. He built a new mansion on the hill as a home for his brother, but Petranilla's gods were not appeased and everything continued to go wrong. Cattle died, the dairy failed, fire destroyed the ripening grain and grasshoppers devoured the crops. The vineyard developed a blight and more. Baldwin was forced to put a mortgage on the property and finally sold the ranch for the amount of the mortgage. The family announced the ranch was cursed and moved away. Then Colonel Griffith J. Griffith purchased the property. Conditions worsened.

The ominous disasters predicted by Petranilla continued their dominion over the property after Griffith's purchase. Great storm clouds gathered in the dark recesses of the Grand Tehunga in March 1884. They crashed together and a flood, in one giant roaring advance, swept down on Rancho Feliz. The waters raged and seethed; the thunder caused the earth to quake and the mountains to rattle. Thunderbolts struck, fires erupted and lightning scorched mighty oaks.

The vast meadow and pastures of the famed Portrero de Los Feliz suffered wreck and desolation. The best of the property was swept out to sea, and the remains were left like a disfigured corpse on a battlefield. Ironically, neighboring orchards and ranchos were left untouched.

Mexican retainers reported seeing the ghost of Petranilla and her uncle, Don Feliz, riding the torrential waves and directing the furious elements against the dissolving margins of the land.

Workmen were dispatched to repair the lands and remains, but they deserted after one night on the property. Their unvarying tale was "Those lands are haunted. A spirit declaring itself to be Jose Antonio Feliz stalks up and down the river and stands on the hill denouncing those who desecrated it."

Griffith went back to the ranch frequently, saying he wouldn't spend another night on it for a million. But the expenses and taxes continued, and he could not find a buyer. There is some speculation as to whether civic mindedness or fear caused Griffith to donate the land to the City of Los Angeles for use as a park, today the largest public park in America.

Even after he gave the land away, the ghostly encroachments

did not stop. His offer was welcomed and the city council agreed to accompany Griffith to the ranch for a great ceremony in the giving and receiving of the 3,000 acres, all that remained of the 8,000 following the flood.

The revelers tarried over the food, liquor and merrymaking. At midnight there appeared a gaunt, sepulchral figure with a fleshless face. His eye sockets emitted sulfurous flashes. Robed in a portion of rotting funeral vestment, he raised his hands to command silence. The skeleton shuffled with bony sound over the concrete floor, seated himself at the head of the noble oaken table, and in the voice of the tomb announced: "Señores, I am Antonio Feliz, come to invite you to dine with me in hell, and I have brought an escort of sub-demons."

An awful din broke loose. Lights went out, gongs and cymbals clashed and demons came dancing into the hall. The party ended as all guests exited.

In the year 1903, there was a sequel to the story that conclusively shows that the curse of Los Feliz is still vindictively in pursuit of all who have profited by the ruin of the ranch. The literal translation of *feliz,* which means "happy," would never apply to this place, for soon an attempted murder was the devastating, demonic second chapter in the course of events confirming the Feliz curse.

William Randolph Hearst's news reporter, Adela Rogers St. Johns, covered the trial of Colonel Griffith when he was charged with the attempted murder of his wife. Said Adela, "Colonel Griffith was one of the most colorful characters Los Angeles has ever known. He did not seem a reality. Rather, he appeared a gnome out of a book of grotesque tales, a human caricature. He was a roly poly, pompous little fellow who held himself to be above public opinion or even that of the courts. He had an exaggerated strut like a turkey gobbler and used an oversized cane as in the fashion of a nobleman. He sported an immense chrysanthemum or dahlia in his buttonhole.

"The tract of land . . . river beds, vales and mountainside . . . that he owned and gave to the City of Los Angeles in 1898, Griffith Park, is today one of the showplaces of the West. Christina, his wife, was the daughter of one of Los Angeles' first families. She was wealthy in her own right, active in civic functions and socially prominent. As a leading member of the Catholic church she was an active social welfare worker.

"She conveyed to Griffith considerable real estate for his use as collateral in a deal he was handling, but, when she requested its return, he became enraged and hated and distrusted her ... which he, nevertheless, concealed with all the cunning of his warped intellect.

"The little turkey has amassed property worth millions, despite his being half drunk all of his waking hours. These excesses filled his mind with weird hallucinations."

Adela related the events, reconstructed at the trial: "While on a month's holiday in the beautiful old Arcadia Hotel on a bluff overlooking the surf on the Pacific Ocean in Santa Monica, he prepared to kill Christina by handing her a prayer book and forcing her to get down on her knees. With her hands on her Bible, he threw imaginary accusations at her, challenging her to defend herself. Brandishing a pistol in her face, he claimed she had improper relations with a porter at the hotel; said she had attempted to poison him for Bishop Conaty, who wanted his property for the Catholic Church; and reminded her that he had to sleep in the bath house to escape the Pope's followers, who, with her aid, wanted him slain.

"As Christina sobbed inarticulately in her attempt to reply, he put the gun to her head. As she watched his finger contact the trigger, she jerked her head to one side; the bullet went through her left temple and eye. She screamed in terror and flung herself through the window, falling upon the roof of the veranda, two stories below. The fall broke one of her legs, but, fearful of her life, she dragged herself through the window into another hotel room. Her screams alerted the hotel manager, who found her stanching the flow of blood from the socket of her eye. She was nearly dead." Petranilla's curse spared no one.

Earl Rogers, Adela's father, was a famous attorney who agreed to defend Griffith. The *Los Angeles Times* headlined, "Rogers will attempt to prove that Mrs. Griffith had too much religion and the Colonel too much champagne."

Griffith was found guilty but was sentenced minimally.

However, his conviction was considered ruinous to Rogers, as it was the first case the brilliant lawyer ever lost. It devastated him.

The earlier residents, the Gabrielinos, understood the curse. If one doesn't do what is right with his fellow man, he can expect punishment by whatever forces can be commanded. Opposite to the Gabrielino word for "good," *dihokon,* Rancho Los Feliz was sworn to have elements that were *tsinukhu,* "bad."

Ill fortune did not cease until the land became a citadel for healing. Part of the land grant is home today to the Hollywood Queen of Angels Presbyterian Hospital.

**Louis Calhern,** 1895–1956. Niche 308 T.3, South Wall, Abbey Foyer.

Calhern was a tall, hawk-nosed actor with a cultured voice. His big roles were in *The Asphalt Jungle* and *The Magnificent Yankee,* for which he received an Oscar nomination. He married four times and died while filming *Teahouse of the August Moon* in 1956. Earlier that same year he had completed his role as a charming, boozy relative to Grace Kelly in *High Society.*

**William A. Clark Jr.,** 1877–1934. In the family mausoleum, built in 1920 at a reported cost of $500,000.

This magnificent mausoleum appears to be a large marble

home. It rests on an island in the middle of a lily pond enjoyed by floating ducks and geese. A visitor reaches the island by crossing a bridge. There one sees a seated nude woman who appears to be pushing back a curtain. On the right is a winged hourglass, sinking out of view. A beast in pursuit charges on the right side. The Latin inscription translates, "The sweet memory of our beloved ones banishes the fear of death; the nature of heavenly things and brings hope

The William A. Clark Jr. family mausoleum.

of new life."The monument honored Hollywood when it was designated by the Architectural Society of America as the most beautiful structure of its type built between 1925 and 1928.

Clark was a brilliant lawyer, a violinist, and a man dedicated to civic and cultural affairs. He was the son of Montana Senator W. A. Clark and was wealthy in his own right from his mining speculations. His wife, **Mabel Foster**, gave birth to their first son, who was known as the "Million Dollar Baby" because his grandfather had pledged that gift to him at his birth. Twenty-three-year-old Mabel died of childbirth fever only days after he was born.

Philanthropist Clark founded the Los Angeles Philharmonic, initiated several other charities, and eventually donated his home and library to UCLA. The Clark Mausoleum is filled with pieces from art collections. For years it was opened upon occasion to the public. Clark rests peacefully between his two wives.

Left at the walkway, turning toward the road, past the Mattoon circular bench near the lake is Section 8. Many film personalities are found in this area, beginning with **Adolph Menjou,** 1890–1963, in Lot 11.

Menjou traded his U.S. Army uniform for the costumes of an actor representing sartorial elegance. The son of a French restaurateur, Menjou began his film career in New York as an extra. His mustaches gained him roles as a nobleman, so he quickly added an ascot, white spats and a walking cane, which later earned him the title of Hollywood's "best dressed man." This fine actor appeared in *The Three Musketeers, A Woman of Paris* and *Little Miss Marker.* In 1969 he made his last film, *Pollyanna.* His explosive portrayal of an editor, based on the life of Charles MacArthur, earned him an Oscar nomination in 1931 for *The Front Page.*

Ten markers from the right and one row toward the lake rests **John Huston,** 1906–1987, and his mother **Rhea Huston,** 1881–1938 (Lot 8).

The marker's pink marble is imported from Ireland, and the names are engraved in gold. Lusty and fun-loving, John was an intense man, a man's man with a great attraction to and by women.

John Huston — Lusty and fun-loving, Hemingway's pal and a master director.

As did his friend Hemingway, John loved big game hunting, drinking, carousing and writing. Before arriving in Hollywood to become a script writer, he had stints in vaudeville and as a newspaper reporter. Married five times, he characterized his wives as "a schoolgirl, a gentlewoman, a motion picture actress, a ballerina, and a crocodile," with no further identification. Huston was a brilliant film maker when he got around to it. His *Prizzi's Honor* won Oscars for both his daughter, actress Anjelica Huston, and his father, Walter Huston. John found his niche in directing classics such as *The Maltese Falcon, The Treasure of the Sierra Madre, The African Queen* with Bogart and Hepburn, *Freud, The Red Badge of Courage, Moby Dick, Reflections in a Golden Eye* and *Chinatown*. An intellectual man, he produced several of these films from well-known literary works.

Huston was a smoker and drinker who became something of a recluse. He spent the last years of his life living with a companion, presumably one of the aforementioned five, in a remote village in Mexico. He died of acute emphysema. His father, famous actor Walter, was cremated, and his ashes were given to the family. Their whereabouts remain a mystery. For more details see the "Chapel of the Pines" section.

Continuing around the lake, you will see the impressive sarcophagi of **Cecil Blount DeMille**, 1881–1959, and his wife, **Constance Adams DeMille**, 1874–1950. They are found directly opposite and across the lake from the monument of DeMille's competitor, Harry Cohn.

The monument features two caskets with crosses on top and two urns in the middle—impressive, but not the spectacle one might expect from the studio head who loved intimate bathtub scenes and great Biblical extravaganzas. The conservative son of a Massachusetts Episcopalian clergyman, DeMille became interested in moviemaking during lunch with Samuel Goldwyn and his brother-in-law, Jesse Lasky. The trio ran into actor Dustin Farnum, who introduced them to the author of *The Squaw Man,* and the Jesse L. Lasky Feature Play Company was born.

Blazing a trail west from New York, DeMille passed over his original destination, Arizona, because he considered the climate unsuitable. California, he decided, provided longer light days and less variable temperatures. For the magnificent sum of $200 a week, he set up shop in a rented barn, which became famous and remains so today. The barn is now located in a park-like setting across from the Hollywood Bowl, having been moved there from its original location on Vine Street. Eventually the barn appeared in many films and TV series, most notably in *Bonanza.*

Actor Buddy Ebsen tells the story of DeMille's annoyance at having to pay the $200 a month rent for the barn, especially after he learned that his secretary was hauling down the munificent sum of $10 a week. "Fire her," he fumed.

As the secretary cleaned out her desk, DeMille asked, "Why is she taking the typewriter?"

"It's hers," was the answer. She kept the typewriter and the job. DeMille arrived in California in 1913, settling in a Hollywood overrun with orange blossoms and rickety boarding houses, that soon would bear signs reading "No dogs or actors allowed." Innovator DeMille devised unique camera effects that immediately caught on with filmgoers. His first production was *The Squaw Man,* which grossed $244,700, and was followed by *The Virginian* and *The Call of the North,* all successful. Throughout his career, he was the persona of "The Movie Director," sartorially elegant in high boots, jodhpurs and a turned-back cap. His leather puttees and his pistol warded off rattlesnakes when on location. His firearms stayed with him on his nightly trips home over the Cahuenga Pass, when he carried his film cans home to better protect them from marauders—and from the Edison Company, which was fighting DeMille over film copyrights.

A physically daring man, he would swim in shark-filled waters and walk naked through snake- and scorpion-infested jungles as examples for his actors. On one occasion he was thrown burned and unconscious into the ocean due to an explosion he created. He valued his stoic courage, which he claimed to have inherited from his father, who died when Cecil was 11. He considered courage, his greatest virtue and had no patience for less valiant actors. He considered Victor Mature not brave enough and derided Cornel Wilde for his acrophobia. When the blind Samson (Victor Mature) brought the Philistine temple crashing down in a scene DeMille was shooting, actor Henry Wilcoxon was struck on the head by a falling column. As Wilcoxon staggered away, with blood pouring down his face, DeMille confronted him with "My God, Henry, clean yourself up. You're holding up production!"

He admired Barbara Stanwyck's bravery when she allowed herself to be chased by a herd of stampeding buffalo, as well as a Dorothy Lamour scene when she hung by her teeth high above the ground.

DeMille's impatience pervaded his personal life as well. When his wife, Constance, for health reasons, locked her bedroom door against him, he allegedly recruited two mistresses, Julia Faye and Jeannie MacPherson, to travel with him on weekends at his ranch, Paradise.

A showman and storyteller, he valued the role he created for himself on his popular weekly series *Lux Radio Theater,* which he personally hosted from 1936 to 1945. A competent actor, DeMille, along with his brother, attended the Academy of Dramatic Arts in New York. There he learned his trade as an actor, stage manager and then playwright under the tutelage of famed impresario David Belasco. Later, he felt qualified to produce motion pictures, which he did on a grand scale. His early features included the *Warrens of Virginia, The Cheat, The Little American* and *The Whispering Chorus.* America welcomed his comedies *Don't Change Your Husband* and *Male and Female.* The latter included a notorious scene of Gloria Swanson in the nude, stepping into her bath. Many actors and actresses became famous under his direction.

Moving from Victorian proprieties to sexy comedies, Hollywood had to defend itself against accusations of being a modern-day Gomorrah. DeMille countered with religious and historical movies such as *The Ten Commandments, The King of Kings, The Sign of the Cross* and *Cleopatra*. He brought us epic westerns, such as *The Plainsman, Union Pacific, The Buccaneer, Reap the Wild Wind, Samson and Delilah* and *The Greatest Show on Earth,* all classics, followed.

Considered Hollywood's "greatest showman" in the mammoth business he helped to build, DeMille died in 1959 at the age of 78. His *Autobiography of Cecil B. DeMille* was published posthumously.

A few rows from DeMille rests the winner of the first Best Actress Oscar for her cumulative work in *Sunrise, Seventh Heaven,* and *Street Angel,* **Janet Gaynor,** 1906–1984, Lot 193.

Sweet, petite and winsome, she was pretty and charismatic, usually demure, but not powerful or inspiring. Originally from San Francisco, she was in Hollywood specifically to get into films. After a few bit parts in Hal Roach comedies and westerns, her career took off when she was teamed with Charles Farrell in the smash hit *Seventh Heaven,* playing a Parisian waif. This success was quickly followed by an additional nine films co-starring with Farrell.

*Daddy Long Legs, State Fair* and *Ladies in Love* were successful, but *A Star is Born* in 1937 was one of her most endearing and persuasive performances. She retired from the screen in 1938, making only occasional radio and TV appearances, but returned to the screen to play the mother's role in *Bernadine.*

She was voted the movies' top box-office female star in 1934. Married to dress designer Gilbert Adrian until his death, she later married producer Paul Gregory and lived with him in Palm Springs. Janet Gaynor died following complications from a car crash that also injured actress Mary Martin.

**Jayne Mansfield,** 1933–1967. Down from Gaynor, near the lake, in Lot 218.

An off-the-rack Marilyn Monroe lookalike, Jayne was in many respects larger than life. She had a voluptuous body that, along with

Jayne Mansfield — Quite a bit larger than life.

a somewhat affected squeaky voice, limited her movie roles. Jayne studied acting in addition to her other courses in college and scored extremely high on IQ tests.

A Monroe parody, *Will Success Spoil Rock Hunter?* first brought her fame in Broadway comedies. She followed with *Illegal, Pete Kelly's Blues, Hell in Frisco Bay* and *The Female Jungle.* Her performances in *The Girl Can't Help It* and the film version of *Rock Hunter* are considered her best. Subsequent roles were mostly decorative. Never out of the spotlight, Jayne was a newspaper man's dream. She posed for *Playboy* magazine, appeared on television, and constantly dreamed up promotion and publicity stunts that kept her public aware of her, such as shopping in a velvet bikini and cutting ribbons at bowling alley openings.

Encouraged by her mother, Jayne grew up wanting to be a movie star. She persuaded her husband, Paul Mansfield, whom she married and had a baby with at 17, to move to Los Angeles when she was 21. After their divorce, she married "Mr. Universe" Mickey Hargitay, who appeared in small roles in her pictures and constructed her pink mansion with a heart-shaped swimming pool.

She divorced Hargitay then married and divorced Matt Cimber. Physical fights between Jayne and the various fathers of her five children were grist for the newspaper mill, as were the altercations between the husbands themselves.

Famous dress designer Mr. Blackwell, noted for his 10 Worst Dressed Women list, announced, "I can't go on designing for an actress who shows off my work by either having the dresses ripped off her or wrestling on the floor with them."

Jayne's career finally deteriorated to playing nightclubs in parody performances of her real life. On the night of her last appearance,

June 28, 1967, she died tragically in a gruesome auto accident. Jayne was a very devoted mother. Her three children, who always traveled with her, were asleep in the back seat and survived the accident. Sam Brody, her latest paramour, who was said to have

had an unsound influence on her, was also in the car. He was killed and is buried at Hillside Memorial Park.

Many theories were advanced as to what caused the accident. Newspapers reported that Jayne was decapitated when her car plowed under a tractor trailer. However, it was later revealed that it was only her wig that was separated from her head. After much debate among her husbands, who thought Jayne should be buried in Hollywood, her family prevailed and she was sent home to Pennsylvania. Her legions of fans still maintain and visit her pink granite heart memorial, which reads "We live to love you more each day." They have brought her flowers and love for more than 30 years.

Jayne would be proud that her daughter, Mariska Hargitay, is an actress who appears on television and in films and presently has her own TV series.

The product of another horrible episode and excruciating death is buried a few plots away from Jayne. Her story is one that created havoc with the film industry and its reputation. **Virginia Rappe,** 1896–1921, is in Lot 257.

Virginia was injured at the party celebrating Roscoe "Fatty" Arbuckle's new $3 million contract with Paramount at the Saint Francis Hotel in San Francisco on a Labor Day weekend. Also present was Maude Demont, a recognized procurer of young women for such parties, who sometimes blackmailed the involved men afterward. Maude accused Fatty of raping the part-time actress with a piece of ice, champagne bottle or some other object. Another theory was that Virginia contracted peritonitis after a botched abortion. From the hotel, she was taken to a hospital where she lapsed into a coma and died of a ruptured bladder five days after the party.

The newspapers had a field day with the resulting trial. Although Arbuckle was funny as a comedian, the public abhorred the thought of the rotund Fatty (who had weighed 16 pounds at birth) violating the young woman. Three trials and two hung juries later, he was acquitted, but his movie career was over.

In spite of Virginia's wanton life, film director **Henry Lehrman,** 1886–1946, loved her and lived the rest of his life around her memory. He laid her to rest at Hollywood Memorial and visited her weekly until he was buried next to her for eternity.

Another eternal love virtually ended by death was that of **Marion Davies,** 1897–1961, and her lifelong love and mentor, newspaper tycoon, William Randolph Hearst.

Buried in a large mausoleum beside the little lake, the name "Douras" (her real name) identifies her final resting place. This engaging, spirited girl swept Hearst off his feet when she was a 20-year-old Ziegfeld Follies showgirl. He was 54. Theirs was a true love affair. They worshiped each other but never married because Hearst was not divorced from his wife, Phoebe. The various versions of the story were never clear about whether Phoebe would grant the divorce, whether Hearst did not wish to deny his sons, or whether the devout Catholic Marion did not insist on his divorce. However, Hearst and Marion remained together until the end of his life.

Hearst spent fortunes, and either built or associated himself with studios, to make Marion a star. A star she became, but not

Davies Mausoleum—Marion *without* WRH.

one of the brightest, because Hearst would never allow her real talent as a dramatic actress or comedienne to surface. Rather, he loved seeing her in costumes and epics that did not suit her type. Still, everyone loved the little scamp who was accepted by the movie industry, society and even royalty as she held court and entertained lavishly at their Santa Monica beach mansion and at Hearst Castle.

Hearst passed away in 1951 at Marion's Beverly Hills home. His family was believed to have had her sedated and refused to tell her where and when the funeral would be held, so she was unable to say her final farewell to him. Shocking the family, Hearst left all editorial and financial control of his publishing empire to her, which required the Hearst family to continue to deal with her. With her business acumen, Marion handled this responsibility successfully. One of her most successful investments was the well-known Desert Inn in Palm Springs, where she spent much time later in her life. (For more on Hearst, see the "Fascinating Funerals" section.)

Ten weeks after Hearst's death, Marion surprised everyone by marrying a former stuntman and sea captain, Horace Brown. He was a younger image of her lover but not a similar man. She filed for divorce twice, but the couple stayed together, and he was at her bedside when she died of cancer of the jaw at 64.

A strange coincidence finds Charlie Chaplin's mother, **Hannah,** 1866–1928, in Lot 260 to the left of the Davies/Douras mausoleum.

When he became successful, the "Little Tramp" brought his mother from England to live in Hollywood. She soon fell ill and died. It was fairly common knowledge that Marion had long had romantic liaisons with Charlie, perhaps unbeknown to Hearst.

Within the Douras mausoleum, boyish, high-voiced **Arthur Lake** also rests.

He was the perpetually perplexed suburban husband Dagwood Bumstead in the series *Blondie.* Although he had appeared in many other films, he would never shake his Dagwood character. Blondie, of course, was played by Penny Singleton, who also became typed.

**Tyrone Power Jr.,** 1914–1958. His memorial bench is to the left of Marion Davies' mausoleum on a grassy knoll, facing the lake where ducks and geese hold court.

One of Hollywood's most popular and handsome actors, his grave is continuously visited by his still-loyal fans. Between bookends on the bench is a single volume showing the masks of Comedy and Tragedy. Lines from Hamlet read:

> There is a special providence in the fall of a sparrow.
> If it be now, 'tis not to come;
> If it be not to come, it will be now;
> if it be not now, yet it will come . . .
> the readiness is all . . . Now cracks a noble heart.
> Good night, sweet prince.
> And flights of angels sing thee to thy rest.

He was the son of silent movie actor Tyrone Power, who died in 1931 after completing his only talkie. Tyrone Jr. resolved at an early age to follow in his father's footsteps, acting on stage while still in his teens and making his movie debut as a cadet in *Tom Brown of Culver* in 1932. Progressing to meatier roles, including three with Loretta Young, he worked with Alice Faye, Norma Shearer, Betty Grable and others. He played a young and handsome lover, a historical figure, the swashbuckling Zorro, an American soldier, a protagonist seeking truth and goodness, an outright rotter, a mind reader and a dramatic and comedic actor.

Power entered the armed services, where he served until the end of World War II, distinguishing himself in action. He returned from the conflict a changed man, more serious and grim. Picking up his career at Fox where he had left off, Power starred in the film version of Somerset Maugham's *The Razor's Edge* in 1946.

A constantly improving actor, Power was at his greatest portraying the famous pianist and orchestra leader in *The Eddie Duchin Story.* He excelled in one of his last on-screen appearances, *Abandon Ship!* Also notable was his role as the tragic protagonist Jake Barnes in Hemingway's classic *The Sun Also Rises* and as a murder suspect in Billy Wilder's *Witness for the Prosecution*, adapted from an Agatha Christie novel.

He became increasingly tired and nervous, drinking heavily and not taking care of his health. Power went overseas to shoot the Biblical epic *Solomon and Sheba* but collapsed and died of a heart attack on location. Subsequently, Yul Brynner re-shot the role.

Two of Power's three wives were actresses: Annabella and Linda Christian. His daughter, Taryn, by the still-beautiful Linda Christian, was an actress during the 1970s. His son, Tyrone, has acted in films such as *Cocoon* and *Shag*. He also had a major role in the long-running, successful TV series *Cheers*.

Film critic and historian Leonard Maltin wrote, "This devilishly handsome star made millions of female hearts flutter every time he appeared on the big screen. He even had that effect on some of his distaff co-stars: Alice Faye once said kissing Power was 'like dying and going to Heaven.'"

Power's obituary in the *New York Times* stated that "Only 100 close friends of the actor could be accommodated in the small chapel at the cemetery." His wife, Deborah Anne Power, sat in front of the open coffin, while actor Cesar Romero gave the eulogy.

Tyrone Power Jr. with Adela Rogers St. Johns. He made millions of female hearts flutter.

He read the essay "The Promises of America" by Thomas Wolfe, which Power himself had planned to read on Thanksgiving Day to Air Force personnel stationed in Spain. Unfortunately, that was about the time he was being buried.

As described earlier, the monument that balances Cecil B. DeMille's is a white marble sarcophagi (Lot 86) that identifies movie mogul **Harry Cohn,** 1891–1958, and his family. Both a Star of David and a cross grace the monument. At his wife's request, Cohn made a deathbed conversion to Christianity.

The film community detested Cohn's display of ego. He raised the desk in his office so that those addressing him had to look up. He shouted indiscriminately over his intercom. When one of his statements was questioned by a visitor with, "Who is that speaking?" Cohn replied, "God." And on the Columbia lot he was God—even though he was disliked and disrespected by his staff and actors.

Originally a song plugger, he formed Columbia Pictures and later its subsidiary, Screen Gems, with his brother Jack. The studios flourished and groomed actors John Wayne, Rita Hayworth, Glenn Ford and Kim Novak, as well as director Frank Capra. Cohn achieved 45 Oscars with classics such as *Mr. Deeds Goes to Town, Mr. Smith Goes to Washington, Lost Horizon, On the Waterfront, All the King's Men* and *Born Yesterday.* Of the last two it was said he modeled the lead characters after his disagreeable self. His ego and love of power led to famous battles with his stars and directors.

Harry Cohn — "Give the people what they want and they'll come."

He was sued by King Vidor for abusive treatment, although the judge ruled in Cohn's favor, citing the nature of the profession and noting that Cohn's abuse was indiscriminate and habitual. In other words, it was forgivable because he treated everyone badly.

His funeral was conducted on converted Columbia Sound Stage 12, with his coffin on a raised platform, just as his desk had always been. Over 1,500 people attended, not all of them mourning his death. Writer Irving Brecher (an Oscar winner for *Meet Me in St. Louis*) heard someone say in amazement, "Look at the crowd that came out."

Brecher replied, "Give the people what they want and they'll come!"

Memorialized by one of the most beautiful tributes in Hollywood Memorial is **Douglas Fairbanks Sr.**, 1883–1939, located in Section 11, Sunken Garden, west of the Cathedral Mausoleum.

The magnificent sunken garden features a long rectangular reflecting pool that mirrors the classical Greek architecture. The centerpiece, fronted by a raised tomb, bears a cameo profile framed by a laurel wreath.

Fairbanks was the screen's first swashbuckling hero, beginning his film career as the prototype of the all-American boy. Energetic, athletic and exuberant, he was one of the first recognized proponents of exercise and a positive mental attitude. Growing up in the west, he attended the Colorado School of Mines and later Harvard University. He worked at various odd jobs before he found a Broadway role in *Her Lord and Master*. But he gave up the stage when his first wife, Manna Beth Sully, asked him to take a job offered by a Wall Street brokerage firm. She craved a kind of security the stage could not provide. Their son, Doug Jr., was born in 1909. Denouncing business, he was drawn back to the stage before moving to Hollywood and films. His stunts and dueling became legendary, even though D.W. Griffith of Triangle Pictures said, "He has the face of a cantaloupe and can't act."

He met, lived with and eventually married America's sweetheart, Mary Pickford, after both divorced their spouses. They became the virtual king and queen of Hollywood. Their palatial residence in Beverly Hills began its life in 1920 as Doug's hunting lodge in the sparsely inhabited area. The couple named it "Pickfair," and it became the unofficial social capital of movieland.

Fairbanks' films soon grew monotonous so he moved on to romantic and adventure films, writing many of them himself. Fairbanks and his wife, Mary, D.W. Griffith and Charlie Chaplin founded their own studio, United Artists Corporation.

Doug and Mary parted over his wanderlust, which kept him away from home and conflicted with her desire to stay put in Pickfair. Reconciling and parting frequently, they kept edging toward the divorce that finally ended their marriage. Both subsequently said it was a mistake, but they were too far along with their differences to stop it.

Fairbanks later married Lady Sylvia Ashley, a chorus girl by trade and a Lady by a previous marriage. In 1936 Mary married the extraordinarily handsome and talented actor-musician Charles "Buddy" Rogers. After meeting and co-starring in a film with her, Buddy had been in love with her for many years. They were together for 43 years until she died.

On the last day of his life, Fairbanks attended a USC-UCLA football game. After returning home, he died of a heart attack. His wake was held in his Santa Monica beach home, where he rested in an ornately carved bed in front of a window facing the Pacific Ocean. Visitors were greeted by Fairbanks' 150-pound mastiff, Marco Polo, who lay by his bed, whining and refusing to move. Mary Pickford, on a musical tour with Buddy Rogers in Chicago, sent her condolences.

**Woody Herman,** 1913–1987. Grounds area, Crypt 6689, Unit 10.

This well-known band leader from Milwaukee, Wisconsin, was educated at Marquette University. Herman played clarinet and sax with dance bands and formed his own band appearing in hotels, theaters, and ballrooms in the United States and Europe. His TV credits include *A Gift of Music, The Nashville Palace, Jazz Alive, Night of 100 Stars* and *Earl Carroll's Vanities.*

Thirteen ten-foot statues guard the hall of the Cathedral Mausoleum. Walk past them and turn right into the second hall. On the right is the crypt of **William Desmond Taylor,** a.k.a. William Deane-Tanner, 1877–1922. The crypt is located to the right as you enter Cathedral Mausoleum. Taylor's tale is one of the most notorious and puzzling of Hollywood's mysteries. He was known as one of Hollywood's finest directors and a perfect gentleman. He was thought to be a man without an enemy, except for the one that shot him dead with one bullet through his heart on the night of February 1, 1922. (For more information on Taylor's death, see the section "Death by Mysterious Circumstance.")

In the alcove across from Taylor, on the left, are **Horace H. Wilcox** (d. 1891) and his widow, **Daeida Wilcox Beveridge** (d. 1914), considered to be the founders of Hollywood.

They envisioned the village as a devoutly Christian community and gave free land to Protestant churches. The sale and imbibing of liquor were prohibited. There are many theories of how Hollywood was named. One story tells how Mrs. Wilcox liked the name of a country estate belonging to someone she met on a train. Another was that the name came from the Holy Wood that was found on the area's hills by the early Spanish priests who first came to the area. If they could see Hollywood now!

In the same area, farther down in the Alcove of Reverence, in a glass compartment on the bottom row, is **Peter Lorre** (Ladislav Loewenstein), 1904–1964.

Lorre's first film role made him a powerful character in motion pictures. He was a peculiar, gnome-like little man with a moon face, bulging eyes and gapped teeth. He was considered one of Hollywood's finest character actors. He fled Germany in the early 1930s and appeared in both British and American films. His roles included a pathetic child murderer in *M,* a mad doctor, a Japanese sleuth, and a sinister but fastidious Joel Cairo in John Huston's *The Maltese Falcon,* which also featured Humphrey Bogart. He also co-starred with Bogart in *Casablanca* and later teamed up with Sydney Greenstreet in several films. During this period he became the most mimicked and caricatured actor in movies and in animated cartoons. In *Arsenic and Old Lace* and *My Favorite Brunette,* he further displayed his comic talents.

He returned to Germany in 1951 to write, direct and act in his own films. In his 50s he seemed to age and became puffy, tired looking and less inspired, walking through his roles rather than acting. During the twilight of his career he teamed with Vincent Price in both *The Comedy of Terrors* and *The Raven.* His performance as a half-man, half-raven endeared Lorre to an entire new generation of fans.

Also in the Hollywood Cathedral Mausoleum is **Eleanor Powell,** 1912–1982, dancing star of the 1930s and 1940s. Her dancing was exuberant and her smile scintillating, but her acting ability was limited. Before she arrived in Hollywood to do a specialty number in *George White's Scandals* (1935), Broadway had already called her the "World's Greatest Tap Dancer."

She delighted depression-era moviegoers with her boundless energy and optimism. She appeared in *The Broadway Melody of 1940* with "the king," Fred Astaire, which attests to her talents. When she married the love of her life, Glenn Ford, she retired from the screen. After 16 years together, she and Ford divorced. She continued to perform, mostly on stage and in nightclubs. She retained her supple figure and pretty appearance well into middle age. In later years, Eleanor Powell became profoundly interested in religion and was ordained a minister of the Unity Church.

**Nelson Eddy**, 1901–1967, Section 8, Lot 89.

A newspaper reporter who possessed a magnificent voice, Eddy signed for a successful career in opera, first with the Philadelphia Civic Opera and later with New York's Metropolitan. Seen and signed by MGM in 1933, Eddy was cast in three films before he was teamed with the popular singing star, Jeanette MacDonald, in the Victor Herbert operetta *Naughty Marietta.*

They were transformed overnight into the nation's favorite couple, ideally mated on-screen with their visions of romantic and requited love. He occasionally appeared with other stars, including Eleanor Powell in *Rosalie,* Ilona Massey in *Balalaika,* Virginia Bruce in *Let Freedom Ring,* and Rise Stevens in *The Chocolate Soldier.* After performing in Universal's *Phantom of the Opera, Knickerbocker Holiday*, and *Northwest Outpost,* he was in great demand for nightclub performances, concert appearances and recordings. In Walt Disney's *Make Mine Music,* Eddy narrated and provided all the voices in a delightful comic tale called "The Whale Who Wanted to Sing at the Met." This film revealed many more of his dramatic dimensions, as well as a sense of humor.

"I'm mad as hell, and I'm not going to take it anymore" was the cry of the TV newsman in *Network* (1976). It was **Peter Finch,** 1916–1977 (Crypt 1244), who shouted the line from the windows of his New York TV station. His performance in that film remains one of the best remembered by moviegoers, and for it he was posthumously awarded an Oscar for Best Actor in 1976.

Finch grew up with his well-to-do parents in France and India. Returning with his parents to their native Australia, he found work in the legitimate theater. Laurence Olivier made him his protégé after he invited Finch to work with him in London. He received good notices and won British Film Academy awards for his work in *A Town Like Alice* and *The Trials of Oscar Wilde.* He was Oscar nominated for his work in the British-U.S. production of *Sunday Bloody Sunday.*

Finch collapsed with a massive heart attack in the lobby of the Beverly Hills Hotel and is buried across the way from Valentino, near the Hollywood Memorial entrance.

Near Finch in the next alcove, finally at rest, is the film star who was known as "The girl who was too beautiful." **Barbara LaMarr** (Reatha Watson), 1896–1926, Vault 1308.

She was a most remarkable, innovative, creative, talented and exquisite person. She found her way into show business and films as a very young girl, but she was sent home by a careful judge who thought she was not safe in Hollywood because she was "too

Barbara LaMarr — The girl who was too beautiful.

beautiful." Her beauty was envied by most other actresses. A genius beyond her years, LaMarr became actress, producer, scriptwriter, poet, author and innovator in all of these forms.

Cub reporter Adela Rogers St. Johns, at that time covering the police beat, took Reatha to her *Herald Examiner* news room after the judge incident and did a feature story on her. Reatha was sent home, but soon she was back in show business. Adela remained her good friend until both her career and her life ended. Reatha, who soon changed her name to Barbara, lived a fast, exhilarating and, some say, wanton life. Several marriages, romances and even suicides and bigamies were committed over her love and rejection. Benito Mussolini was rumored to be in love with her and even appeared, with his army, in a movie that LaMarr produced in Italy. She was a superb actress; her acting skills stand up today, but like many in Hollywood, her life ended too soon.

Some of her classic films include *Thy Name is Woman, Three Musketeers* (the biggest hit of 1921), *Shooting of Dan McGrew, Prisoner of Zenda* and *The Eternal City.*

LaMarr's life was cut short by her fast living, drugs and alcohol, which led to a nervous breakdown. Her greatest love was a little boy she adopted, and when she died, she left him in the care of her close friend, Zasu Pitts. A book is presently being written about LaMarr's life and her son, Don Gallery. This narrative reveals more about the "adoption" and who is thought to be Don's father.

I'm the Sheik of Araby.
Your heart belongs to me.
At night when you're asleep,
Into your tent I'll creep . . .
The stars that shine above
Will light our way to love.
You'll rule the world with me,
The Sheik of Araby!

Most of the world knows that the above identifies **Rudolph Valentino,** formerly known as Rodolpho Guglielmi, 1895–1926. He rests in compartment 1205 in the Cathedral Mausoleum, through the main lobby on the third right hall.

Valentino—romantic, menacing and haughty with hot, piercing eyes—changed the leading man look for the American cinema. Audiences, especially female, loved it. He hated it. He could not appear anywhere without women tearing his clothing off and looting his home, office or hotel rooms for souvenirs of this example of "sheikish love."

His father was a veterinarian in the remote village of Castellaneta in Italy, a poor section where villagers' teeth, for lack of good food and water, turned black and rotted in their mouths. When he got in trouble with his family and the law, his mother arranged steerage for him to New York, where he arrived in 1913. He worked as a landscape gardener, dishwasher, waiter, gigolo and petty criminal before establishing a minor career as a ballroom dancer. However, this man would one day own a 1,000 pairs of socks, 300 ties and over 40 suits. Along with these, he had certain assets that would eventually help him achieve worldwide fame, specifically his smoldering good looks and fluid grace on the dance floor.

He met Alla Nazimova, an established dancer, and toured with her on stage before going to Hollywood in 1917. A few "oily Latin villain" roles brought him to screenwriter June Mathis's attention. She introduced him to director Rex Ingram, who cast him in *The Four Horseman of the Apocalypse* and then in *The Conquering Power.* In each film he danced, and, voilà—each was a big hit. He became the "sheik" sensation, although he transcended the common version. A decent actor with charm and humor, he was

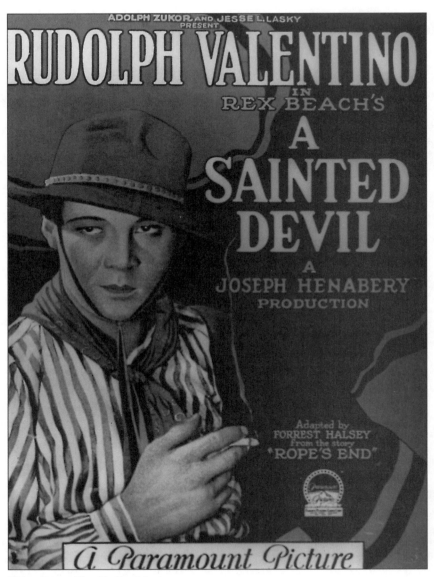

Valentino — The Sheik of Araby.

soon America's most popular star, exciting moviegoers with his swashbuckling athleticism, as well as his bedside manner. He became a sex symbol and idol to millions of women throughout the world, stirring in them dreams of adventure, skullduggery and illicit sex.

His first marriage in 1919, to actress Jean Acker, ended on their wedding night when she slammed the hotel door in his face and told him it was "a horrible mistake." Later, Acker insinuated that he abandoned her. In 1922 he married dancer and set designer Natacha Rambova (nee Winifred Hudnut of the famous cosmetic family); the marriage did not last because of her attempts to dominate him.

She "took charge" of his career because she thought he was not getting the roles she imagined for him, although he was at the peak of his career. She became such a nuisance of herself that Paramount barred her from his sets. Both quit the studio in protest and set out on an extended personal appearance tour. Both his career and his marriage waned. He was single again. It was rumored that neither of his marriages were consummated.

Adela Rogers St. Johns recounts how she was in New York in the same hotel where Valentino spent his last days. He visited her in her suite and for several days complained that he was in escalating pain. She encouraged him to see a doctor, which he refused. Soon he was rushed to Manhattan's Polyclinic Hospital with a perforated ulcer and ruptured appendix, which caused acute peritonitis and his death. For seven days, Valentino's condition was headlined in national newspapers while the world worried over him. He died in 1926 at the age of 31.

Valentino's body lay in state in a bronze coffin at the Frank E. Campbell Funeral Chapel. Soon a crowd of 15,000 people, mostly women, was standing outside the chapel in a driving rainstorm. The crowd soon turned into an angry mob, and with mounted police trying to push them back, they charged the chapel, shattering its huge plate-glass windows. Dozens of injured people, mostly women and children, had to be treated in an emergency hospital set up in another of the chapel's rooms.

Finally the doors opened and the growing mob stormed forward again. They invaded the Gold Room where Valentino was lying in state, tearing the room to pieces. When order was finally restored, 40,000 waiting fans were allowed two-second glances at the body. Many attempted to kiss the protective glass before being forced back into the street, which was now littered with ripped clothing, mashed hats, shoes and other debris. The day had been a catastrophe. The doctor helping the injured turned out to be a con man with no medical training, while the honor guard of black-shirted men from Mussolini's Fascist League were really actors hired by the funeral parlor's press agent. These "Black Shirts" were later attacked by a violent group of anti-facists, adding more broken glass and debris to the streets.

Pola Negri had arrived via train from Los Angeles where, from her bungalow in the Ambassador Hotel, she very dramatically posed for the press, "admitting" that she and Valentino had been engaged. More pandemonium ensued when she arrived at Valentino's bier, screaming and fainting on command for the New York press.

Rumors soon surfaced that Valentino had been poisoned or shot by a jealous husband. Strangely, an autopsy was never performed, and no irate husband was ever found.

Across the nation, tens of thousands turned out at every train station to stare at the car carrying his body back to California. After the funeral, all his possessions were auctioned off, including his clothes. During the months that followed, popular singer Rudy Vallee released a commemorative record entitled *There's a New Star in Heaven Tonight—Rudy Valentino*.

The arrival of the train bearing Valentino and the subsequent funeral in Hollywood created more emotional pandemonium. Thousands attended the rite, with people screaming and crying and being trampled in the crush.

Meanwhile, blueprints for a magnificent monument were drawn up by architect Matlock Price. They included a large statue of Valentino as "the Sheik," set in a semicircle of Roman columns. Each column would feature a bas relief of Valentino in his six greatest films: *The Four Horsemen of the Apocalypse, The Sheik, Monsieur Beaucaire, Blood and Sand, The Eagle* and his biggest hit, *Son of Sheik*. The monument was never built, so at the request of Valentino's old mentor, June Mathis Balboni, he was placed in her husband's crypt next to her own. Later Valentino's brother purchased the vault from Sylvano Balboni, making sure his brother had a permanent resting place. June later died tragically in a fire.

Frequently, souvenir hunters have attacked the tomb in Hollywood Memorial Park, breaking off pieces of marble to keep or sell. Once five men tried to steal the body. Pola Negri received numerous proposals of marriage from men who claimed that Rudy's spirit was now inhabiting their bodies. And who doesn't know of the ritual of the mysterious "women in black" who constantly visit his grave, always with floral gifts?

On May 6, 1930, a statue of Valentino, by sculptor Roger Noble Burnam, was placed in DeLongpre Park in Hollywood. The four-foot bronze figure, entitled *Aspiration,* shows a nude male with head upturned toward heaven. It sits on a green marble base. The inscription reads, in part, "Presented by his friends and admirers from every walk of life in all parts of the world in appreciation of the happiness brought to them by his cinema portrayals." For many years, on Memorial Day, a woman placed a wreath at the foot of the statue. The statue was stolen in the 1950s then recovered and stored until 1976, when it was replaced on its pedestal.

It is strange, when one considers Valentino's popularity and his effect on the world of film, that his career spanned less than six years, and for two of those years he was off the screen altogether. Seventy years later, his fans are still legion and fiercely loyal.

The masks of Comedy and Tragedy, circled by a reel of film, represent the famous producer, **Jesse Lasky,** 1880–1958.

Located in the Abbey of the Psalms, in the extreme left hallway, Sanctuary of Lights. His epitaph reads, "Beloved son of California who, in 1913, headed the company that produced the first feature-length film made in Hollywood. His greatness never lacked simplicity. Carry the song along the passage, you the soul of all there is in glory forevermore."

One day Lasky went to the Beverly Hills Hotel to give a lecture about his book, *I Blow My Own Horn.* He told how he went from being a coronet player for picnics to becoming a film producer. He spent time in the Alaska gold rush and promoted his own Lasky Quintet, which included four female cellists and a male bass playing romantic music from inside a giant shell. Later Lasky teamed up with his brother-in-law, Samuel Goldfish (later Goldwyn), and Cecil B. DeMille to produce *The Squaw Man* in 1913. He joined Adolph Zukor in creating Paramount Pictures, which wound up in temporary receivership in 1932. Then he produced *Sergeant York, Rhapsody in Blue* and *The Great Caruso*. According to Lasky, his two greatest mistakes were not producing the very successful Irving Berlin musical, *Alexander's Ragtime Band*, and turning down moppet Frances Gumm, who became Judy Garland.

Lasky collapsed following his speech; he died in the Beverly Hills Hotel, as did Peter Finch and Clifton Webb.

Bachelor **Clifton Webb**, 1889–1966, Abbey of the Psalms, Crypt 2350, corridor G.6, is marked with an urn and eternal flame in the Sanctuary of Peace.

A very dapper man, who always escorted his mother to his social and film events, Webb achieved stardom with *Sitting Pretty, Cheaper by the Dozen, Titanic* and *Satan Never Sleeps*. He was nominated three times for an Academy Award. He is remembered for his great fashion sense: the double-breasted vest, the white mess coat dinner jacket and the ever-present red carnation boutonniere.

Webb's spirit is said to haunt his corridor of the mausoleum, as well as his former Beverly Hills home. After his mother died in the house in 1960, Webb encountered her ghost many times, as well as that of opera and movie star Grace Moore, who had previously lived there and died in a plane crash. In death as in life, his mother, Maybelle, is at his side.

Three famous sisters, **Norma Talmadge**, 1897–1957, **Constance**, 1898–1974, and **Natalie**, 1899–1969, are also united in death as they were in life. They have their own alcove located in the Sanctuary of Eternal Love. A stained-glass window of Jesus and two worshiping angels is inside the alcove, overlooking a marble bench.

The most famous of the three sisters, Norma, earned over $5 million between 1922 and 1930 in silent films. At that time her husband was movie mogul Joseph Schenck. Anita Loos describes the couple as she "looking like Snow White and he an overgrown dwarf." Schenck idolized Norma and he built the luxurious apartment house on Wilshire Boulevard, known as "The Talmadge," for her. It is located just east of the Ambassador Hotel. She left Schenck when she fell in love with actor Gilbert Roland. When they did not marry, she married Georgie Jessel in 1934. That lasted five years, after which she married the physician who had been supplying her the drugs to which she had become addicted.

Constance was a pretty, gifted comedienne during the silent era, but she left films with the advent of sound. She married four times, became an alcoholic and finally died wealthy and alone. The bulk of her $1 million estate went to her nephews, Bobby and Jimmy Keaton.

Natalie married Buster Keaton and starred with him in several of his films. She did not achieve the same fame that her sisters did, nor did she aggressively pursue a career. After divorcing Keaton, she raised their two sons alone, without money or Keaton. She later became an alcoholic and a recluse. She died alone in her Santa Monica apartment.

Charlie Chaplin's mother is buried at Hollywood Memorial, and so is his son, **Charlie Jr.,** located in the Abbey of the Psalms. Charlie Jr. is one of two sons born to Charlie's second wife, Lita Grey, whom he married when she was 16. Lita won a $1 million divorce settlement after their forced marriage and miserable life together.

**Edward G. Robinson,** 1893–1973, lies in the Abbey of the Psalms.

Unattractive, short and squat, with a pudgy face, large mouth, and nasal voice, he nevertheless reached stardom because of his dramatic acting ability. As a youthful immigrant he considered becoming a rabbi, but his love of the theater drew him to the American Academy of Dramatic Arts and then to a stage and screen career. He was first seen on screen in the 1923 silent *Bright Shawl,* followed by *Hole in the Wall* opposite Claudette Colbert. He literally became the role he played in *Little Caesar*, which launched his very successful career that lasted for decades.

The quality of Robinson's performances was always excellent, dynamic and aggressive, though he could also be tender and sensitive when the role demanded. Although he was never nominated for an Oscar, he was presented posthumously with an honorary Academy Award.

He experienced many personal problems, including his blacklisting during the Hollywood witch hunt days. His collection of artwork was renowned. His autobiography, *All My Yesterdays,* was published after his death from cancer in 1973.

**Bebe Daniels,** 1901–1971. Niche 7-8, T-3 upper North wall.

She lies in the columbarium with her husband. One of the silent screen's finest light comediennes, she co-starred with Harold Lloyd in dozens of short comedies and then was signed by Paramount and appeared in several Cecil B. DeMille films. She possessed a keen sense of timing and could match double takes and pratfalls with the best of them. After Paramount she signed with RKO, co-starring with Douglas Fairbanks and Edward G. Robinson in a series of super-musicals.

In 1936 she moved to England with her husband, Ben Lyon, and played the London Palladium. She and Lyon appeared in several movies and founded the radio show *Life With the Lyons,* which became extraordinarily successful and helpful to England's war effort. Ben Lyon was a successful movie personality who later worked as a casting director. He is credited with discovering Marilyn Monroe in the Ambassador Hotel while she was still a model with the Emmaline Snively Agency.

**Benjamin "Bugsy" Siegel,** 1906–1947. In the mausoleum at Beth Olam.

His marker is inscribed, "In Loving Memory from the Family." Siegel was quoted as saying, "My friends call me Ben; strangers call me Mr. Siegel; and guys I don't like call me Bugsy, but not to my face."

Siegel first appeared on the west coast in the 1940s and soon became very popular with the Hollywood crowd, especially George Raft, who had been a boyhood pal. Jailed in 1940 for the murder of "Big Greeny" Greenburg, Bugsy lived it up in style in his cell, with his own chef, wine and women delivered to the door. He was released after the only two witnesses against him conveniently died.

Called "the most dangerous man in America" by "Joey A." Adonis,

Bugsy was Meyer Lasky's protégé and pals with Mob bosses Lucky Luciano, Frank Costello, Tony Accardo and Joey A. (For more on Bugsy Siegel, see the section on "Death by Mysterious Circumstance.")

"The Great Aquarius," astrologer **Carroll Righter,** 1900–1988, is buried in an unknown location in Hollywood Memorial.

Born in Philadelphia in 1900, Righter was 14 when Evangeline Adams, the grand old lady of American astrology, read his horoscope. She advised him to seek his future in the stars. He did, and at the height of his career his astrology columns were read in 30 million homes. His phone never stopped ringing. Stars, moguls and politicians called at all hours, day and night, for consultations on what directions to take with their lives.

After graduating from the University of Pennsylvania and the Dickerson School of Law, Righter worked for a year in a Philadelphia law firm. But his heart wasn't in it, emotionally or physically. After his doctors told him he had only six months to live, he consulted his own horoscope, which told him he would find "physical protection in the Southwest." He moved to California.

In Hollywood, Righter's amateur horoscopes were such a hit he turned pro in 1939. He drew up charts for stars and others, including Dietrich, Susan Hayward, Robert Cummings, Tyrone Power, Ronald Colman and Ronald Reagan. His many books include *Dollar Signs* and *How to Increase Your Worth by Astrology.* This grand old man truly was "a friend to the stars."

California's Governor (and one of our favorites) **Goodwin Knight,** 1896–1970, was originally buried here, next to his daughter, Carol. However, his wife, Virginia, removed the body and he is now believed to be buried in Forest Lawn.

In the Abbey of the Psalms is Broadway actress and former fashion model **Joan Hackett,** 1942–1983. Outspoken, truthful and enchanting, she played straightforward, strong women and was well known as a comedic performer. She was married to actor Richard Mulligan (from the sitcom *Empty Nest)* and she died from cancer. Her marker reads, "Go Away, I'm Asleep."

Ever vigilant.

# 27

## Holy Cross Cemetery

Located at 5835 West Slauson Avenue, Culver City, Holy Cross is one of the Catholic cemeteries of the Archdiocese of Los Angeles. Like a theme park, it is divided into subdivisions: Mother of Mercy, Mother of Good Hope, Precious Blood, Mother of Sorrows, Holy Redeemer, Divine Savior, Assumption, Holy Rosary, Good Shepherd and more. It is set on gentle, rolling hills covered with tall marble crucifixes, a Pieta and several Madonnas. The cemetery's most visible feature is its Grotto, up the hill and to the left of the main building. In Europe a grotto, a kind of religious cave, is believed to be where many miracles take place. Holy Cross's grotto is made of rock, its roof open to the sky, its focus an altar and a statue of the Virgin Mary in prayer before a shawled woman with clasped hands.

The famous interred at Holy Cross include Bing Crosby; Sharon Tate, buried with her unborn son, Richard Paul (for more on Sharon Tate, see the section "Death by Mysterious Circumstance"); Rosalind Russell; Bela Lugosi (buried in his cape); and Gloria Vanderbilt Sr., mother of "the richest little girl in the world." Also here is Mario Lanza, rumored to have died either as the victim of a mob hit ordered by Lucky Luciano or from extreme dieting and overeating.

**Edward "Kid" Ory,** 1886–1973. Facing north, he is to the left of the Grotto and halfway down the hill.

His marker reads, "Father of Dixieland Jazz." Ory was born in LaPlace, Louisiana, to Creole parents. By the age of 13, he had formed his own band. At 14 he had moved to New Orleans, where he starred with his band for the next nine years. A trombonist, Ory's brand of Dixieland jazz attracted such future stars as "King" Oliver, Sidney Bichet and Johnny Dodds on clarinet. When Oliver, to whom Ory had given the nickname "King," left the band, the "Kid" replaced him with another master of the cornet: 17-year-old Louie "Satchmo" Armstrong. Satchmo would go on to form his own band

and become America's "Ambassador of Jazz"—and one of the world's most beloved entertainers. When jazz moved north to Chicago, Ory followed, playing for both "King" Oliver and Armstrong in their bands from 1925 to 1929. During this time he wrote the famous "Muskrat Ramble," which was recorded by Armstrong's Hot Five.

In the 1930s Ory moved to California where, semi-retired, he played with several groups, including one formed by drummer Barney Bigard. Bigard played drums for Louie Armstrong, Duke Ellington and Earl "Fatha" Hines. He recruited Ory, Armstrong and Hines, and with himself on drums, formed the All Star Jazz Group that played on Orson Welles' radio show. Their traditional jazz music caused their popularity to soar.

Ory starred in two motion pictures during this time. Known as a "tailgate" trombonist, he was best at using his horn as a rallying point to lift the other musicians to play their best. Along with Jack Teagarden, Ory may have been the finest, most creative trombonist to ever play Dixieland jazz.

**Jack Haley,** 1898-1979. Three rows above Ory.

An affable comedian, singer and dancer, Haley is best remembered for playing the Tin Man in *The Wizard of Oz.* Haley enjoyed a long career in vaudeville, radio and in the movies. His other features included *Poor Little Rich Girl* and *Wake Up and Live* with Alice Faye. His son is producer/director Jack Haley Jr. and his widow, Flo, was a Ziegfeld Follies star.

**Harry Lillis "Bing" Crosby,** 1901-1977. His black marker with white letters is in the fourth row down from the Grotto. His first wife, **Wilma "Dixie Lee" Crosby,** 1911-1952, and his parents are next to him. Crosby is buried nine feet down in case his second wife, Kathryn, wishes to join him here.

Crosby was born in Tacoma, Washington, and studied law at Gonzaga University, a Catholic school in Spokane, before beginning his career in show business. He and another singer, Al Rinker, toured the west coast as "Two Boys and a Piano." From the beginning Crosby had a laid-back, easygoing singing style, and most of his contemporaries in the music business would credit him with being the first to use the "crooner" style.

In 1927, Crosby and Rinker were joined by singer/songwriter Harry Barris ("Mississippi Mud" was one of his songs), and the three became "The Rhythm Boys." In the late 1920s they joined the Gus Arnheim Band, a popular group that played the Cocoanut Grove at the Ambassador Hotel in Los Angeles. Arnheim's band was known because of its popularity as a great stepping stone for young musicians and singers. Still billing themselves as "The Rhythm Boys," Crosby and the others sang with Paul Whitman's band when they were introduced to the movies and were featured in *The King of Jazz* in 1930. In 1931 Bing made the first of a string of six two-reelers for Mack Sennett. It was called *I Surrender Dear* and was based on a Barris song.

Crosby then left "The Rhythm Boys" and continued to make musical shorts, including some with "America's Sweetheart," Mary Pickford. Pickford helped him get an important part in Doug Fairbanks' 1931 picture *Reaching for the Moon,* in which Crosby sang "There's No Low-Down Lower Than That." A CBS 15-minute radio show that followed made Crosby a household name.

In 1932, he starred in the feature *The Big Broadcast.* Now a

Bing Crosby with his sons — Call him lucky.

major film star, Crosby made a string of glitzy pictures such as *Going Hollywood* and *Anything Goes.* Then in 1940, he teamed up with Bob Hope in the first of the "Road" pictures. *The Road to Singapore* introduced a blend of songs, romance, in-jokes, pratfalls, and leaving your buddy behind to take the heat. Over the next 20 years, the "Road," also including Dorothy Lamour, would lead to *Zanzibar* in 1941, *Morocco* in 1942, *Utopia* in 1945, *Rio* in 1947 and *Bali* in 1952. All this without ever leaving Hollywood's back lots, except to go to England for *Hong Kong* in 1962 with Peter Sellers.

Crosby's first wife, Dixie Lee, bore him four children, all boys, and died at 40 of ovarian cancer. After four postponements, Crosby married his second wife, Kathryn Grant, in 1957. Kathryn wisely figured out that Bing was a man of many interests who had a lot of guy pals available for golf, horse racing, hunting, ranching, fishing, investments, radio, TV and film making. She planned their home activities around his schedule.

*Holiday Inn* in 1942 paired Crosby with Fred Astaire. Bing sang Irving Berlin's "White Christmas" in the picture, and it became the highest-selling record of its time. He would team with Astaire again in 1946 for Berlin's *Blue Skies.* As Father O'Malley in the sentimental *Going My Way* in 1944, Crosby sang the Oscar-winning song of the same title, while earning a Best Actor Oscar for himself. One year later he was nominated again for an Oscar in the sequel, *The Bells of St. Mary's.* He got his third Oscar nomination for a drama, *The Country Girl,* in 1954. His remaining musical in the 1950s was *High Society,* a remake of the stage play *The Philadelphia Story. High Society* gave him a last musical hurrah with Louie Armstrong and Frank Sinatra and a chance to sing the beautiful love song, "True Love" with Grace Kelly.

On television, Crosby was a frequent host of ABC's *Hollywood Palace,* and starred in a sitcom, *The Bing Crosby Show.* His Bing Crosby Productions was a major supplier of product to the TV networks. In 1958, Crosby published his autobiography, *Call Me Lucky.* He died while enjoying his favorite pastime, golf, on a course in Spain.

**Bela Lugosi** (Bela Blasko), 1882–1956. In the center of the same row of markers as Crosby. His marker reads, "Beloved father."

Lugosi first took to the stage in Budapest in 1901. He made one Hungarian movie, *The Leopard,* in 1917 and another in Germany in 1919. He came to the United States and in 1927 landed the part on Broadway that would brand him for life as Dracula. Burdened with a heavy accent, and handsome in a somewhat frightening way, Lugosi's type was set in cement with the movie public when he made *Dracula* for Universal in 1931.

Lugosi was the bogeyman who appeared in such roles in *Murders in the Rue Morgue* and *Chandu the Magician,* both in 1932. He made both *The Return of Chandu* and *The Black Cat* in 1934, the latter with Boris Karloff. *Black Friday* followed in 1940 and *The Wolf Man* in 1941. Firmly entrenched in these "B" horror pictures, Lugosi starred in *The Ghost of Frankenstein* in 1942 and *The Body Snatcher* in 1945. However, in 1948 Lugosi starred in the surprisingly funny *Abbot and Costello Meet Frankenstein.* Then in 1955, a director named Ed D. Wood appeared on the scene. Wood loved to dress in women's clothing and honestly thought he was writing and directing wonderfully creative movies instead of the disturbingly hilarious messes they were. He cast Lugosi in *Plan Nine from Outer Space.* The plot concerned pompous aliens who intended to take over the earth by bringing the dead back to life. Lugosi died two days after shooting began, and Wood replaced him with his dentist, who was a full head taller and had to run around the set with his cape covering his face.

Lugosi loved attention and drove five wives to divorce him with his 24-hour-a-day needs to be pampered. The pressure of trying to keep a career alive with so few acting opportunities, plus the pain from an old World War I injury, led Lugosi to use morphine, Demerol, Methadone and other drugs. In 1955, he went through a drug rehabilitation program and remained drug-free until he died in 1956 clutching a movie script, *The Final Curtain.* (For details of his wake, including remarks from Peter Lorre and Boris Karloff, see "Fascinating Funerals and Wakes.")

**Charles Boyer,** 1897–1978, his actress wife, **Patricia,** 1910–1978, and **Michael Charles Boyer,** 1943–1965, whose marker reads, "Our Beloved Son," are buried side by side in the level garden behind the Grotto.

Boyer's marvelous French accent and wonderful continental charm enchanted American audiences throughout a film career spanning more than 65 pictures in the United States. Boyer made films in France and Germany during the 1920s and made his American film debut in *The Magnificent Lie* in 1931. Other films in which he delighted his audiences included *The Garden of Allah, History is Made at Night* and *Algiers* in which he appeared as the delightful rogue, Pepe le Moko. It was in *Algiers* that Boyer was widely quoted using the line, "Come with me to the Casbah," words that were never actually used in the picture. Boyer's other films included *All This and Heaven Too* and the delightful *Tales of Manhattan,* which follows the adventures of a formal suit with tails as it moves through New York City from owner to owner. He made *Gaslight* in 1944 and *Barefoot in the Park* in 1969.

Boyer suffered through his son Michael's suicide and his wife's painful death from cancer after 44 years of marriage. Alone, two days after his wife's death, Boyer took an overdose of Seconal and joined them.

**Jim Jordan,** 1896–1988, and wife **Marian I. Jordan,** 1898–1961, lie side by side, buried to the right of Sharon Tate

Better known as Fibber McGee and Mollie from the show of the same name, this popular and well-liked pair starred in the well-loved show, which ran throughout the golden years of radio, from 1935 through 1957. Their favorite running joke was Fibber's closet, which was constantly being opened by someone who had no idea what was coming. The unsuspecting innocent would be subjected to the McGees' howls of "Don't!" before being buried by two minutes of falling, clattering and clanging junk that Fibber had packed into it.

**Jimmy Durante,** 1893–1980. Marked by a standing cross and rosary, behind the Grotto.

Durante was one of a kind, possibly the most beloved entertainer by other show biz people. His Brooklyn-accented, gravely voice charmed audiences while he crooned his signature song, "Inka Dinka Doo." He pounded it out, along with other tunes, in a raucous, honky-tonk piano style. Other Durante "signatures" included

Jimmy Durante — "Good night Mrs. Calabash, wherever you are."

a beat-up felt hat pushed up on his forehead; a large nose, which was shown in profile or being shaken at the camera head on; and a way of mispronouncing words that he slid past his audiences with audacity. His famous, mysterious sign-off line was "Good night, Mrs. Calabash, wherever you are!" Calabash was the Chicago suburb where both his grammar school sweetheart and first wife, Jean Olsen, were from. Was he referring to one or both? He never said.

Durante started out as a honky-tonk piano player at Coney Island before moving into vaudeville in 1919. As one-third of Clayton, Jackson and Durante, he appeared in Ziegfeld's 1929 show, *Show Girl.* His first motion picture was *Roadhouse Nights* in 1930. Then Durante teamed with a fading Buster Keaton in three MGM pictures, all unsuccessful, including the last one, *What! No Beer?* in 1933. His memorable films included *Joe Palooka,* in which he played manager Knobby Walsh and introduced "Inka Dinka Doo," his theme song. He made *Melody Ranch* in 1940 with Gene Autry and Ann Miller and was the co-star of *Billy Rose's Jumbo* in 1962, where he stole the show. His last screen role, and a fitting one, was as Smiler Grogan in *It's a Mad, Mad, Mad, Mad World* in 1963, where he literally kicked the bucket when he died on screen.

In the early days on TV, Durante was a fixture on variety shows, including his own series, for which he won an Emmy. In 1993, the movie love story *Sleepless in Seattle* featured two of Durante's songs, "As Time Goes By" and "Make Someone Happy." These old tunes helped create the picture's poignant mood and made the soundtrack a hit.

When Durante was 67, he married a second time, and he and his wife, Marge, adopted an infant daughter. Always in the company of old and dear friends, his philosophy was "I know there are more good people than bad ones in the world. I don't mind if a gentleman scratches a match on the furniture, so long as he is careful with the grain."

**Rita Hayworth** (Margarita Carmen Cansino), 1918–1987. In front of the Grotto, under a kneeling angel covered by a dwarf-like tree. Her marker reads, "To yesterday's companionship and tomorrow's reunion."

Rita Hayworth, the great American love goddess, with Sybil Brand, philanthropist.

Using the name Rita Cansino, Hayworth, a dark-haired Spanish dancer, made less-than-memorable movies, including *Under the Pampas Moon*, "B" westerns such as *Hit the Saddle*, and the thriller *The Shadow*. She married businessman Edward Judson at the age of 19. Judson gave her the stage name Rita Hayworth and made her a beautiful redhead. *Life* magazine called her "The Great American Love Goddess," and she became the dream girl of several million servicemen during World War II.

Rita danced her way into "A" pictures with *Over Broadway*. This was followed by the musical *You'll Never Get Rich*, in which her voice was dubbed, although she later used her own voice in pictures. She first danced with Fred Astaire in *Strawberry Blond* in 1941. She then made *Cover Girl* in 1944 with Gene Kelly and starred in *Gilda* with Glenn Ford, in which she sang the steamy "Put the Blame on Mame." Hayworth married Orson Welles in 1946, leaving him in 1948 to marry Muslim playboy Aga Kahn, with whom she had one daughter, Princess Yasmin Aga Kahn.

In 1948 she starred in *The Lady from Shanghai*, which her ex-husband Orson Welles directed and co-starred in. Hayworth's next husbands were singer Dick Haymes and director James Hill, who made pictures with animal themes, including *Born Free* and *Black Beauty*.

She suffered from Alzheimer's disease and by 1970 was unable to memorize lines. She died at the age of 68. During her last days, she was lovingly cared for by her daughter.

**Bonita Granville,** 1923–1988. Close to Rita Hayworth.

Granville, at the age of 15, starred in the Nancy Drew detective series. These Warner "B" movies, made in 1938–1939, were *Nancy Drew, Detective; Nancy Drew—Trouble Shooter; Nancy Drew, Reporter;* and *Nancy Drew and the Hidden Staircase.*

Granville was born to show people and, as a toddler, appeared on stage in 1932. In 1936 she was nominated for an Oscar in *These Three,* an adaptation of Lillian Hellman's *The Children's Hour.* Granville played an ingenue and other supporting roles until the late 1940s, when her millionaire husband, Jack Wrather, bought the rights to both the "Lassie" and "Lone Ranger" characters and she elected to work behind the camera. She was supervising producer of the long-running *Lassie* TV series and made her last on-screen appearances in *The Lone Ranger* in 1956 and *The Legend of the Lone Ranger* in 1981. Her husband, Jack, 1918–1984, rests next to her.

**Pat O'Brien** (William Joseph Patrick O'Brien), 1899–1983. Just west of Jimmy Durante.

O'Brien was known as a member of the "Irish Mafia," which included his childhood friend, Spencer Tracy. A vaudeville hoofer in the 1920s, O'Brien played mostly cops, priests and servicemen in the movies. He was Hildy Johnson in *The Front Page* in 1931. Then he made *Oil for the Lamps of China* in 1935 and *The Great O'Malley* in 1937. After that he went to Warner's, where he starred with James Cagney in *Angels with Dirty Faces.* In 1940, he starred again in the remake of *The Front Page* with Adolph Menjou.

His two most memorable movies, also made in 1940, were *The Fighting 69th* with James Cagney and *Knute Rockne—All American,* in which he played the famous Notre Dame football coach and Ronald Reagan played "The Gipper." Here Reagan had his famous line, "Win one for the Gipper." O'Brien made *The People Against O'Hara* in 1951, *The Last Hurrah* in 1958 and *Ragtime* in 1981, with his old friend, James Cagney. He appeared in some TV shows, including the short-lived sitcom *Harrigan and Son* from 1960–1961. His autobiography, *The Wind at my Back,* was published in 1964.

**John Leslie "Jackie" Coogan,** 1914–1984. Just south of O'Brien.

The movies' first real child star appeared as a tattered little waif in films with Charlie Chaplin. Coogan was discovered by Chaplin when he was four years old, working in an outdoor review with swimming star Annette Kellerman. Chaplin used him first in the 1919 short *A Day's Pleasure* and then in the feature film *The Kid*. This picture skillfully blended comedy and pathos. It established Chaplin as an artist and Coogan as a star.

He appeared in many other features in the 1920s until his popularity declined because of his age. In the 1930s he starred in *Tom Sawyer and Huckleberry Finn*. Later he and then-wife Betty Grable made *College Swing* together.

Before he was 12, he had earned more than $4 million, most of which was spent by his family. Ultimately only $250,000 remained, of which he received half, as ordered by the court. His case led to passage of the Child Actors bill, also known as the Coogan Act, which has curtailed similar abuses to child actors.

Coogan did achieve latter-day stardom as the bald-headed Uncle Fester on the *Addams Family* TV series.

**Barney Oldfield,** 1878–1946. Southeast of Jackie Coogan.

Cigar-chomping Oldfield was an American racing legend who inspired a legion of motorcycle cops to ask speeders, "Who do you think you are, Barney Oldfield?" Oldfield was the first man to drive a mile in a minute in 1903. By 1910, despite bad dirt tracks, poor-handling cars and huge, heavy engines, he was piloting his Blitzen Benz at speeds of over 130 miles per hour.

Adored by children whose scooters and wagons were named after his cars, "999," "Big Ben," "Green Dragon," and "Golden Submarine," Oldfield retired in 1918, lucky to have lived through the many injuries and crashes he suffered while racing. A popular speaker, Oldfield nourished the dream of someday breaking the world speed record, which at the time was over 130 miles per hour. He never succeeded.

**Louella O. Parsons,** 1881–1972. Just below and to the left of Oldfield.

Parsons and her bitter enemy, Hedda Hopper, were the two most powerful gossip columnists covering Hollywood. Louella worked for the powerful Hearst papers and their INS wire service and was a close personal friend of William Randolph Hearst, the publisher, and his girlfriend, Marion Davies. Parsons joined the Hearst organization in 1925 and soon was famous for her "scoops" of Hollywood gossip. She loved the parties that Hearst and Davies threw at his estate, San Simeon, and was not amused when Hopper described one party, "It was like a visit to Never-Never Land. Never have we seen its like and never will again."

Parsons could make or break the biggest stars in Hollywood with her column, which was carried by 70 newspapers with a combined circulation of over 20 million. Because of her mood swings, Hollywood watched her with great trepidation, not knowing if she would greet their latest news or escapades with warmth, with her claws out or possibly worse—a wall of stony silence.

Her husband, Dr. Harry "Docky" Martin, was head of the Twentieth Century Fox medical department and a heavy drinker. When he passed out at one party, Louella remarked, "Oh, let Docky rest. He has to operate in the morning."

**Gloria Morgan Vanderbilt,** 1904–1965, and **Thelma Viscountess Furness,** 1904–1970. Close by Louella Parsons.

Christened the "Magnificent Morgans" by society, the twins were born in Switzerland and educated in French convents before coming to Manhattan where they were the toast of the town. At 18, Gloria married Reginald Vanderbilt, 48, who died 18 months later. Thelma's second husband was the English shipping executive, Viscount Furness. Ten years passed after their marriages before the twins made the papers again. Then Gloria became involved in a custody battle for her daughter Gloria, a battle that the daughter's paternal aunt, Gertrude Whitney, would ultimately win. Thelma caught the public's attention when she left her boyfriend, Edward, Prince of Wales, with her friend, Wallis Warfield Simpson. Upon leaving the two of them, she remarked, "Well, Dear, look after him for me while I'm away, and see that he doesn't get into any mischief." Sure. Bye, Edward.

In their later years, the twins moved to California, where they were highly successful in business, including cosmetics and fashion. Many years later, daughter Gloria published her autobiography, *Little Gloria, Happy at Last.*

**Edgar Kennedy,** 1890–1948. Near the road, to the right, under a tree.

His bronze marker has a three-cross crucifixion scene. Kennedy, famous for his "slow burn" when angry, started with Mack Sennett in 1914 as a Keystone Kop. From there he joined Hal Roach for a series of Laurel and Hardy comedies, including *Two Tars, From Soup to Nuts* and *You're Darn Tootin',* all in 1928. With the "Our Gang" kids, he made several comedies, including *Moan and Groan, Inc.* At RKO, Kennedy made the first of his own two-reelers under the title *Mr. Average Man.* These were so successful, he made 103 of them between 1941 and 1948. Kennedy made many movies during the 1930s and 1940s. His last picture was *My Dream is Yours* with Doris Day.

**Gene Lockhart**, 1891–1957. Just south of Edgar Kennedy.

Puffy-faced and jowly, Lockhart was at home playing a cheery cherub or a villain. His most memorable parts included Lushin in *Crime and Punishment* in 1935 and Regis in *Algiers* in 1938, for which he received an Oscar nomination. He played Stephen Douglas in *Abe Lincoln in Illinois* in 1940. His wife, Kathleen, was also an actress. She appeared with Gene and their daughter, June Lockhart, in *A Christmas Carol,* in which Gene played Bob Cratchit. June, besides playing in several motion pictures, starred for six years in the TV series *Lassie.* She later appeared in *Lost in Space.* Gene Lockhart starred in the memorable *Miracle on 34th Street* and *The Man in the Gray Flannel Suit.*

**Rosalind Russell Brisson,** 1908–1976. Located northeast of Lockhart in Section M, by a large crucifix.

Russell, a devout Catholic and a very funny lady, referred to her parish in Beverly Hills as "Our Lady of the Cadillacs." Rosalind began

Rosalind Russell, she named her parish in Beverly Hills, "Our Lady of the Cadillacs."

her career in 1934 as the neglected wife in *Evelyn Prentice*. She then turned in a fine performance as another neglected wife opposite Robert Donat in *The Citadel* in 1938. Also in that year, she played a wise-cracking scribe in *Four's a Crowd*. She then co-starred with a wonderful cast of women, including Joan Crawford and Norma Shearer, in *The Women*, a hilarious adaptation of Clare Boothe Luce's play about divorce, cattiness and competition among a group of female friends.

In 1940, Rosalind landed the plum role of reporter Hildy Johnson in the high-spirited comedy, *His Girl Friday*. She played opposite Cary Grant in this remake of *The Front Page*. She followed up with *My Sister Eileen* in 1942 and *Panic* in 1955. Then in 1958, Rosalind starred in what many of her peers thought was her best role, playing the zany, off-the-wall, high spirited, hilarious Mame in *Auntie Mame*. The role fit her perfectly. Rosalind *was* Mame.

Russell was married to the same man, Frederick Brisson, for 35 years. His devotion to her earned him the nickname "The Wizard of Roz." In 1972, the Academy presented Russell with the Jean Hersholt Humanitarian Award for her charity work. In her later years she suffered from severe arthritis. She published her autobiography, *Life's a Banquet,* in 1976.

**Gia Scala** (Giovanna Scoglio), 1935–1972. Just below Rosalind Russell.

Scala died when she was just 37, from an overdose of alcohol and alcohol-related medications. A tall, sultry brunette with green eyes, she appeared with Glenn Ford in *Don't Go Near the Water* in

1956. She did *The Guns of Navarone* in 1961, with Gregory Peck, David Niven and Anthony Quinn, a big budget World War II story of allied commandos destroying a German gun emplacement. Her best picture was *The Garment Jungle* in 1957, with Lee J. Cobb, for which she received fine reviews from the critics. Unfortunately, this would be her last picture because of her drinking problem.

**Evelyn Florence Nesbit,** 1884–1967. To the east and slightly down from Rosalind Russell, near the curb.

Her marker is a plain granite stone with a cross in the center and the word "Mother." Nesbit first appeared on the glittering New York party scene in the early 1900s. Barely 16, she was gorgeous with an ingenue look that soon made her one of the most sought-after models in New York. Charles Dana Gibson had her pose for his drawings, famous photographers fought over her, and she even became one of the Floradora dancing girls.

It wasn't long before she caught the eye of Stanford White, one of America's most famous architects, who in 1880 had joined the firm of McKim, Mead and White as a partner. White designed most of the decorative detail of the Villard Houses, Madison Square Garden, the Century Club and Herald Building. White preferred his sex a bit kinky and was famous for the Red Velvet Swing that hung from the ceiling in his studio. Evelyn would not be the first sweet thing to use the swing, but she would become the best known "Girl in the Red Velvet Swing." She would swing up to the ceiling and kick out the paper panels of rotating Japanese parasols. It was here, in this room with the swing, red velvet walls, and four-poster bed encircled with tiny colored lights, that White would have his way with Evelyn. Some would say she lost her virginity here; others said, "Oh, get real, she's a pavement princess."

Soon Nesbit swung out of White's life and into the arms and bed of swinger Harry Thaw, a rich, debased and deranged playboy from Pittsburgh. Thaw was filled with a crazed rage that manifested itself in uncontrolled jealousy, paranoia and self-degradation. Thaw would go from beating Nesbit with whips and canes to begging her forgiveness with tears, baby talk, and kisses.

Evelyn married Thaw, and the two shared their mutual hatred

for White, because of the well-publicized talk about the rides Nesbit took on his swing and in his bed. No longer able to control his hatred, Thaw shot and killed White, who was watching *Mamzelle Champagne* at Madison Square Garden. Thaw was tried twice for Nesbit's murder. The second time he was acquitted by reason of insanity and sentenced to a hospital for the criminally insane.

Nesbit did not fare well without Thaw's money. She began a long slide from fancy ballrooms to a room over a grocery store. She attempted several unsuccessful stage comebacks. For a brief time she was a consultant on the movie *The Girl in the Red Velvet Swing* in 1955, with Ray Milland, Joan Collins and Farley Granger. She attempted suicide twice and said about her life, "Stanny White was killed, but my fate was worse, I lived."

**John Ford** (Sean Aloysius O'Fienne), 1895–1973. Four rows below the crucifix where Rosalind Russell is buried and about 25 markers to the west. Ford's stone is marked, "Portland, Maine to Hollywood." Next to Ford is his wife, **Mary Ford,** 1890–1960, whose marker reads, "His Beloved Wife for 49 years."

John Ford described himself simply as "A hard-nosed director." His peers spoke of him as a man of poetic vision who could paint on film like a brush on canvas. Ford did more for the western than any other director. He loved the rolling sands of Utah's Monument Valley. Here he used his technique of "don't take the camera to the action, bring the action to the camera," to film the beauty of both men and horses in action. He captured the wild loneliness of the sprawling, unforgiving, but breathtakingly beautiful land. Of all the directors to step behind the camera in Hollywood, Ford was the only one whose films were instantly recognizable for being his and his alone.

Ford's early films in the 1920s were westerns, and most of them starred Harry Carey. His natural ability to film the outdoors allowed him to direct the top screen cowboys, Hoot Gibson, Buck Jones and Tom Mix, at Universal and Fox. *The Iron Horse* in 1924, an epic western about the building of the transcontinental railroad, was followed by the large-scale *Three Bad Men* in 1926, which used the Oklahoma land rush as its background. These two films quickly cemented Ford's reputation as one of Hollywood's top directors. Ford continued to develop his unique directing style in the 1930s, and in 1935 he made *The Informer,* set in Ireland and starring Victor McLaglen as an informer on the IRA. He won his first directing Oscar for *Informer.* Ford's biggest year yet was 1939, with the release of *Drums along the Mohawk,* which starred Henry Fonda and Claudette Colbert. That same year he released *Young Mr. Lincoln,* again with Fonda, and what many of his contemporaries think may be the best western ever made, *Stagecoach,* which made a star of John Wayne and earned Ford another Oscar nomination.

Ford, who was proud of his Irish heritage, was often shown wearing tweed jackets and a neatly creased fedora in publicity shots. On location, however, he preferred khakis, a baseball cap and a neckerchief, which was also used for chewing. He was contemptuous of authority and hated pretension. As he entered the 1940s, the members of what would become known as his "stock company" of actors began to emerge. Ford was loyal to his crew. His actors included Fonda, Wayne, Harry Carey and McLaglen, and later he added real cowboy Ben Johnson, Harry Carey Jr., George O'Brien, Ward Bond and one woman—the beautiful and fiery Maureen O'Hara, a red-haired green-eyed gift from Ireland.

Ford opened the 1940s with back-to-back Oscars for *The Grapes of Wrath* and *How Green Was My Valley,* stories of close families struggling against adversity. World War II found him making documentaries, two of which won Oscars, before he returned to Hollywood. In 1945 he made *They Were Expendable* with John Wayne and Robert Montgomery, and then returned to his beloved westerns with Henry Fonda as Wyatt Earp in *My Darling Clementine.*

In the late 1940s he formed Argosy Productions with producer Merian C. Cooper and directed what may have been his best pictures, and certainly his most personal, his unofficial cavalry trilogy. These were *Fort Apache* in 1948, *She Wore a Yellow Ribbon* in 1949 and *Rio Grande* in 1950, all starring John Wayne and the rest of Ford's "regulars." In 1952, Ford made *The Quiet Man,* again starring Wayne. But this was no western. Instead, Wayne played an American boxer of Irish descent who settles on the

Emerald Isle to claim an inheritance and finds a wife, Maureen O'Hara, both of whom infuriate the natives. It was a beautiful, sensitive picture that won Ford his fourth Oscar. Only two other pictures in the 1950s seemed to still have Ford's magic: *The Searchers* and *The Man Who Shot Liberty Valance.* Ford was the first recipient of the American Film Institute's Life Achievement Award.

**Frank Lovejoy,** 1914–1962. Section P, directly in front of the mausoleum.

Roughhewn, with a deep, tough voice, Lovejoy probably did his best work in 1930s and 1940s radio. In films, he played servicemen and cops, and on TV he starred in the series *Man Against Crime* and *Meet McGraw.*

**Walter F. O'Malley,** 1903–1979, and his wife **Katherine H.,** 1907–1979. Top of Section P in the second row of markers.

Probably the most powerful team owner in baseball, O'Malley got tired of fighting with the politicians in Brooklyn for a new stadium and, in a surprise move, brought his team to Los Angeles after the 1957 season. Famous for being a man who watches his money, O'Malley was not one to waste it on inflated players' salaries or overcompensated management. He did, however, have a reputation for stability and a family atmosphere within his team. O'Malley was known to take a personal interest in his players, such as picking up Roy Campanella's medical expenses after he was paralyzed in a car accident.

O'Malley was an engineer who later practiced as an attorney. He became a director of the Dodgers at the age of 29 and bought the team, along with partner Branch Rickey, in the 1940s. He became the sole owner in 1950. Under his guidance, the Dodgers would win 11 pennants and four World Series. O'Malley's wife, Kay, who died the same year he did, was his childhood sweetheart. During their engagement, she was operated on for cancer of the larynx, which left her unable to speak. This made no difference to O'Malley, who said, "She's still the same girl I fell in love with."

**Zasu Pitts,** 1898–1963. At the rear of the Grotto, near Sharon Tate.

Mary Pickford gave Pitts her start with small parts in *A Little*

*Princess* and *Rebecca of Sunnybrook Farm,* both in 1917. Erich Von Stroheim called her the screen's greatest tragedienne and used her in two films, including *Greed* in 1924.

Because of her fluttery hands and high-pitched, cracking voice, when the sound era came, she was used almost exclusively as a comedienne. During the 1930s, Hal Roach starred her in a string of short subjects, and she had supporting roles in many pictures, including *Ruggles of Red Gap* in 1935. Zasu also played sleuth Hildegarde Withers in two RKO pictures, *The Plot Thickens* and *Forty Naughty Girls.* As film roles became scarce, Pitts turned to the stage and TV, where she was a sidekick on *Oh Susanna/The Gale Storm Show* in 1956-1960. Zasu's last film was *It's a Mad, Mad, Mad, Mad World* in 1963. She wrote the book *Candy Hits by Zasu Pitts.* On the personal side, she adopted and raised Barbara LaMarr's son upon the actress's death.

## The Holy Cross Mausoleum

The mausoleum is a long white building whose entrance is dominated by a large Art Deco sculpture of the crucifixion, with Jesus and two mourners set against a shining gold background. The inscription reads, "We adore Thee, O Christ, and we bless Thee because by Thy holy cross Thou has redeemed the world." The inscription over the door reads, "Behold the tabernacle of God with men and He will dwell with them. And they shall be His people and God himself shall be their God. And God shall wipe away all tears from their eyes. And death shall be no more. Nor mourning. Nor crying. Nor sorrow shall be any more . . . Behold I make all things new." Inside, the interior of the mausoleum is finished in light marble, with stained glass windows depicting biblical themes in a modern design.

**Jose Iturbi,** 1895-1980. To the left of the entrance in Section 16.

Iturbi was a child prodigy of the piano from Valencia, Spain. As an adult, he made his U.S. debut with the Philadelphia Orchestra in 1929. In the 1930s he became the conductor of the Rochester Philharmonic. After eight years he moved to Hollywood where he played himself in many movies. He was popular with the public, but his peers found that his overbearing, brazen attitude and outspoken put-downs of women for what he considered to be their limited temperament left them cold. In spite of his chauvinism, he and his sister made a wonderful musical team, playing duets on their twin pianos.

**Jack La Rue** (Gaspare Biondolillo), 1902–1984. Section 69, on the right, two markers up and two to the right.

Slick-haired, dark and swarthy, LaRue played mostly gangsters. He appeared in a few westerns and period pieces, always as a villain. His most memorable part was as the sadistic rapist in *The Story of Temple Drake,* an adaptation of William Faulkner's story *The Sanctuary.*

**Spike Jones,** 1911–1965. Section 70, at the top near a stained-glass window.

His marker reads, "Beloved husband and father." "Spike Jones and his City Slickers" was the zaniest, craziest band ever created. He attacked all music, including his own theme song, "Cocktails for Two," with musical and not-so-musical instruments. He "played" saws, toy guns, real guns, bells and instruments of his own design, including a Flit gun tuned to E flat, doorbells, a live goat, automobile horns and more. He even featured a pretty lady who did nothing but knit. This innovative craziness made him extremely popular. He toured the country with his show, *The Musical Depreciation Review,* in the 1940s. Although he was popular on both radio and TV in the 1940s and 1950s, rock music finally killed his brand of zaniness in the 1960s. "How can you make fun of that mess?" he asked.

Jones' biggest hit came in 1942, when he recorded "Der Fuerher's Face," mocking Adolph Hitler. It sold one-and-a-half million copies. At his funeral, he was eulogized as "a genius in the clothes of a musical satirist."

**Joan Davis,** 1907–1961. To the right of the altar and facing it.

Davis was a physical comedienne, with long legs and a rubber face. Her film debut was in Mack Sennett's *Way Up Thar* in 1935. She continued to do her comedy dance routine, complete with pratfalls, in films through the late 1930s and 1940s, including *Sun Valley Serenade.* Known also for her wry sense of humor, Davis held her own while trading dialog through a string of "B" comedies with stars such as Eddie Cantor, Lou Costello and Leon Errol. Her TV series, *I Remember Joan,* played on NBC from 1952 to 1955.

**Mario Lanza** (Alfredo Arnold Cocozza), 1921–1959, and his wife, **Betty Lanza,** 1922–1960. Located next to Joan Davis.

A high school dropout, Lanza had a big voice and an even bigger body. A commanding tenor, he sang for conductor Serge Koussevitzky in 1942. Lanza earned a music scholarship, performed at the Berkshire Summer Music Festival and toured in concert. After serving in World War II, Lanza signed a four-picture contract with MGM. He made two films with Katherine Grayson, *That Midnight Kiss,* in which he sang the hit song, "They Didn't Believe Me"; and *The Toast of New Orleans,* where he sang another hit, "Be My Love," plus a duet with Grayson of segments from *Madame Butterfly.* Extremely popular with the public, Lanza suffered from his ballooning weight. His poundage went up when he needed his voice and then down, on a studio-induced diet of grapefruit and little else, before facing the camera. *The Great Caruso* in 1951 was a big hit. However, due to Lanza's difficult personality and extreme self-importance, along with his use of alcohol, barbiturates, and his ballooning weight, he was not used on screen for his next picture, *The Student Prince.* Instead the part went to Edmund Purdom, with Lanza used only as the voice on the soundtracks.

Lanza appeared in only three more films, including *The Seven Hills of Rome* in 1958. He died a year later in Rome at the age of 38. Rumors alleged that he had been killed by gangster Lucky Luciano for not singing at a charity event in Naples in which Luciano was involved. Betty, Lanza's wife, a long-time abuser of alcohol and amphetamines, died a year later and was laid to rest beside him.

**Ray Bolger,** 1904–1987. Toward the back of the chapel in Section 35.

Bolger was a rubber-legged dancer, singer and comedian who will forever be known as the scarecrow in *The Wizard of Oz,* despite his having had a long and varied career on stage and screen.

Bolger started in vaudeville as half of "Sanford and Bolger" and appeared in many Broadway shows, including George White's *Scandals. The Great Ziegfeld* in 1936 was his first film, followed by *Rosalie* and *Sweethearts*. In the film version of *Where's Charlie?* in 1952 he sang his signature song from Broadway, "Once in Love with Amy." He starred in several other films including *The Harvey Girls* in 1946, in which he was reunited with Judy Garland, followed by *April in Paris* and *Babes in Toyland*. Bolger was popular on TV, appearing on all the popular variety shows, including Garland's 1963 series. He also starred briefly in 1963 in his own sitcom, *Where's Raymond?* which later became *The Ray Bolger Show*.

## Holy Cross, Outside the Mausoleum

**Mack Sennett,** 1880–1960. To the right of the mausoleum, Section N, down ten rows.

His epitaph reads, "King of Comedy." Sennett was certainly the king of pie-throwing and other slapstick visuals popular in the physical comedy of the 1920s silent film era. Sennett got into the film business in 1908 when he joined Biograph, which was owned by D.W. Griffith. He soon began directing films.

He moved to California in 1912 and formed the Keystone Company with his girlfriend, Mabel Normand, and star comedian Fred Mace. His first year, Sennett made over 100 one-reelers, comedies that relied on stock situations such as a jealous wife or a stroll in the park. One film, *A Muddy Romance*, was built around the actual draining of a lake. During this time, Sennett was able to show his disdain of cops by creating the *Keystone Kops,* with performers such as "slow burn" Edgar Kennedy (also buried at Holy Cross), Mack Swain and Slim Summerville. His scantily clad "Mack Sennett Bathing Beauties" never did well on screen but brought him tons of publicity. Features were never Sennett's strength, but he made a few good ones, including *Molly O* in 1923, with Mabel Normand, and *The Sheik of Araby* that same year, with Ben Turpin.

Sennett was a genius at finding talent. He introduced Charlie Chaplin, "Fatty" Arbuckle, Wallace Beery, Gloria Swanson, Charlie Chase, Harry Langdon and Carole Lombard to pictures. Mabel

Normand, his longtime love, came back to him in the 1920s, following a murder scandal involving William Desmond Taylor. (See the section "Death by Mysterious Circumstance.")

By the 1930s, Mack Sennett was pretty much eclipsed by Hal Roach, whose comedies were extremely well made. Sennett did manage to continue finding new talent, such as Bing Crosby and W. C. Fields, with whom he made two pictures. He directed Joan Davis in his last short, *Way Up Thar,* in 1935. Although he was finished in pictures, Sennett was given an honorary Academy Award in 1937. In 1954, he wrote his autobiography, *King of Comedy,* a funny, if fanciful, story of his zany, freewheeling days in the world of silent comedies.

**Conrad N. Hilton, Jr.,** 1926–1969. Near the Madonna with child, in Section T.

His grave is marked by a memorial left by his children and reads, "In memory of our loving father." The son of the chairman of the Hilton Hotels Corporation, "Nicky" died tragically at the age of 42 of cardiac arrest. His marriage to Elizabeth Taylor, when she was 19, lasted only one year.

**Richard Arlen** (Cornelius van Mattimore), 1899–1976. Right of the Madonna in Tier 56, Grave 130.

Arlen starred in the Oscar-winning *Wings* in 1928 and *The Virginian* in 1930, two of the early "talkies." Both were big hits and made him an immediate star. During the rest of his career the very handsome Arlen, scion of a wealthy, socially prominent family and an ex-journalist and pilot, would never again match the popularity he enjoyed in his earlier pictures.

His other pictures included *The Four Feathers* in 1929, *Island of Lost Souls* in 1932, and *Come on Marines* in 1934. In 1939, Universal teamed him with Andy Devine in a string of 14 "B" films, including *Mutiny on the Blackhawk.* In 1941, Arlen moved to Pine-Thomas for another string of "B" pictures, including *Power Dive* with Chester Morris. Arlen continued to work sporadically in the 1940s and 1950s, and in 1970 he appeared in the film *Won Ton Ton, the Dog Who Saved Hollywood.*

**Mary Astor** (Lucille Vasconcellos Langhanke), 1906–1987. Location in Holy Cross is not known.

Cool, ruthless and beautiful, Mary Astor retained her reputation throughout her career as one of the screen's greatest femme fatales. Off screen this sophisticated, versatile leading lady led a private life that was even more eventful, truth being stranger than fiction. As a very young ingenue, she was rehearsing in John Barrymore's private suite for a leading role with him. Their romance became torrid, and her very controlling mother and father encouraged their affair to teach Mary skills as an actress and in affairs of the heart.

After many successful films, Mary Astor was in the process of a divorce and custody battle with her physician husband when her diary became public as evidence in the trial. It revealed frank descriptions of her many affairs, especially with playwright George S. Kaufman. Newspapers carried daily bizarre details, which distinguished her as a notorious figure.

That same year she appeared with Walter Huston in *Dodsworth,* which revitalized her career and attracted audiences in droves. She won an Oscar for her supporting role in *The Great Lie.* This very versatile actress was capable of performing in dramatic, romantic,scatterbrained and intellectual roles, later settling into older, more motherly characterizations.

In her later years, she turned to writing. She produced five novels, her autobiography entitled *My Story,* and *A Life on Film,* one of the best accounts of working in Hollywood. She died alone at the Motion Picture Country Home.

**Fred MacMurray**, 1908–1991.

MacMurray was both a light comedian and a good dramatic actor. In the 1920s and early 1930s, he played the saxophone in various bands. He made his film debut in 1935 in *The Gilded*

Fred MacMurray — A saxophone player who could act.

*Lily* and had his first big hit with *Double Indemnity* in 1944. He continued to star in dramas, comedies and musicals through the 1940s and part of the 1950s. In the mid-1950s he turned to playing the aging leading man in westerns, including *Good Day for a Hanging*.

In 1959 his career began to improve with his starring role in Walt Disney's *Shaggy Dog*, the first of a string of comedies he would make for Disney over the next 12 years. His 1960s hit, *The Apartment,* is considered by many to be his best work. Also for Disney, he starred in the popular TV series *My Three Sons,* which ran for 12 years. He married actress June Haver in 1954.

**Vince Edwards** (Vincenzo Eduardo Zoino), 1926–1996.

Edwards is remembered for his portrayal of the brooding TV doctor in *Ben Casey,* a television hit in the 1960s. Both before Ben Casey and after, he toiled in second banana roles in motion pictures and TV. Throughout his life, he struggled with a gambling problem. His wife, Janet, is presently finishing his autobiography, in which he talks candidly about his addiction and how he ultimately beat it.

**Lawrence Welk**, 1903–1992.

Welk was an enigma to the other bands of his era. How could anyone with an accordion, a bubble machine, and a North Dakota farmer's voice cooing "Wun-a-ful, a-wun-a-ful," hit it big on national TV and stay there for close to 40 years? Welk was born on a farm near Strasburg, North Dakota. He taught himself to play a mail-order accordion, formed a band and began playing any gig in the Dakotas that liked his brand of . . . well, let's say bubbly swing.

His first radio broadcast was over WNAX in Yankton, South Dakota, with his band called "Welk's Novelty Orchestra." Welk stayed with WNAX into the 1930s. The station had a good reach in plains country. What's to stop a radio signal—a barbed wire fence? Over the years his radio popularity helped to build a solid following in the area. By the 1950s, Welk was enjoying a successful career playing ballrooms and hotels. In 1951 he began a weekly TV show from the Aragon Ballroom at Pacific Ocean Park in Santa Monica, calling his band the "Champagne Music Makers" and using "Bubbles in the Wine," as his theme song. By 1955 his show had gone national on ABC-TV and his theme was now "Champagne Music." Welk stayed with ABC until 1971, enjoying a vast popularity. He then joined with a national syndicator who put his show in more cities, delivering an even larger audience than he had at ABC.

Over the years, Welk became known for being tight with a buck, and many of the singers and dancers who had become famous on his show, such as Julius LaRosa and the Lennon Sisters, complained bitterly about their wages. But Welk just kept bubbling on, playing his accordion and giving his audiences a "Wun-a-ful, a wun-a-ful" time. He had a good time, and his fans loved him.

# 28

## Home of Peace Memorial Park

Located across from Calvary Cemetery on Whittier Boulevard in East Los Angeles, Home of Peace is a Jewish cemetery dominated by carved menorahs and an Art Deco mausoleum.

Inside the Mausoleum is the marble drawer containing **Shemp Howard** (Samuel Horwitz), 1895–1955, of "The Three Stooges." He is found halfway down the Corridor of Eternal Life. The other original Stooges were Shemp's brothers, **Moe Howard** (Moses Horwitz), 1897–1975, located at Hillside Memorial Cemetery; and **Jerome "Curly" Howard** (Jerome Lester Horwitz), 1903–1952, located in Home of Peace, behind the mausoleum.

The Stooges made their debut in 1922 when vaudevillian Ted Healy first featured his boyhood pal, Moe, as his stooge and straight man. Shemp soon joined the act, followed in 1925 by violinist Larry Fine. After a move to Hollywood in the 1930s, Shemp was replaced by kid brother Curly. Soon, movie audiences were roaring at the trio's madcap mayhem and physical abuse of each other in on-screen anarchy.

The Three Stooges — Planning ahead.

In 1946, Curly suffered a stroke; he died six years later at age 48. Shemp, who replaced Curly, died in 1955, and his role was taken over by Joe Besser and later Joe DeRita. Both Moe and Larry died in 1975. In total, the Stooges made over 200 short subjects and full-length films.

Curly's crazed antics inspired writer Jack Kerouac to take a playful swipe at him in his novel *Visions of Cody:* "All big dumb convict Curly does is muckle and yukkle and squeal, pressing his lips, shaking his old butt like jelly, knotting his Jell-O fists, eyeing Moe, who looks back at him with that lowered and surly 'Well, what are you gonna do about it?'"

**Jerome "Curly" Howard** (Jerome Lester Horwitz), 1903–1952. Row 5, southwestern corner of the cemetery.

Probably the funniest and most loved of the Three Stooges, Curly is buried in this far-flung corner of the 30-acre cemetery. Fans of the Stooges are still legion, and reruns of their zany antics appear in syndication in major markets throughout the country.

**Fanny Brice** (Fanny Borach), 1891–1951. Compartment E1109 in the Corridor of Memory Mausoleum.

From 1938 until she died in 1951, Brice, a homely Jewish girl from New York's Lower East Side, played the obnoxious and enormously popular Baby Snooks on the radio show of the same name. Brice broke into vaudeville at the age of 13 as both a singer and comedienne. She was also known for her stormy marriage to racketeer Nicky Arnstein, who during their marriage did time at Leavenworth for stealing a reported $6 million. In 1968, Barbra Streisand played Fanny in the romantic movie *Funny Girl.*

**Louis B. Mayer,** 1885–1957. Drawer S-405, Corridor of Immortality Mausoleum.

Mayer came into prominence when he joined Marcus Loew of Metro and Sam Goldwyn to form Metro Goldwyn Meyer (MGM) in 1924. As head of production, the short, belligerent cigar-smoking Mayer churned out 100 pictures that first year. During the next ten years, he increased the size of the studio to 23 sound stages occupying 117 acres. Mayer's number two man was "Boy Genius" Irving Thalberg, who many industry figures credited with being the creative genius that made MGM's dominance of the movie industry possible. Known as the studio with "More Stars Than There Are in Heaven," MGM had under contract artists such as Keaton, Garbo, Harlow, Gable, Wallace Beery, Grant, Tracy, Rooney, Myrna Loy and

William Powell. MGM's hits under Mayer include *Grand Hotel,* the *Thin Man* series, *Gone With the Wind, The Philadelphia Story, Easter Parade, Adam's Rib* and *The Red Badge of Courage.* For many years MGM dominated the movie industry.

Samuel Goldwyn is quoted as saying about Louis Mayer, "The reason so many people showed up at his funeral was that they wanted to make sure he was dead."

**Carl Laemmle,** 1867–1939. In the Laemmle Family Room Mausoleum.

Carl was a member of the large Laemmle family, about which humorist Ogden Nash wrote, "Uncle Carl Laemmle, has a very large faemmle," referring to the large number of family members Carl had on the Universal Studios payroll. Laemmle made 250 pictures during the first year after he opened Universal in 1915.

Today the sprawling Universal complex occupies several hundred acres, including stages, the MCA (Music Corporation of America) building, and Universal City. The complex attracts tourists with its Universal Studios Tours and City Walk, which has dozens of stores and restaurants. Tourists can dine at Gladstones, B.B. King's Blues restaurant and club, and the Hard Rock Cafe, among others, or visit a multi-screen movie theater or several on-site hotels.

**The Warners**

**Harry Warner,** 1881–1958. Third Mausoleum back in Section D.

Harry was one of 11 children born to Polish immigrants Benjamin Warner and his wife, Pearl. Benjamin was a cobbler by trade who tried everything from selling pots and pans to groceries in his struggle to avoid poverty. Harry, along with his brothers, Sam and Jack, started with a single print of *The Great Train Robbery* and built a modestly successful film distribution company. By 1918, they were making films under their own company, Warner Brothers, at a Hollywood studio located at Sunset and Bronson. In 1957, Harry and Jack made a pact with each other to sell their stock in the company. Jack held back and was able to gain control of Warner Brothers. Feeling betrayed, Harry never spoke to Jack again.

**Charles Vidor**, 1900–1959, with father-in-law Harry Warner.

Vidor was a Hungarian director who worked mostly for Columbia Pictures. He was best known for the engrossing musical bio *Love Me or Leave Me*. It was the story of singer Ruth Etting, played by Doris Day, and her love affair with a gangster called "The Gimp," played by James Cagney.

**Jack Warner**, 1892–1978. In an underground crypt marked by a fountain, near the family mausoleums.

While Harry Warner was the president, it was Jack who ran the studio. Tough and scrappy with a uncompromising attitude concerning money, the talent he had under contract referred to Warner Brothers as the "Buchenwald of Burbank." However, Jack Warner, despite his reputation for crudeness, turned out such pictures as *Public Enemy, Petrified Forest, The Maltese Falcon, Casablanca, Treasure of the Sierra Madre, Rebel without a Cause* and *The Searchers*.

# 29

## Inglewood Park Cemetery

Inglewood Park is located at 720 East Florence Avenue in Inglewood. Founded in 1905, the buildings are Spanish Mission in style. Their orange tile roofs, sweeping arches and stucco walls, along with dozens of palm trees, give the place a somewhat tropical Baja California look. Even the names of the various areas in the park have an exotic flavor, such as Garden of Verses, Mausoleum of the Golden West, Sanctuary of Faith, Miramar and Sequoia.

East of the gate, on the first road in the cemetery, is the Mausoleum of the Golden West. The inside is bathed with warm light from the colored-glass roof and stained-glass windows at the end of each hall. Many of the windows provide a garden-like effect, such as the one at the end of Sanctuary of Dawn. Here you can enjoy a view of the San Luis Rey Mission, with an explosion of colors from the flowers and bushes surrounding it.

Babes at rest.

**Betty Grable** (Ruth Elizabeth Grable), 1916–1973. Crypt A78 in the Sanctuary of Dawn.

Grable hit Hollywood at the age of 14. This talented, extroverted child, with the soon-to-be world-famous legs, sang and danced in chorus lines such as *Whoopee!* with Eddie Cantor. Grable made three forgettable pictures with producer Sam Goldwyn. Then, billed as Francis Dean, she worked in low-budget shorts and movies until she landed a featured spot in the Astaire-Rogers musical *The Gay Divorcee* in 1934, doing the delightful novelty number, "Let's K-nock K-nees."

As the wholesome, vivacious, all-American co-ed, Grable made many movies throughout the 1930s, but they took her nowhere. Her brief marriage to Jackie Coogan in the late 1930s brought her some notoriety, but it was a part on Broadway in 1939, in Cole Porter's *DuBarry Was a Lady,* that finally got her a *Life* magazine cover.

In 1940, Grable was signed by Fox and got her big break when Alice Faye was sidelined with appendicitis and Grable took her place in *Down Argentine Way.* This led to a string of hit musicals. In a 1943 bathing suit photo she looked over her shoulder with a wicked smile, knowing full well her shapely rear and long, beautiful legs would knock the guys dead. Grable became the Hollywood sex symbol. That picture became the number one pinup for American servicemen in World War II. (Little did they know that the backward pose was so designed because she was pregnant!) Fox, in a publicity move, immediately insured her legs for a million dollars with Lloyd's of London.

Grable's career declined throughout the rest of the 1940s, with the exception of *Mother Wore Tights,* made in 1947 with Dan Dailey. In the 1950s, an aging, slightly overweight Grable fought to hang onto her star power, but her only successes were *How to Marry a Millionaire* and *How to be Very Very Popular,* pictures that owed most of their success to the younger female co-stars, Marilyn Monroe and Sheree North.

A great, vivacious and beautiful actress, she performed in many stage musicals and was most popular as Dolly Levi in *Hello, Dolly.* Grable married band leader Harry James in 1943. Their common interest was raising and racing horses. They had two children and divorced in 1965. A heavy smoker, she died of lung cancer.

**Ferde Grofé,** 1892–1972. Also in the Sanctuary of Faith.

In addition to being one of the top sidemen in the 1920s jazz era, Grofé also had a genius for arranging and composing music. He began his career as a kid in his teens, playing piano in bawdy houses. Grofé then joined Paul Whiteman's band in 1919, and together the two musicians developed the style known as symphonic jazz. After a successful tour in Europe, Whiteman, on February 12, 1924, staged a symphonic jazz concert in New York's Aeolian Hall, the city's sanctuary of classical music. Victor Herbert was on the program along with George Gershwin, who played Grofé's arrangement of *Rhapsody in Blue* on the piano. This arrangement was done by Grofé because Gershwin at the time did not have the experience to fully orchestrate the piece. Grofé's arrangement became the immortalized *Rhapsody in Blue.*

Grofé's own scores were popular in his day. The best known was *Grand Canyon Suite,* which was the first piece of American music ever recorded by Toscanini. For those old enough to remember, the section of the suite entitled "On the Trail" was used in the Phillip Morris commercials on radio, followed by Johnny, the bellhop, saying, "Call for Phillip Mor-r-r-ris!"

**Paul Bern,** 1890–1932. Niche F96 in the Mausoleum.

Paul Bern was a scriptwriter-turned-producer for MGM. Bern, an extremely sensitive man, was known as "Father Confessor" and "Saint Francis of Hollywood" around the studio. It was this sensitivity that attracted movie star Jean Harlow to Paul. Harlow, the "Platinum Venus," was a gorgeous woman at the height of her career, starring in movies with Gable, Tracy and Cagney, among others. She spoke of Bern as one of "the great influences of my life." Harlow married Bern on July 2, 1932. Burdened with a sexual problem that destroyed his marriage, mounting financial debts, and the reappearance of his first wife from whom he had not obtained a divorce, Bern committed suicide. (For more details, see the section "Death by Mysterious Circumstance" and Jean Harlow in the "Forest Lawn, Glendale" section.)

**Edgar Bergen,** 1903–1978. In the Bergen family marker, Miramar Section. The stone is flanked by two arborvitae.

Bergen was a ventriloquist who became famous through his wildly popular dummy, tuxedo-clad, top-hatted gravely-voiced Charlie McCarthy. Bergen, a rather pale man with slicked-back hair and a Swedish accent, took his dummy Charlie, who always wore a monocle, on the vaudeville circuit in the 1920s. The pair finally went on radio in 1936, where they became extremely popular as *The Edgar Bergen and Charlie McCarthy Show*. As sometimes happens with ventriloquists, the characters of the dummies, Charlie and Mortimer Snerd—a dim-bulb hayseed—were stronger than that of their creator. Charlie once said in an interview, "Bergen is nothing without me." Charlie's personality was so pervasive that Bergen's daughter, Candice Bergen of the *Murphy Brown* TV series, thought Charlie was her brother when she was a little girl.

Bergen acted in several movies without Charlie, including *I Remember Mama* in 1948 and *The Hanged Man* in 1964. He died in his sleep at the age of 75 and was buried alone. Charlie was sent to the Smithsonian, after quipping, "Well, I won't be the only dummy in Washington."

Francis, Bergen's beautiful wife, revived her acting career in the 1990s and has appeared in such films as *Eating* and *Made in America*. Daughter Candice, who strongly resembles her mother, published her autobiography in 1984, called appropriately *Knock Wood*.

**Lillian Leitzel and Alfredo Codona.** Also in the Miramar section. Their graves are marked by a statue of them, with Lillian portrayed as an angel slipping out of Alfredo's arms. Below the sculpture is a bas-relief of two trapeze rings, one with a broken rope, and the words, "In Everlasting Memory of My Beloved Leitzel Codona, Copenhagen, Denmark, February 15, 1931. Built by her beloved husband, Alfredo Codona." Alfredo's monument is on the ground below, and reads, "Alfredo Codona" with the dates, "October 7, 1893– July 30, 1937."

The Codonas were circus performers who played their acts separately. In Copenhagen, Denmark, in 1937, waif-like Lillian fell

45 feet to her death with no safety net. Alfredo rushed to her side from Germany where he had been performing as part of an acrobatic act. Only 44 when he passed away, there is no record of what caused Alfredo's death, but if you're a romantic, wouldn't you believe it was probably from a broken heart?

**William B. Thomas,** 1931–1980. In the Acacia Section.

Thomas played the character "Buckwheat" in the Hal Roach *Our Gang* comedy series. The series started in the 1920s but made the transition to talkies in the 1930s. Thomas joined them in 1934 at the age of three and played "Buckwheat" for over ten years.

**Lyman Wesley Bostock Jr.,** 1950–1978. Located at the center of the Parkview Section.

His marker reads "Beloved Son" and has a baseball player hitting a ball and the California Angels logo engraved on it. Bostock, a star outfielder for the Angels, died at the age of 28. He was gunned down by an assailant who was trying to kill the woman riding with Bostock in his car.

**Willie Mae "Big Mama" Thornton,** 1926–1984. Located in Section M.

When Thornton was a young woman belting out the blues, she got the nickname "Big Mama" because of her weight, which was over 200 pounds. In addition to singing the blues, Thornton played a mean set of drums and a harmonica, Cajun-country style. Thornton wrote the hit songs "Hound Dog" and "Ball and Chain," which were made popular by Elvis Presley and Janis Joplin.

**James J. Jeffries,** 1875–1953. In the Sequoia section, near the entrance to the cemetery.

His bronze marker reads, "World Heavyweight Boxing Champion from 1899–1906." Jeffries was most famous for knocking out Gentleman Jim Corbett twice. In 1910, he came out of retirement and was immediately dubbed "The Great White Hope." He went up against Jack Johnson, who was black, in Reno, where Johnson quickly knocked him out. Jeffries got the message and quit boxing to open a saloon in Los Angeles. It was closed down by Prohibition in 1919. That was it for Jeffries. He retired to a farm in Burbank, where he lived until his death in 1953.

**Norman Spenser Chaplin,** July 7, 1919–July 10, 1919. Located in the section reserved for babies and young children.

His grave is near a statue of two angelic children reading a book. Below is this inscription:

I have just to shut my eyes,
To go sailing through the skies.
To go sailing far away
To the pleasant land of play.

Norman Spenser Chaplin was the son of Charlie Chaplin. He was born badly deformed and only lived for four days. His marker has only three words, but they speak volumes, "The Little Mouse, July 7–July 10, 1919."

**Cesar Romero,** 1907–1994.

A suave Latin, Romero entered show business first as a dancer. A very versatile actor, he played a gangster in *The Thin Man,* a lover to Marlene Dietrich in *The Devil Is a Woman,* and an Afghan leader to Shirley Temple in *Wee Willie Winkie.* In the 1940s, he appeared in a string of Fox musicals, including *Springtime in the Rockies,* where he danced with Betty Grable. By the 1950s his career slowed down and he made few movies but did appear as the "Joker" on the *Batman* series from 1966 to 1968. He joined the cast of *Falcon Crest* at the age of 78 and stayed for two years. In all, Romero made over 100 pictures. A bachelor, he was Hollywood's favorite escort of beautiful film stars. His grandfather, poet Jose Marti, liberated Cuba from Spain.

# 30

◆

## Mission Hills Cemetery

Located in the Mission Hills area of Los Angeles, the entrance to the cemetery is at 11160 Stranwood Avenue. This is a modern cemetery that is divided into sections. In the largest, Section C, is the Statue of the Sacred Heart of Jesus.

**William Frawley,** 1887–1966. Section C, curb number 64.

Stocky, balding and growly voiced, Frawley is best known for the part of Fred Mertz, Lucille Ball and Desi Arnaz's landlord on *I Love Lucy*. He was a prolific actor, appearing in over 150 movies, mostly in comedic roles. He appeared in both the 1934 and 1951 versions of *The Lemon Drop Kid*. His last acting role was as "Uncle Bub," Steve Douglas's (Fred MacMurray) father-in-law, in the 1960's sitcom *My Three Sons*.

**Lee DeForest,** 1873–1961. Row 416, near curb marker 409.

DeForest was a pioneer in wireless telegraphy and radio. He held over 300 patents, including a vacuum tube called a triode. The tube, which amplifies weak sounds, was basic to the development of radio and television.

**Ritchie Valens** (Richard Valenzuela), 1941–1959. Plot 247, near curb number 409.

His marker has five notes from his 1958 hit single, "Come on— Let's Go," and the words, "Beloved Son." Valens was a rock star of the 1950s, whose hits include "La Bamba" and "Donna," based on a fight he had with his Anglo girlfriend. Valens was a Mexican teenager who grew up in Pacoima. When he died, he was on a 13-city tour with fellow rocker Buddy Holly, ("Peggy Sue Got Married," "That'll Be the Day"). Holly, who hated their unheated bus, chartered a plane to make the trip from Clear Lake, Iowa, to the next stop on their tour, Moorehead, Minnesota. Aboard the plane were Holly, 22, Valens, 17, and J.P. Richardson, known as "The Big Bopper." Valens won his seat in a coin toss with one of Holly's "Crickets." They were all killed when the plane crashed in a farmer's field in a light snow storm.

In 1987, a movie biography of Valens was made. *La Bamba* starred Lou Diamond Phillips as Valens. Valens's music was used on the soundtrack and featured Los Lobos, who also appeared in the movie as a Tijuana band.

**William Bendix,** 1906–1964. Section D, near curb number 241.

A beefy, common-man type, Bendix played likable, sometimes not bright tough guys, including some with a Brooklyn accent. Despite his looks and the roles he played, Bendix came from a cultured family. His father had been a conductor with the New York Metropolitan Opera orchestra. Bendix left Broadway for Hollywood in 1942 and was nominated for a Best Supporting Actor award for his performance in *Wake Island* that same year. His best performances include those in *The Glass Key, Hairy Ape* and *Lifeboat.* From 1953 to 1958, he played the likable Chester A. Riley in the hit TV show *The Life of Riley.*

**Chuck Connors,** (Kevin Joseph Connors), 1921–1992.

Connors was a big, lanky man with a hatchet face. His appearance made him a natural to play cops and cowboys, after a less than successful career playing pro baseball with the Los Angeles Dodgers. He is best remembered as Lucas McCain, the moralistic rancher raising his motherless son (played by Johnny Crawford) in the hit TV series *The Rifleman.* He was strongly identified in the series because he carried a rifle instead of a pistol. It was a .44-40 Winchester, which he twirled in a circle by its lever to cock it.

His other TV series included the documentary drama *Crossroads* and *Branded,* in which he played a cashiered calvary officer roaming the West, looking for the men who had framed him. His 1963 series, *Arrest and Trial,* was unique because the first half of the program was devoted to catching the bad guy and the second half was the trial. (Sounds a little like the law-and-order formula.) Connors played a defending attorney in the series. He appeared in many mediocre pictures, but he did show his gift for humor in *Airplane II—The Sequel.*

## San Fernando Mission

The San Fernando Mission, originally named San Fernando Rey de España, is up the road from the Mission Hills Cemetery at 11160 Stranwood Avenue. It is just off San Fernando Mission Boulevard in the Mission Hills area of Los Angeles.

The first missionaries to the United States came from Spain in the 1500s. Members of the Franciscan order of the Roman Catholic Church founded most of the Spanish missions. At these missions, Indians were taught many things, such as farming, stock raising, citizenship, trades and other social tools, along with religion. Many of the Indians chose to live around the missions, which functioned like small towns for their inhabitants. The first California mission was established in San Diego in 1769.

The San Fernando Mission was founded in 1797 and includes a small cemetery whose size is surprising because some 2,500 people have been buried there, including Indians and priests. The graves are marked with crude wooden crosses and pieces of slate.

The two largest markers there are for the Menendez family. The first is dedicated to Maria Esprito Capigaras, 1836–1906, with the words, *"En paz descanse recuerdo de su hijo."* The other marker is for Luisa Straube, 1876–1906, and reads "In peaceful rest."

# 31

◆

## Mt. Sinai Memorial Park

Located at the edge of Burbank, Mt. Sinai Memorial Park seems to belong right where it is, high on a hill in this land of movies and movie-makers, directly across from the Walt Disney Studios. And while the magic at Disney is the weaving of make-believe with reality, Mt. Sinai's magic is the weaving of Jewish history with a place to be buried with dignity.

Here you will find sights such as the Heritage, a 145-foot mosaic commemorating the Jew in American history. Its depiction ranges from the Revolutionary War through the Gold Rush to the mass migration to New York City, including scenes of Hester Street and the Lower East Side. Also striking is the Memorial Monument, a dark, frightening sculpture commemorating the victims of the Holocaust. Mt. Sinai is located at 5950 Forest Lawn Drive in Los Angeles.

**Billy Halop,** 1920–1976. Along the wall in Crypt 6418.

As a teenager, Halop played Billy, the Dead End Kid, in the play and movie *Dead End* in 1937. Several other *Dead End Kid* movies followed through 1938, at which time Halop's career began to decline and he was only able to get bit parts.

**Phil Silvers,** 1912–1985. Vault 1004, Heritage Garden, next to the Heritage mosaic.

Silvers is probably best remembered as Sergeant Bilko, the ingratiating fraud with the pearly smile in the TV hit show *You'll Never Get Rich,* also known as *The Phil Silvers Show,* which ran from 1954 through 1959.

Phil, always ready to give you a big "Glad to see ya," started in show business in Minsky's Burlesque in 1934. During the 1940s, he had ten small but very funny parts in movies, including *Cover Girl* and *Summer Stock.* In 1951, he starred in the big Broadway hit *Top*

*Banana* and sang the hit song of the same name. The song's famous first line declared, "If you want to be a top banana, you've got to start at the bottom of the bunch." Silvers made several more movies in the 1960s, including *It's a Mad, Mad, Mad, Mad World* in 1963. His biography, *The Laugh's on Me,* was published in 1973.

**Lee J. Cobb** (Leo Jacoby), 1911–1976. In the Garden of Shemot, opposite a zodiac mosaic.

His epitaph, "Aye, every inch a king," is taken from Shakespeare's *King Lear,* a part Cobb played on the stage at Lincoln Center in 1969. His other major stage success was playing Willy Loman in *Death of a Salesman* in 1949. His first motion picture was *North of the Rio Grand* in 1937. Cobb played many meaty supporting roles in the 1940s and 1950s and received Oscar nominations for *On the Waterfront* in 1954 and *The Brothers Karamazov* in 1958. From 1962 through 1966, he played Judge Garth on the TV series *The Virginian,* and in the early 1970s he appeared in the TV series *The Young Lawyers.*

**Bruce Geller,** 1930–1978. In an individual garden, near a wall mural.

Geller was the creator/producer of the hit TV series *Mission Impossible,* in which he introduced the famous line, "Your mission, should you decide to accept it . . . " Geller died in an airplane crash near Santa Barbara in 1978.

**Herschel Bernardi,** 1923–1986. In Crypt 52250 in the Courts of Tanach.

His inscription, a tribute from his wife, Teri, reads "Hershy, you were the greatest moment in my life." Bernardi was a character actor who made many "B" movies, such as *Gangs, Inc.* with young Alan Ladd and *Stakeout on Dope Street* with Abby Dalton. From 1958 through 1961, he was a regular on the TV series *Peter Gunn* and later provided the voice of "Charlie the Tuna" on a series of TV commercials.

**Irwin Allen,** 1916–1991.

Allen was the producer/director of disaster movies and is probably best remembered for *Voyage to the Bottom of the Sea, The Poseidon Adventure* and the monster hit, *The Towering Inferno,* for which he received an Oscar nomination in 1974. His TV adventures included *Voyage to the Bottom of the Sea, Lost in Space* and *Land of the Giants.* Allen came to show business after a successful literary career as a writer, agent and editor.

The Richard Nixon Library and his resting place.

# 32

## The Richard Nixon Presidential Library and Birthplace
## The Center for Peace and Freedom

With history at your fingertips and the future to be explored, the Nixon Library and Birthplace is open daily from 10:00 A.M. to 5:00 P.M. at 18001 Yorba Linda Boulevard, Yorba Linda, California.

Not too far from most Angelinos' homes, these nine acres encompass 22 high-tech Presidential Museum galleries, movie and interactive video theaters. Here also is the spectacular First Lady's Garden, the President's faithfully restored 1910 birthplace, and the flower-ringed memorial burial sites of President and Mrs. Nixon.

In the library's first five years, it has operated according to President Nixon's mandate that it become a dynamic performing arts center for public affairs. It was his vision that all nine acres be devoted to the presidency, the U.S. system of government, and the life and legacy of Richard Nixon as an architect of peace. According

The presidents and their wives at the dedication of the library.

to the library director, John Taylor, "The Library has accomplished it all without accepting one cent of government funds."

The educational foundation is chaired by President and Mrs. Nixon's daughters, Tricia Nixon Cox and Julie Nixon Eisenhower. Financial support comes from admission fees and gift shop revenue, the $1,000-a-year President's Council and a 2,215-member Associates Club, private rentals, an annual Architect of Peace Award dinner and other charitable grants.

The library features many attractions including special exhibitions, issues forums, a speaker's series, personal appearances by associates of First Families, town meetings, and free student tours.

A history of American government, along with a history of the presidency and its achievements, is a focal point. There is a recreation of the Lincoln Sitting Room and an exhibit of gifts Nixon received during his presidency. Other exhibits include a moon rock, the telephone Nixon used to talk with Apollo XI astronauts while they were in space, and the famous gift pistol from Elvis Presley. Visitors can enjoy the First Lady's Rose Garden, and The Memorial Garden—the final resting place of President and Mrs. Nixon, located just a few steps away from our 37th president's birthplace.

Many of President Nixon's good and fast friends continue to support his goals and dreams. They serve as docents, volunteers and contributors. Library Director John Taylor and Kathy O'Connor, Assistant to the Library Director, have been associated with Nixon since 1980. Loie Gaunt, the Library's controller, has been an associate since the early 1950s.

# 33

### Oakwood Memorial Cemetery

Oakwood is located in the San Fernando Valley, at Andora Avenue and Lassen Street in Chatsworth.

**Bob Crane,** 1937–1978.

Bob Crane was born in Waterbury, Connecticut. He first aspired to be a drummer, but it was radio that gave him his start in show business. In the 1950s, Crane came to Los Angeles, where his radio show became the number one in morning ratings on KNX. The show ran for ten years and featured a creative mixture of humor, on-air interviews and records. He made over $100,000 a year, an excellent income for a radio performer at that time.

He moved into television and starred in the popular series *Hogan's Heroes* from 1965 to 1971. His movies, including Disney's *Superdad,* were mediocre. While filming that picture, rumors began to surface about the dark side of Crane's life, which was said to involve pornography. (For more information on Crane's death, see the section on "Death by Mysterious Circumstance.")

Fred Astaire — Elegance and style.

**Fred Astaire,** 1899–1987. Exact location in Oakwood is not known.

His screen test read, "Can't sing. Can't act. Slightly balding. Can dance a little." Teamed with his sister Adele, Astaire starred in hit musicals for nearly 15 years on Broadway. Then in 1933, he teamed with Ginger Rogers in the hit movie, *Flying Down to*

*Rio,* where their fancy footwork in "The Carioca" stole the show. Astaire and Rogers continued to star together in eight more musicals for RKO, including *Top Hat* in 1935. Rogers left the team to pursue her acting career, while the debonair, always immaculately dressed Astaire continued his fabulous acting/singing/dancing in musicals. He played opposite stars such as Eleanor Powell, Rita Hayworth, Bing Crosby, Gene Kelly, Judy Garland, Jane Powell and Audrey Hepburn in pictures that included *Blue Skies, Easter Parade, The Band Wagon,* and *Funny Face.* When musicals began to decline in popularity, Astaire played straight acting roles, such as in *The Towering Inferno,* for which he received an Oscar nomination in 1974. His television musical specials won him two Emmys, and the Academy gave him a special Oscar in 1949.

In any medium, including life itself, Astaire brought an elegance and style that has never been matched by any actor or dancer. He was expected to marry a movie star because of his close working relationship with so many of them. In fact, he married a young woman jockey named Robin and lived happily with her until he died in 1987. There was no feuding between Astaire and Rogers as the gossip wags frequently suggested. However, when Astaire received raves for his dancing performances, Rogers was heard to remark, "Sure, he's great—but don't forget—I do everything he does, and I do it backward, in high heels!"

# 34

## Pacific View Memorial Park

Founded in 1959, Pacific View is located on a hill above Newport Beach, California. With a majestic view of the harbor areas filled with yachts and of the blue Pacific Ocean, on a clear day you can see Catalina and the San Clemente Islands in the distance. The park accommodates all faiths and offers a mortuary and crematory, cemetery lots, crypts, niches, urn gardens, a mausoleum and a chapel.

Pacific View has provided its services to many people, including celebrities who are not interred here, such as **Andy Devine,** the gravel-voiced character actor who many remember as Roy Rogers' sidekick, Cookie Bullfincher, in 1940 movies and from 1950's TV. Devine's ashes were scattered at sea.

Pacific View Park is located at 3500 Pacific View Drive in Newport Beach, California.

One of the more than 30,000 Southern Californians buried in the park near his beloved Pacific Ocean and his home is the cemetery's most famous occupant, **John Wayne.** (The Duke is buried in an unmarked grave, but if you go to the cemetery office and ask, they may point you in Wayne's direction.)

**John Wayne** (Marion Michael Morrison), 1907-1979. John Wayne is the only actor about whom it can be said, "He is truly an 'American Legend' as big as Buffalo Bill, Davey Crockett, John Paul Jones, and other true-life heroes who share a special place in America's heart and memories."

Wayne came to represent the values Americans respect most. He was honest, direct, decisive, solitary and reverent. The character that the "Duke" played in almost every movie he ever made was one whose belief in his own abilities, sense of justice and values enabled him to take action when needed to right wrongs and

The Duke — An American legend.

protect people being treated badly. It was a character he believed in because it *was* him. It is hard to think of Wayne without director John Ford and his pals Ben Johnson, Harry Carey Jr., Victor McLaglen and Maureen O'Hara and the movies Wayne made, *Stagecoach, Red River, Fort Apache, Sands of Iwo Jima, The Quiet Man, True Grit* and *The Shootist*.

In 1979, he accepted an Academy Award while masking his approaching death by cancer behind his quiet courage. He loved his family and country and took great pride in his ranching, love of the outdoors and skippering his converted mine sweeper, *Wild Goose*, through the heaviest of seas.

**Ray Malavasi**, 1930–1987, was the football coach of the Los Angeles Rams during the hectic days of the 1979 season after the Rams' owner died. Malavasi coached them all the way through Super Bowl XV, their only appearance in any of the bowls, an appearance they won as a wild card team in the playoffs. Facing the Steelers led by quarterback Terry Bradshaw, who had led them to victory in the three preceding bowls, Pittsburgh figured slicing up the Rams would be quick, painless and easy. Not so, the game seesawed back and forth with both teams scoring points through the third quarter. The Steelers finally won the game 31 to 19.

**Freddy Martin**, 1906–1983, started his musical career demonstrating saxophones in a Cleveland music store. Raised in an orphanage until he was 16, Martin played with several nondescript bands before forming his own band with the encouragement of his friend Guy Lombardo. Martin opened with his band on October 1, 1931, at the Marine Roof of the Bossert Hotel in New York, before playing Chicago and San Francisco. Martin played his first engagement at the Cocoanut Grove in Los Angeles, a place that he would play so often his fans gave him the name "Mr. Cocoanut Grove." In the 1940s he introduced his theme song "Tonight We Love." He continued to play at the Grove and on the radio well into the 1960s, until a change in Grove management and philosophy caused him to retire to the Balboa Bay Club in Newport Beach in the early 1970s.

In 1972, Martin went on tour with Bob Crosby, Frankie Karle and Margaret Whiting as the "Big Band Cavalcade," which was a big success, with each of them alternating as leader of Martin's band. In 1977, Martin was asked to front his friend Guy Lombardo's band on tour after Guy was hospitalized with a heart condition that would eventually kill him.

In 1947, **Myford "Mike" Irvine,** 1899–1959, a talented musician and composer, took over the family business. Mike's father, J.I., had died in an accident while on a Montana fishing trip. The powerful Irvine Company was then valued at more than $1 billion. While Mike did not possess the fierce "Irvine lover of the ranch" that his father did, he was an able businessman. He ran the company for several years until his sister Joan, joined by her mother, pooled their stock and took control of the company.

# 35

◆

## Rose Hills Memorial Park

Rose Hills is located just south of Los Angeles in the city of Whittier, the birthplace of Richard Milhouse Nixon. Several Nixon family members are buried here. At 2,600 acres, it is the world's largest cemetery at a single location, four times the size of Arlington National Cemetery. Rose Hills may also be one of the most beautiful cemeteries in the country, located on rolling hillsides and graced with thousands of rose bushes. It includes the famous Pageant of Roses Garden, which has over 7,000 bushes featuring 600 varieties of roses spread over three acres. Annually, the public is invited to select rose clippings for their personal gardens.

This cemetery was born on land acquired by Augustus "Gus" H. Gregg's pioneer family. The first interment took place in 1895 on the original 18 acres of land. Under Gregg's leadership, the cemetery was named Whittier Heights Memorial Park. In addition to owning the cemetery, Gregg had extensive holdings in real estate, gravel, livestock and a savings and loan. He continued to develop the cemetery and added the first mausoleum, which he called the Little Mausoleum, in 1916, followed by another, El Portal de la Paz, in 1930.

The architectural style of Rose Hills is early California mission, and today there are four nondenominational chapels: the Rainbow Chapel, Hillside Church, Sky Church and the Memorial Chapel. Mausoleums include the Terrace of Memories, Court of Eternal Light, Mausoleum of the Valley and Lakeview Mausoleum.

In addition to their regular grave locations, Rose Hills has set aside special gardens for groups, including Masons, Mormons, Lutherans, Jews, Catholics, Buddhists, Chinese, Koreans and Japanese, whose garden includes an *azumaya*, a "meditation house."

Veterans are honored with a special place called the National

Academy Award winner Dr. Haing Ngor with Robert Wagner.

Shrine at Rose Hills, which features an Arch of Freedom Memorial and an All Services Memorial. Special services are held at the National Shrine on Memorial and Veterans Days.

Cambodian native **Dr. Haing Ngor**, a Cambodian war victim, movie star and Academy Award winner, is buried here (see "Death by Mysterious Circumstance").

Rose Hills Memorial Park is located at 3988 South Workman Mill Road in Whittier.

# 36

## Valhalla Memorial Park

Valhalla is located at 10621 Victory Boulevard in North Hollywood. Like Forest Lawn and other modern cemeteries, Valhalla uses large sculptures to denote areas for specific groups. A large bronze piece with a helmet and rifle marks the area for military veterans. The baroque, circular Heritage Fountain denotes a European style. The Portal of the Folded Wings, an ornate Byzantine memorial highlighted by a tiled dome, was built to honor the pioneers of American aviation. The portal has memorial plaques to famous flyers such as Amelia Earhart.

**Oliver Hardy,** 1892-1957. Near the Heritage Fountain in the Garden of Hope.

His plaque reads, "A genius of comedy. His talent brought joy and laughter to all the world." Oliver Hardy and Stan Laurel were two great comedic actors who, when paired together, created magic in their brilliantly crafted roles as "Stan" and "Ollie." One

Oliver Hardy with Stan Laurel — Comedy at its best.

was fat, the other thin. Stan had an English accent, Ollie's was Southern. Together, and guided by the comedic genius of Hal Roach, they made a series of films destined to be classics. Their comedic bag of tricks included tit-for-tat destructive techniques, which they used to destroy automobiles, buildings and their own homes; Ollie's long, slow burns; their too-small bowler hats; Stan's blank looks when something he did went wrong; and Ollie's fastidious gestures, which he used when trying to sell his "get rich" schemes to anyone who would listen.

The highlights of Laurel and Hardy's silent films include *The Battle of the Century*, which featured the classic pie fight that grew until half the city was involved; and *Two Tars,* which included a tit-for-tat scene where, in an escalating adventure of rampant destruction, a whole line of motorists rip each other's cars apart.

Stan and Ollie made the transition to talkies with ease. *The Music Box* in 1932, a picture in which they try to deliver a piano up an enormous flight of stairs, earned them an Academy Award. Other hits included *Sons of the Desert* and *Babes in Toyland.* In the 1940s, they moved to MGM where the pictures they made were second-rate. They never recaptured the greatness of the comedic vehicles of the 1920s and 1930s that made them stars.

The two men loved each other like brothers. Hardy died of complications from a stroke in 1957, while Laurel, despite his own heart problems, lived until 1965. Their fans, even today, number in the millions.

**Gorgeous George** (George Raymond Wagner), 1915–1963. Section D, Plot 6657.

His marker reads, "Love to Our Daddy." Gorgeous George was the unchallenged king of the theatrical wrestlers of his time. His contemporaries included the Masked Marvel, Andre the Giant and the Swedish Angel. Dressed in purple, his favorite color, with his long bleached-blonde, carefully curled locks bouncing on his shoulders, George would prance toward the ring to the strains of "Pomp and Circumstance." He would remove his robe with its mink collar and enter the ring after his valet had sprayed it with perfume. Despite his years as a champion in the game of theatrical wrestling,

George died broke. His friends had him buried here in a coffin covered with orchids—purple ones.

**Gail Russell**, 1924–1961.

Russell was a classic, dark-haired beauty of the Hedy Lamarr school. She made her film debut in *Henry Aldrich Gets Glamour* in 1943. The next year she made *The Uninvited,* which got rave reviews, and in 1947, opposite John Wayne, she played the strong-willed Quaker girl in *Angel and the Badman.* Wayne's interest in her reportedly extended beyond their acting relationship. She starred again with Wayne in *Wake of the Red Witch* and continued to make a few pictures, none memorable, until her last in 1961.

Russell suffered greatly from stage fright and over the years turned to drinking for the courage needed to face the camera. When she died, her body was found surrounded by empty liquor bottles.

Also at Valhalla are **Cliff Edwards,** 1895–1971, in Section D. Character actor Cliff was the voice of Jiminy Cricket in Disney's animated feature *Pinocchio.* Next to him is **Mitty Morris,** 1874–1953. Known as Mother Morris, she founded the Faith Home Missions. Near the Mausoleum of Hope is **Bea Benaderet,** 1894–1968. Bea played the mother on the TV series *Petticoat Junction* in the 1960s and was the voice of Betty Rubble in the animated TV series *The Flinstones* from 1960 to 1964. In her radio days, she was the next-door neighbor on *The Burns and Allen Show.*

Dean Martin — "A man's got to stand for something. I'll stand for another round of drinks."

# 37

## Westwood Memorial Park

This "postage stamp" jewel of a cemetery, located at 1218 Glendon Avenue in Westwood, is surrounded by tall office buildings and condominiums just a few blocks from the UCLA campus. It is a quiet haven in the midst of this very urban spot.

Westwood is the final resting place of many luminaries, and there is room for more at about $13,000 per plot. It is famous for housing the remains of Marilyn Monroe. Cemetery staff used to tape letters to her crypt and, if return addresses were available, took a photograph of the letter and sent it to the writer. Over the years some of the pink marble stone has had to be replaced three times because of lipstick stains from the many kisses of her fans.

**Dean Martin** (Dino Crocetti), 1917–1996. He was tall, with dark, wavy hair, a slow drawl, a relaxed attitude and an absolutely engaging personality. Dino could both croon and wisecrack with equal ease. He spent his early years as half of the Martin-Lewis team, with rubber-faced comedian Jerry Lewis.

Following his split with Lewis, his career accelerated with club performances, TV shows, record sales and movie roles. In motion pictures he proved himself to be a richly talented actor in films such as James Jones' *Some Came Running* (with Frank Sinatra), *Rio Bravo,* and *Airport.* At times, however, he seemed bored with himself, especially during his TV series, *The Dean Martin Show,* which ran from 1965 to 1974. Still, he was effortlessly engaging, charming and sexy.

In the 1960s, Martin joined the "secret agent" craze and made a series of *Matt Helm* spy spoofs, including *The Silencers.* Also, as part of the famed "Rat Pack" with Sinatra, Sammy Davis Jr., and Peter Lawford, he made the intriguing *Ocean's Eleven.* It is amazing that with all his club appearances, recordings and TV work, he still made over 40 motion pictures during his career.

The Armand Hammer Family Mausoleum.

The death of his son, a military pilot, in a jet crash near Palm Springs devastated Martin. After this tragedy, he seemed to withdraw into his own world.

**Armand Hammer,** Chairman of Occidental Petroleum, 1898–1990.

The Hammer mausoleum, just to the left of the entrance, features black wrought iron with an Egyptian motif. Hammer was one of the most controversial industrial tycoons of this century. His desire was for the world to picture him as its greatest benefactor and as a leader of humanitarian causes. But there was a darker side to Hammer that peeked through his life, and it suggested that his methods and intents were more like those of a 16th century robber baron. On a plaque in Hammer's bedroom appeared his version of the golden rule: "He who hath the gold maketh the rule."

At the time of his death, Hammer was CEO of the mammoth and far-reaching Occidental Petroleum. He was also a medical doctor, pharmacist, major art collector and adviser to presidents of the United States and foreign heads of state, particularly Russia.

On December 11, 1990, the morning after Hammer's death, the public woke up to find Hammer's passing front-page news. The *New York Times* called him the only man to "tell Mikhail Gorbachev first hand what Lenin was like." The *Los Angeles Times* hailed him as a man whose "new idea was to see beyond ideology to what business could accomplish." The *Wall Street Journal* described him as "one of the most colorful and forceful entrepreneurs of the 20th Century." Probably the most on-target description came from the *Orange County Register,* which said he was "living proof that with enough money, charm, philanthropy, and carefully crafted public relations, a persistent apologist for communism in its brutal phases can buy his way into conservative and Republican circles."

Hammer's total compensation for 1990 was revealed to be $28.7 million, making him the highest paid executive in California. At first considered a prime takeover target, insiders soon labeled Occidental as an "over-leveraged chemical company, with an $8.5 billion long term debt." Financial analysts stated that Occidental's only chance to survive was to sell off subsidiaries and write off $2 billion in debt in order to recover from Hammer's disastrous management. Despite this financial bad news, the fact remained that Hammer had turned a corporate shell called Occidental Petroleum into the 16th largest industrial company in America.

Also buried in the Hammer mausoleum are his father, Julius, a doctor and pharmacist; his mother, Rose; and brother Victor, an art collector and expert whose legend reads, "The only time Victor made anyone sad was the day he died."

**Heather O'Rourke,** 1975–1988. First outdoor mausoleum east of the Hammers.

She was the beautiful little fair-haired girl who played in the *Poltergeist* series of films in the 1980s. Her only other film credits were for *Happy Days*. Her tragic death at such a young age was caused by a congenital deformity of the intestines. She died during an operation from septic shock and cardiac arrest. Her marker reads, "Star of Poltergeist One, Two and Three."

**Harry S. Warren** (Salvatore Guaragna), 1894–1981. In the Sanctuary of Tenderness, just east of Heather O'Rourke.

Warren's plaque is decorated with a musical staff and the opening notes from his hit song, "You'll Never Know Just How Much I Love You" along with the words "Beloved husband, father, composer." Warren was a self-taught musician who came from a large and poor family in Brooklyn. A composer, he is best known for the work he did with lyric writers Al Dubin and Mack Gordon. His three Academy Awards were for "Lullaby of Broadway," "You'll Never Know" and "On the Atchison, Topeka and the Santa Fe." His other hits include "Serenade in Blue" and "I Only Have Eyes for You."

**Buddy Rich,** 1917–1987. Continuing east, in the Sanctuary of Tranquillity.

His marker reads, "One of a Kind." And one of a kind he was. Rich was probably the greatest of all big band drummers. Born in Brooklyn, he broke into vaudeville in his parent's act and by 1930 was playing with Joe Marsala's sextet at the Hickory House in New York. Although he was dubbed "Mr. Warmth" by his fan, Johnny Carson, Rich was known for his quick temper and even quicker fists. Late in 1938, he joined Bunny Barigan's band. He then moved on to play with Artie Shaw and finally with Tommy Dorsey from 1939 until late in 1942 when he joined the Marines.

Out of the service in 1944, he rejoined Dorsey and two years later started his own band. His band stayed together only a couple of years, which forced him to tour with Norman Granz and his "Jazz at the Philharmonic." In the 1950s, he alternated between playing for Dorsey and Harry James while trying again to start his own band. In the late 1950s he settled down with James for a reported $35,000 a year—big money for those times—where he stayed until he had a heart attack in 1959. He returned to James in 1961 after a brief try at a singing career and stayed there as James' most publicized sideman until 1966. That year, Rich finally formed another band. It was a driving, swinging big jazz band with a sound that caught on with the public and was always booked for months ahead. Rich was credited with reviving the big band sound, and the band, still using his name, is alive and well today.

**Nunnally Johnson**, 1897–1977. Sanctuary of Tranquillity.

Nunnally was a screenwriter, producer and director with a great sense of humor. He was famous for his put-downs of Hollywood such as, "Let's show the movies in the street—and drive the people back into the theaters." He was also known for his literate screenplays, including the Oscar-nominated *The Grapes of Wrath,* directed by John Ford. As a writer and producer for Fox, he made another Oscar-nominated picture, *Holy Matrimony,* in 1943. In 1953 he made *How to Marry a Millionaire* for Marilyn Monroe, a woman he greatly admired.

As a director he never achieved the success he had in writing

Marilyn Monroe — The reason why gentlemen prefer blondes.

and producing, but he did turn out *The Three Faces of Eve* in 1957. In 1964 he collaborated with his daughter Nora in turning her comic novel, *The World of Henry Orient,* into a delightful movie starring Peter Sellers. It was directed by George Roy Hill. Johnson says about Marilyn Monroe (who is interred near him), "Marilyn Monroe is a natural phenomenon, like Niagara Falls or the Grand Canyon. You can't talk to it. It can't talk to you. All you can do is stand back and be awed by it."

**Marilyn Monroe,** 1926-1962. Crypt located in the Corridor of Memories, in the northeast corner.

Formerly known as Norma Jean Mortenson, Marilyn Monroe began her movie career in the 1950s with parts in *Asphalt Jungle, Gentlemen Prefer Blondes, How to Marry a Millionaire* and *The Seven Year Itch.* (For more information on Marilyn Monroe's life and death, see the section "Death by Mysterious Circumstance.")

**Oscar Levant,** 1906-1972. Just south, along the east wall in the Sanctuary of Love.

Levant was famous as a mental basket case who just couldn't shut up. In motion pictures such as *An American in Paris,* he always played himself, a man filled with a biting, scattering of put-down thoughts that continually rattled around in his mind. He was definitely the dog who bit the hand that fed him, as shown by his comment, "Strip the phony tinsel off Hollywood and you'll find the real tinsel underneath." Yet at times in some pictures, such as *The Band Wagon,* he displayed his flair as a brilliant pianist and a wonderful comedian.

Levant quit high school at 15 to study piano in New York. As word of his talent spread, he found himself in great demand and played at dozens of different places from road houses to elegant supper clubs. In New York, he became a friend and champion of George Gershwin. In the 1930s, while studying with Arnold Shoenberg, he was asked to display his talent for the German conductor Otto Klemperer. Always self-destructive, Levant obliged with a bawdy rendition of *When Irish Eyes Are Smiling*, bellowing out the lyrics to an unamused Klemperer.

Levant was also a composer whose pieces were played by the world's leading symphony orchestras. Over 100 recordings of his music were made by major record companies. During the 1940s he began radio and TV appearances on various shows, including six years on *Information Please*. The audiences loved him for his humorous, biting remarks, which he aimed at anything and anyone whose name popped into his head. And while the fans loved it, the sponsors sweated bullets and fired him often for his off-color and often slanderous barbs. However, he continued to be a favorite on shows such as Jack Paar's, where he made the remark, "As a child, my main aspiration was to be an orphan."

"So little time. So little to do," was one of Levant's famous remarks. However, in the early 1950s, he suffered from nervous exhaustion, which he unsuccessfully tried to treat with drugs. The combination of drugs and his worsening mental condition led to a series of voluntary and enforced stays at mental hospitals over several years. He continued to take heavy doses of drugs, despite wife June Gale's threat to kill the doctor who was supplying him. In the 1960s Levant retired, exhausted from his battles with his mind and drugs. Always difficult, he summed up his life: "In some situations I was difficult, in odd moments, impossible, in rare moments, loathsome, but at my best, unapproachably great."

**Richard Conte** (Nicholas Peter Conte), 1914–1975. In the center of the cemetery.

Conte's Italian look caused him to be cast in gangster roles, although he did appear in several war dramas such as *Guadalcanal Diary* in 1943. He often appeared in gritty melodramas such as *Call*

*Northside* 777. After 1950, Conte played mostly supporting roles, the most memorable of which was *The Godfather* in 1972.

His cemetery marker has a pyramid in each corner and a tree trunk with roots in the center. It reads, "Actor-Writer-Painter-Composer-Poet," and is followed by a lengthy poem that begins:

A man of many talents and graces,
Loved by a thousand unknown faces . . .

**Darryl F. Zanuck,** 1902–1979, lies beside his wife, **Virginia Zanuck,** 1906–1982, in the center, six rows down from the north wall.

Zanuck's plaque, with the Twentieth Century Fox logo on it, lists his achievements, including those in the military as a soldier in World War I and colonel in World War II, when he led a combat camera crew. His plaque also reads "A man who used his imaginative creative genius to deliver inspiration through his celebrated motion pictures. He imparted a lifetime message of decency, love, patriotism, equality and hope throughout the nation and the world." Virginia's plaque begins with her achievements and ends with a poem that says, "With a cheerful smile and a wave of her small hand. She has just wandered off into unknown land."

Zanuck was the only early movie mogul who came from the white-bread middle west of America. He was born in Wahoo, Nebraska, to a roguish, gambling father and a tubercular mother and was raised mostly by his grandfather, Henry Torpin, in Oakdale, Nebraska. Torpin, while teaching Zanuck hunting and horsemanship, regaled him with stories of his own youth as an engineer, building the great transcontinental Canadian Pacific railroad. There, during an Indian uprising, he fought bravely, receiving no less than 21 arrow wounds. With Torpin as his hero, Zanuck, only 14 years old, five feet, six inches tall, and a mere 104 pounds (which he was able to get up to the required 107 pounds by drinking water), enlisted in the U.S. Army to fight in World War I. He was posted to France as a private in the 37th "Buckeye" Division from Ohio, an outfit that had taken many casualties in battle. Zanuck served bravely, had several close calls from enemy fire, and returned home as a PFC. During this time, several of his letters were published in his hometown paper by his grandfather, as well as in *Stars and Stripes.*

Zanuck's greatest talent was the ability to create and find stories that could be translated into motion pictures. He also had the gift of being a fine editor, which served him well in saving several films that had been declared "disasters." He first tried his hand at writing for the pulps but had no luck until he wrote a book containing four stories, three of which sold to motion picture companies. These early stories revealed what Zanuck thought was the "stuff of good movies." One was a Western adventure. Another was a musical, *Alexander's Ragtime Band*, and the third concerned a mute Chinese man who witnesses a murder. All of these stories carried a common theme: the romanticized stories of people and their struggles with life. "Only make stories about people, not places or things," would be his continuing film philosophy. He was 23 and on his way as a studio writer. He eventually wrote many films for the dog Rin Tin Tin, of which he was very fond.

"Darryl was a very light sleeper. I pinned his side and mine with a great big safety pin to keep him from falling out of bed," his wife Virginia once said.

By 1923 he was at Warner's. Here he was such a prolific writer that he had to use four different pen names so his name wouldn't appear so often on their pictures. He was promoted to head of production at Warner that same year, and while there he made two of his best pictures, *The Public Enemy* with James Cagney and *I Am a Fugitive from a Chain Gang.* Zanuck left Warner in 1933 over a dispute about wages for his people. He was making $5,000 a week, a fortune in those days. Joe Schenck quickly snapped him up and Zanuck formed a new company—20th Century. He also became well known as a polo player, a safari hunter and a practical joker. In 1935, in a merger, the company became 20th Century Fox, and Zanuck now had his own source of distribution. His two best films made with the new company were John Ford's *How Green Was My Valley* and *The Grapes of Wrath.*

In January of 1942, Zanuck was commissioned as a lieutenant colonel in the Signal Corps and a few weeks later became an observer on a British commando raid on radar stations at St. Valery,

France. From there he went to Algiers as a full colonel to command a combat film crew. While there he made the documentary film *At the Front* and escaped some close calls during German air raids. During one such incident he emptied his machine gun at one of the planes, claiming he was sure he had hit it.

While working for him as a producer, George Jessel said of Zanuck, "When I die, I want to be cremated and have my ashes sprinkled on Mr. Zanuck's driveway so his car won't skid."

Zanuck returned to 20th Century Fox, where he made such notable pictures as *Laura, Gentleman's Agreement,* and *The Sun Also Rises,* based on his close friend Ernest Hemingway's novel.

In 1962, Zanuck made his most adventurous picture, *The Longest Day,* based on Cornelius Ryan's book about D-Day, the 6th of June. To make this film, he fought Ryan, his own board of directors, the weather and almost insurmountable logistical problems. Zanuck courted former military leaders of both the Allied and German armies, including his friend Ike, for their support in lending him everything from ships and planes to men and weapons.

For the huge cast, he called on Wayne, Fonda, Eddie Albert, Mitchum, Robert Ryan, Peter Lawford, Fabian, Connery, Burton, and more. With a budget of $8.5 million, Zanuck set out to tell the story of the world's most complex invasion, as seen through the eyes and stories of the leaders, their subordinate officers, the GIs and combined Allied soldiers. He made the film centered around what Irwin Rommel said on hearing of the landings: "This could be our longest day." At Zanuck's funeral, following his instructions, the only music played was the theme from *The Longest Day.*

After flings in Europe over the years with exotic women such as Bella Darvi, Juliette Greco and Genevieve Gilles, he finally came home to his wife, Virginia, a West Virginia coal miner's daughter, whom he married in 1924. Together they had three children. She hated his flings but never deserted him. Their son Richard is now one of Hollywood's most successful directors.

**Natalie Wood,** 1938–1981. Located southeast of the entrance, just south of the Hammer Mausoleum.

She was first known for her performance, at age nine, in

*Miracle on 34th Street.* She gained notoriety as a teenager, with James Dean, in *Rebel Without a Cause.* Wife of Robert Wagner, Natalie died mysteriously on a boat off the Catalina coastline. (For more of Natalie Wood's story, see the section "Death by Mysterious Circumstance.")

**Donna Reed** (Donna Belle Mullenger), 1921–1986. South of Natalie Wood, in the center of the cemetery.

Reed will always be with us in memory as the heartwarming wife of Jimmy Stewart in Frank Capra's *It's a Wonderful Life.* We could scarcely celebrate Christmas without this film.

She was born on a farm and was a genuine campus queen. Her first real break in films was as John Wayne's navy nurse love interest in John Ford's *They Were Expendable* in 1946. She played a contrasting role as a prostitute in *From Here to Eternity,* earning a Best Supporting Actress Oscar. On TV, Reed starred in *The Donna Reed Show* from 1958 to 1966, a series produced by her husband, Tony Owen.

**Sebastian Cabot,** 1918–1977. In the Urn Garden in the southwest corner of the cemetery.

An English actor of substantial girth, Cabot was famous for his beard and rich, deep voice. A very likable bear of a man, he played in just a few movies, such as *Ivanhoe,* and on two TV series. *Checkmate,* a 1960s mystery show, featured Cabot as one of the three detectives. Anthony George and Doug McClure played the others. From 1966 to 1971, he played the "gentleman's gentleman" on *Family Affair,* a series about a bachelor, played by Brian Keith, who inherits his brother's three children. With Keith often gone for long periods, Cabot more or less raised the kids.

**Victor Killian,** 1891–1979. His ashes were scattered in the Rose Garden.

Killian worked as a villain in a string of forgettable films. This character actor is probably best remembered as the Fernwood Flasher in the sitcom *Mary Hartman, Mary Hartman,* starring Louise Lasser.

Dorothy Stratten — Beauty and the Beast.

**Dorothy Stratten,** 1960–1980. East of Cabot, in the fifth row.

Her prominent marker contains a passage from Hemingway's *A Farewell to Arms,* which reads, "If people bring so much courage to this world, the world has to kill them to break them, so of course it kills them . . . it kills the very good and the very gentle and the very brave impartially. If you are none of these, you can be sure that it will kill you too, but there will be no special hurry. We love you, D.R."

Stratten was a beautiful Canadian woman who married Paul Snider who took advantage of and murdered her. Snider, who pictured Stratten as his ticket to becoming one of Hollywood's movers and shakers, brought her to the attention of *Playboy* magazine, where she became the 1980 "Playmate of the Year." In *Playboy* she was spotted by producer/director Peter Bogdanovich, who co-starred her in a colorful romantic comedy, *They All Laughed,* in 1981. During the filming, Bogdanovich and Stratten fell in love, and she became his companion.

On August 14, 1980, Stratten went to Snider's house to explain to him that their marriage was over. Snider took the news badly, and within the hour he raped, tortured and killed Stratten with a shot gun, which he later used to kill himself. The beautiful young woman, who was looking forward to life with someone who loved her and whom she loved, was gone.

**Will Durant,** 1885–1981, and **Ariel Durant,** 1898–1981. Just north of Stratten, under a big tree.

Will was 28 and Ariel just 15 when they married in New York City. In their autobiography, Ariel is described as arriving at New York's City Hall for her wedding on roller skates. They became famous for their work as historians and writers of their *Story of Civilization* book series, a concept of Will's that began in 1927. At first, Ariel was not involved, but then she became a partner in the writing, research, and editing of the 11-book series. They won a Pulitzer Prize for their tenth book, *Rousseau and the Revolution.* The series was completed in 1975. While there was a 13-year difference in their ages, they died within two weeks of each other. Will was 96 and Ariel 83.

Among other notables found at Westwood Memorial are **Stan Kenton**, popular composer and big band leader of the 1950s, whose style of music he named "progressive jazz" and who attracted many of the finest jazz musicians to his band, such as Maynard Ferguson, Jerry Mulligan, Shorty Rogers and singer June Christy; **Lewis Milestone,** a film director who won an Oscar for *All Quiet on the Western Front;* **Roy Orbison,** a rock singer whose hits include "Only the Lonely" and "Pretty Woman"; **James Backus**, the actor who starred as the millionaire on the 1960s TV series *Gilligan's Island* and who was the voice of Mr. Magoo in the animated cartoon series.

Another notable at Westwood is **John Cassavetes**, an actor and innovative film maker. He was nominated for Oscars three times, including for *The Dirty Dozen.* As a director he made modest, gritty little pictures using his own stock company, which included his wife, Gena Rowlands, and his friend Ben Gazzara.

**Irving "Swifty" Lazar,** a Hollywood talent agent made famous for his "Oscar Night" parties, but even better known for his quick deal making, which caused Humphrey Bogart to give him the name "Swifty"; and **Sammy Cahn,** lyricist, who wrote hits such as "High Hopes" and "Love and Marriage."

**Don Defore,** film and TV actor, rests here. He was best known for playing Mr. Baxter in the 1950s series *Hazel.* He was also Ozzie Nelson's neighbor, Thorny, in the *The Adventures of Ozzie and Harriet.*

Others include **Frank Zappa,** a "flower child" rocker who was the leader of the eclectic band The Mothers of Invention from the 1960s through the 1970s; **J. C. Flippen,** the film and TV character actor; **James Wong Howe,** a cinematographer credited with being Hollywood's greatest and most creative director of photography; **Dominique Dunn,** a film actress who appeared in the 1982 film *Poltergeist* and who was strangled by her boyfriend; her father is the famous author, Dominick Dunn; and **Christopher George,** a motion picture and TV actor who starred in the late 1960s TV series *The Rat Patrol.* He was married to actress Linda Day George.

**Richard Basehart** is here, the actor with the deep, rich voice who is best remembered for his mid–1960s TV series, *Voyage to the Bottom of the Sea*; along with **Brooks West**, an actor/artist, and his wife **Eve Arden**, of *Our Miss Brooks*, who are buried together.

**Peter Lawford** was a British actor who began his career in musicals. In later years, he became a member of Frank Sinatra's legendary "Rat Pack," starring with other Pack members in such forgettable films as *Ocean's Eleven*. He was once entombed in a crypt in a mausoleum near Truman Capote, but in 1988 his ashes were removed and scattered at sea by his wife, Patricia Kennedy Lawford.

**Truman Capote** is here. He was the boy genius writer who grew up and wrote the romantic classic *Breakfast at Tiffany's* and the true crime drama *In Cold Blood.*

**Lloyd Nolan,** an actor from northern California, was known for his Bronx accent, which found him lots of work in gangster pictures in the 1930s and 1940s. He made some westerns in the 1960s and then made the transition to TV, playing the grumpy Dr. Chegly on the series *Julia,* from 1968 to 1971.

**Harold Hecht** was a motion picture producer whose main collaboration was with Burt Lancaster on films such as *Marty* and *Cat Ballou*.

**Gregor Piatigorsky,** a cellist, came to the U.S. in 1929 and for the next 20 years toured the world as one of its most famous classical performers.

**Mario Castelnuovo-Tedesco,** a composer, fled Mussolini's Italy for the United States in 1939. He composed overtures for seven Shakespeare plays, as well as operas, concertos and other pieces.

**Minnie Ripperton Rudolph,** a singer with a 5-1/2 octave range, is best remembered for her 1973 hit record, "Loving You."

**Helen Traubel** joined the Metropolitan Opera as a soloist at the age of 23 and soon left to perform popular music with stars such as Jimmy Durante.

**Eva Gabor,** Zsa Zsa's sister, appeared on the stage in plays such as *Blythe Spirit* and in motion pictures such as *Gigi.* She is best remembered as the star of the TV sitcom *Green Acres,* with Eddie Albert.

Eva Gabor — A glamorous Gabor.

# 38

◆

## Woodlawn Cemetery

Woodlawn started out as a district cemetery for Santa Monica and was taken over by the city in 1897. This non-denominational cemetery is located on 26.6 acres, 14 blocks from the Santa Monica Freeway at 1847 Fourteenth Street. A mausoleum was built in 1928, and the cemetery stopped offering cremating services in the mid–1960s.

**Charles Bickford,** 1889–1967.

Bickford was a bushy-haired character actor with piercing eyes. After working as a sailor and an engineer, he spent ten years on Broadway. In the 1940s he was at the peak of his film career. He received Oscar nominations for *The Song of Bernadette* in 1943, *The Farmer's Daughter* in 1947, and *Johnny Belinda* the following year. In the 1960s he starred in *The Virginian.* His autobiography, *Bulls, Balls, Bicycles and Actors,* was published in 1965.

**Paul Henreid** (Paul Henreid Ritter), 1908–1992.

Henreid is best remembered as freedom fighter Victor Laszlo in *Casablanca.* He was born in Trieste and made his first films in England during the 1930s, including *Goodbye, Mr. Chips.* He starred in a number of pictures, surprisingly as a swashbuckler and sword-and-sandal type. In the 1950s he turned to directing and made several movies, as well as episodes for TV series. His autobiography, *Ladies Man,* was published in 1984.

**Leo Carrillo,** 1880–1961. In Section 2, near Fourteenth Street.

Carrillo was graduated from St. Vincent of Loyola. He worked as a newspaper man and cartoonist before becoming a dialect comedian, first in vaudeville and later on the legitimate stage. He started his work in films in the 1920s, and in the 1950s he played

Leo Carrillo — Actor and member of a distinguished pioneer family.

the role of Pancho, Renaldo's sidekick in *The Cisco Kid* television series. He was married to stage actress Edith Hazelbarth.

Carrillo was a member of one of the oldest and most respected pioneer families in California. He was born on Bell Block, a long row of adobe dwellings on the east side of Los Angeles Street between Aliso and First. This was "the Plaza," near what is now known as Olvera Street, a replica of Old California. In later years Carrillo contributed a great deal to the restoration of Olvera Street.

His family history is quite impressive; his ancestry can be traced to the Spanish Castilians as far back as 1260. The Carrillos were military leaders, attorneys, governors and judges. Leo's great-grandfather, Carlos Antonio, received Santa Rosa Island, off the coast of Santa Barbara, in payment for his services as governor of California. He later traded the island for 1,500 head of cattle. It is now known as Vail Ranch Operations.

Leo's great-great-grandfather, Jose Raimundo Carrillo, founded the new colony of Alta (upper) California in Baja (lower) California. One family member received the Coronado Peninsula as a wedding gift, including Coronado Island. After the wedding, the bride sold the peninsula and island for about $1,000. Later, a part of the estate known as North Island was sold to the U.S. Navy for $7 million.

The Carrillos are related by marriage to Pio Pico, the last governor of California under Mexican rule. The home belonging to Leo's great uncle, Jose Antonio Carrillo, was located across from Pico House, Los Angeles' first hotel. Pio Pico, having fallen into debt, gave his sisters the vast Santa Margarita Ranch where Camp Pendleton now stands. Another great uncle, Andres Machado, owned a ranch covering thousands of acres in Santa Monica. He met his tax obligations by selling off portions of the land. Finally he was left with just enough land to accommodate his house. Although Andres never knew it, the land he sold later became part of the Great Baldwin Hills Oil Discovery.

Another of Leo's relatives, his great aunt, married Colonel R.S. Baker, after whom Bakersfield is named. The pair purchased the entire Santa Monica area in 1874 and later subdivided it and sold off the lots. They donated 300 acres of the property for a soldiers' home at Sawtelle, now the National Veterans Administration facility.

Leo himself lived in Santa Monica Canyon, near the Malibu Sequit Canyon. He later bought 1,700 acres in Carlsbad on El Camino Real, which he purchased for $17 an acre. The property was later valued at $3,500 to $4,000 an acre. After Leo's wife died, he disposed of a portion of this land and lived out his life comfortably in his daughter's home.

# Epilogue

**You Know . . .**
You know one night the stars will shine
Upon your cold gravestone,
And find a name, a silver line
And it will be your own.

That night beneath a star-filled sky
You'll find your time ran out,
That mortal life had passed you by
That you had lost the bout.

Cheer up, you had your share of laughs
You loved and lived your dreams,
And those who cared wrote epitaphs
On the stone with silver beams.
**— Gary Hudson**

So, in the immortal words of Mel Blanc, "That's all, folks!" If you have any unique stories of fascinating funerals, unusual tombstones (send pictures), mysterious deaths, entertaining epitaphs, celebrity grave locations or anything on death or dying you'd like to share with us for the next edition of *Final Curtain,* please contact:

Margaret Burk
*Final Curtain*
860 Fifth Avenue
Los Angeles, CA 90005

# Appendix

## Cemetery Locations

**Angeles-Rosedale**
1831 W. Washington Blvd., Los Angeles, 90007     (213) 734-3155

**Calvary Cemetery**
4201 Whittier Blvd., Los Angeles, 90023     (213) 261-3106

**Chapel of the Pines**
1605 S. Catalina, Los Angeles, 90006     unpublished

**Crystal Cathedral**
12141 Lewis St., Garden Grove, 92840     (714) 971-4000

**Eden Memorial Park**
11500 Sepulveda Blvd., Mission Hills, 91345     (818) 361-7161

**Forest Lawn, Covina**
21300 Via Verde Dr., Covina, 91724     (818) 966-3671

**Forest Lawn, Cypress**
4471 Lincoln Ave., Cypress, 90630     (714) 828-3131

**Forest Lawn, Glendale**
1712 South Glendale Ave., Glendale, 91205     (818) 241-4151

**Forest Lawn, Hollywood Hills**
6300 Forest Lawn Dr., Los Angeles, 90068     (818) 984-1711

**Forest Lawn, Long Beach**
1500 E. San Antonio Dr., Long Beach, 90807     (310) 424-1631

**Hillside Memorial Park**
6001 Centinela Ave., Los Angeles, 90045     (310) 641-0707

**Hollywood Memorial Park,**
6000 Santa Monica Blvd., Los Angeles, 90038     (213) 469-1181

**Holy Cross Cemetery**
5835 West Slauson Ave., Culver City, 90230     (213) 776-1855

**Home of Peace Memorial Park**
4334 Whittier Blvd., Los Angeles, 90023     (213) 261-6135

**Inglewood Park Cemetery**
720 East Florence Ave., Inglewood, 90301      (310) 412-6500

**Mission Hills Cemetery**
11160 Stranwood Ave., Mission Hills, 91345      (818) 361-7387

**Mt. Sinai Memorial Park**
5950 Forest Lawn Dr., Los Angeles, 90068      (213) 469-6000

**Oakwood Memorial Cemetery**
22601 Lassen St., Chatsworth, 91311      (818) 341-0344

**Pacific View Memorial Park**
3500 Pacific View Dr., Corona Del Mar, 92625      (714) 644-2700

**The Richard Nixon Presidential
Library and Birthplace**
18001 Yorba Linda Blvd., Yorba Linda, 92686      (714) 993-3393

**Rose Hills Memorial Park**
3888 South Workman Mill Rd., Whittier, 90601      (310) 699-0921

**Valhalla Memorial Park**
10621 Victory Blvd., North Hollywood, 91606      (818) 763-9121

**Westwood Memorial Park**
1218 Glendon Ave., Los Angeles, 90024      (310) 474-1579

**Woodlawn Cemetery**
1847 14th St., Santa Monica, 90404      (310) 450-0781

# Glossary

**Cemetery** - A place for burying the dead. A graveyard.

**Cinerary Urn** - A container in which to save the ashes of the dead.

**Columbarium** - A vault with niches for urns containing ashes of the dead.

**Crematorium** - A furnace or establishment for the incineration of corpses.

**Crypt** - An underground vault or chamber, especially one beneath a church that is used as a burial place.

**Mausoleum** - A large, stately tomb or a building housing such a tomb or several tombs.

**Sarcophagus** - A stone coffin, often inscribed or decorated with sculpture.

**Tomb** - A grave or other burial place. A monument commemorating the dead.

**Vault** - A burial chamber, especially when underground.

# Index

Abbott, Bud, 117
Accardo, Tony, 26, 269
Acker, Jean, 263
Adams, Edie, 212-213
Adams, Evangeline, 269
Adams, Franklin P., 108
Addario, Daniel, 57
Adler, Buddy, 150
Adonis, Joey, 26, 268-269
Adrian, Gilbert, 246
Akins, Claude, 79-80
Albert, Eddie, 337, 342
Albright, Lola, 173
Alda, Alan, 154
Alda, Robert, 154
Alexei, Prince, 105-106
Alland, William, 7
Allen, Gracie, xiv, 180-181
Allen, Irwin, 313
Allen, Steve, 123
Allen, Woody, 4
Allensworth, Allen, 107
Ambrosi, Justinus, 46
Anderson, Eddie, 228
Anderson, Mary Ann, 78
Andrews, Laverne, 173-174
Andrews, Maxine, 173
Andrews, Patty, 173
Antonio, Carlos, 344
Arbuckle, Fatty, 190, 199-200, 249, 292
Arbuckle, Minta Durfee, 190
Arden, Eve, 341
Arlen, Richard, 293
Arliss, George, 202
Armstrong, Bruce, 83
Armstrong, Louie, 271-272, 274
Armstrong, Robert, 6
Arnaz, Desi, 197-199, 307
Arnaz, Desi, Jr., 199
Arnaz, Lucie, 199
Arnstein, Nicky, 298

Arrouge, Marty, 172
Ashby, Hal, 113
Ashley, Lady Sylvia, 168, 256
Astaire, Fred, 258, 274, 279, 317-318
Astor, Mary, 294
Atkins, Susan, 35
Austin, Gene, 161
Autry, Gene, 69, 215, 278
Bacall, Lauren, 116, 149
Backus, James, 340
Bacon, James, ix, 11, 14, 28
Baer, Max, 5
Baillie, Hugh, 10
Baker, R. S., 345
Balboni, June Mathis, 264
Balboni, Sylvano, 265
Baldwin, Leon, 237-238
Ball, Lucille, 188, 197-199, 228, 236, 307
Ballard, Lucien, 153
Banning, Phineas, 104
Bara, Theda, 173
Barham, Patte, 107
Barigan, Bunny, 332
Barker, Lex, 78
Barnes, George, 138
Barrett, Rona, 15
Barris, Harry, 273
Barrymore, Ethel, 11, 115-117, 141
Barrymore, Georgie Drew, 115
Barrymore, John, 3, 10-11, 114-115, 134, 294
Barrymore, Lionel, 1, 115-116
Barrymore, Maurice, 115
Bartholomew, Freddie, 136
Baruch, Bernard, 10
Basehart, Richard, 341
Baum, Frank, 186
Baum, Maud Gage, 186
Bavetta, John, 20
Baxter, Anne, 118
Baxter, Warner, 1, 146

Beatty, Clyde, 205
Beatty, Warren, 31
Beaulieu, Priscilla, 56
Beckett, Samuel, 200
Beery, Wallace, 39, 149, 292, 298
Belasco, David, 245
Bell, Rex, 175, 177
Belushi, John, 51
Benaderet, Bea, 327
Bendix, William, 308
Bennett, Constance, 1, 63
Bennett, Joan, 63-64
Benny, Jack, xiv, 170, 181, 227-228
Benny, Mary Livingston, 227-228
Bergen, Candice, 304
Bergen, Edgar, 159, 304
Bergen, Francis, 304
Berger, Anita Louise Adler, 150
Berle, Milton, 15
Berlin, Irving, 266, 274
Bern, Paul, 3, 38-39, 171, 303
Bernardi, Herschel, 312
Besser, Joe, 297
Beveridge, Daeida Wilcox, 257
Bichet, Sidney, 271
Bickford, Charles, 7, 343
Bigard, Barney, 272
Bigelow, Gloria, 18
Bigsby, Carl Morgan, 236
Blair, Nicky, 15
Blake, Eubie, 107
Blanc, Mel, xiii, 346-347
Blanchard, Frederick W., 237
Blandick, Clara, 163
Bliss, William, 25
Block, Karl M., 10
Block, Sherman, 98-99
Blondell, Joan, 138
Bogart, Humphrey, 7, 60, 74, 81, 116,
    136, 147-149, 209, 217, 243, 257, 340
Bogdanovich, Peter, 64, 339
Boland, Paul, 91
Bolger, Ray, 291-292
Bond, Carrie Jacobs, 164
Bond, Ward, 287
Boone, Daniel, 48-49
Booth, John Wilkes, 47
Borglum, Gutzon, 164
Borzage, Frank, 137

Bostock, Lyman Wesley, Jr., 305
Bow, Clara, 175-177
Boyd, Benjamin, 47-48
Boyd, William, 161
Boyer, Charles, 275-276
Boyer, Michael Charles, 275-276
Boyer, Patricia, 275
Bradshaw, Terry, 321
Brand, Sybil, 279
Brando, Marlon, 4, 28
Brecher, Irving, 255
Breeson, Chalk, 60
Brennan, Walter, 210
Brett, Dorothy, 51
Brett, Mabel Dodge, 50
Brice, Fanny, 298
Brisson, Frederick, 284
Britt, May, 142
Brody, Sam, 248
Brooks, Mel, 204
Brown, Clarence, 139
Brown, Don Evan, 182
Brown, Horace, 251
Brown, Joe E., 170, 182-183
Brown, Johnny Mack, 144
Brown, Lansing, 169
Browning, Victor, Jr., 13
Browning, Victor, Sr., 13-14
Browning, Victor "Shane," 13
Bruce, Lenny, 123
Bruce, Nigel, 111, 133
Bruce, Virginia, 259
Bruckheimer, Jerry, 12
Brynner, Yul, 253
Burch, Rosabella, 17-18
Burk, Margaret, 156-157, 194, 347, 367
Burnam, Roger Noble, 265
Burnette, Lester "Smiley," 215
Burns, Bob, 190
Burns, George, 170, 180-181
Burton, Richard, 337
Burton, Tim, 74
Busch, Mae, 117
Bushman, Francis X., 189
Buttram, Pat, 69
Bynner, Witter, 51
Byrd, Ralph M., 154
Cabot, Sebastian, 338
Caesar, Arthur, 4

Cagney, James, 6-7, 37, 138, 171, 280, 300, 303, 336
Cahn, Sammy, 340
Calhern, Louis, 241
Calhoun, Rory, 65
Callender, Marie, 122
Cambridge, Godfrey M., 215
Campa, Betty, 85
Campanella, Roy, 288
Cannon, Phil, 19
Cano, Ray, 19
Canova, Diana, 150
Canova, Judy, 150
Canova, Leon, 150
Canton, Mark, 12
Cantor, Eddie, 197, 228-229, 291, 302
Capigaras, Maria Esprito, 309
Capone, Al, 27
Capote, Truman, 341
Capra, Frank, 77, 116, 236, 254, 338
Carey, Harry, 286-287
Carey, Harry, Jr., 287, 321
Carney, Art, 215
Carol, Sue, 174
Carpenter, Karen, 221-222
Carr, Patrick, 70
Carrier, Dona Lee, 140
Carrillo, Jose Antonio, 344
Carrillo, Jose Raimundo, 344
Carrillo, Leo, 343-345
Carroll, Earl, 144-145, 256
Carson, Jack, 172
Carson, Johnny, 15, 332
Carter, President Jimmy, 24
Cassavetes, John, 340
Castelnuovo-Tedesco, Mario, 342
Cather, Willa, 50
Chance, Frank, 108
Chandler, Buffy, 235
Chandler, Harry, 235
Chandler, Jeff, 229
Chandler, Marion Otis, 235
Chandler, Norman, 235
Chandler, Otis, 235
Chaney, Lon, Sr., 163
Channing, Carol, 63
Chaplin, Charlie, 21, 62, 81, 118, 200, 202, 251, 256, 267, 281, 292, 306
Chaplin, Charlie, Jr., 267
Chaplin, Hannah, 251

Chaplin, Norman Spenser, 306
Chase, Borden, 203
Chase, Charlie, 292
Chasen, David, 11
Cher, 6
Chevalier, Maurice, 160, 179
Christian, Linda, 253
Christie, Agatha, 252
Christy, June, 340
Cimber, Matt, 248
Claiborne, Billy, 60
Clanton, Ike, 60
Clark, Eli, 186
Clark, Hatti, 104
Clark, John, 145
Clark, Luci, 186
Clark, Robert, 192
Clark, Scott, 85
Clark, William A., Jr., 241-242
Clemmons, Jack, 30
Clifford, Belene, 18
Clift, Montgomery, 6, 168
Clooney, Rosemary, 67
Cobain, Kurt, 71
Cobb, Lee J., 285, 312
Cochrane, Kathy, 24
Codona, Alfredo, 304
Codona, Lillian Leitzel, 304
Cohen, Mickey, 81, 230
Cohn, Harry, 243, 254-255
Colbert, Claudette, 167, 267, 287
Cole, Cornelius, 236
Cole, George Townsend, 236-237
Cole, Nat King, 178-179
Cole, Natalie, 178-179
Collins, Joan, 286
Collins, Ray Bidwell, 203
Colman, Ronald, 6, 63, 269
Columbo, Russ, 199
Como, Perry, 153
Condon, Robert, 25
Connolly, Sheilah, 65
Connors, Chuck, 308-309
Connery, Sean, 337
Conrad, William, 216
Conte, Richard, 334-335
Convy, Bert, 217
Coogan, Jackie, 281, 302
Cooke, Sam, 17, 41, 141
Cooper, Gary, 175, 210

Cooper, Merian C., 287
Corbett, Jim, 305
Corman, Roger, 74
Coronel, Don Antonio, 237
Cosby, Bill, 17
Costello, Frank, 26, 269
Costello, Lou, 117, 291
Cotten, Joseph, 6, 68-69, 169, 174
Coward, Noel, 63, 160
Cox, Tricia Nixon, 316
Crane, Bob, 40-41, 317
Crane, Cheryl, 78
Crane, Hart, 5
Crawford, Joan, 141, 144, 167, 170, 284
Crawford, Johnny, 308
Cregar, Samuel Laird, 138
Crosby, Bing, 1, 65, 169-170, 173,
    272-274, 293, 318
Crosby, Bob, 322
Crosby, Dixie Lee, 272, 274
Crothers, Scatman, 204
Crystal, Billy, 17
Cukor, George, 140-141
Cummings, Robert, 269
Curtis, Tony, 183
Curtiz, Michael, 190
D'Abo, Ursula, 18
Dailey, Dan, 143, 302
Dalton, Abby, 312
Daly, Bob, 12
Damita, Lily, 134
Dandridge, Dorothy Jean, 181-182
Daniels, Bebe, 268
Danton, Ray, 209
Danza, Tony, 16
Darrow, Clarence, 4, 234
Darvi, Bella, 337
Darwell, Jane, 187
Dastigar, Sabu, 214
Dastigar, Sheik, 214
David, Paul, 58
Davies, Marion, 8-10, 250-252, 282
Davis, Bette, 62, 200-202
Davis, Joan, 290-291, 293
Davis, Sammy, Jr., 15-17, 41, 141-142,
    329
Davis, Larry, 122
Davis, Tracey, 16-17
Day, Doris, 4, 206, 283, 300
Day, J. Dabney, 236

Dean, James, 31, 52-53, 338
Dee, Francis, 59
Defore, Don, 340
DeForest, Lee, 307
de Havilland, Olivia, 133
DeHaven, Gloria, 73
DeMille, Cecil Blount, 243-246, 254,
    266, 268
DeMille, Constance Adams, 243, 245
Demont, Maude, 249
Dempsey, Dean A., 87
DeRita, Joe, 297
DeSylva, George G., 191
Devine, Andy, 293, 319
DeVoe, Daisy, 177
Dickinson, Angie, 15
Dietrich, Marlene, 7, 269, 306
DiLeo, Lia, 174
Diller, Phyllis, 208
Dillon, Josephine, 165, 167
DiMaggio, Joe, 28, 30
Disney, Edna Frances, 214
Disney, Roy, 131-132, 214
Disney, Walt, 131-133, 259, 295, 311
Dodds, Johnny, 271
Dolgen, Jonathan, 12
Dolly, Roszika "Rosie," 170
Dolly, Yansci "Jenny," 170
Donat, Robert, 133, 284
D'orsay, Fifi, 191
Dorsey, Tommy, 332
Dougherty, Bill, 19
Dougherty, Jim, 28
Douglas, Lloyd C., 191
Dreyfuss, Richard, 13
Dubin, Al, 331
Duff, Howard, 78
Dumont, Margaret, 124
Duncan, Isadora, 204
Duncan, Rosetta, 186
Duncan, Vivian, 186
Dunn, Dominick, 341
Dunn, Dominique, 341
Durant, Ariel, 339-340
Durant, Will, 339-340
Durante, Jimmy, 67, 276-278, 280, 342
Durer, Albrecht, 192
Eager-Tanner, Johnny, 211
Earhart, Amelia, 325
Earp, Jim, 60

Earp, Morgan, 60
Earp, Virgil, 60
Earp, Wyatt, 59-60, 287
Eason, Sam, 19-20
Eaton, Hubert, xiv, 127-129, 144-145, 157, 165, 195, 197, 221
Ebsen, Buddy, 244
Eddington, Nora, 134
Eddy, Nelson, 164, 179, 258-259
Eden, Barbara, 63
Edward I, Prince, 47
Edward, Prince of Wales, 282
Edwards, Cliff, 327
Edwards, Vince, 295
Eichler, John, 20
Eisenhower, Julie Nixon, 316
Eisner, Michael, 12
Elizabeth, Queen, 63
Ellington, Duke, 178, 272
Emmanuel, Victor, 97
Epstein, Joseph, 27
Errol, Leon, 291
Estephan, Elie, 92
Esterhazy, Prince Nicolaus II, 45
Esterhazy, Prince Paul, 46
Etting, Ruth, 300
Evans, Dale, 82
Evans, Linda, 15
Evans, Robert, 172
Ewell, Tom, 77
Fabian, 337
Fairbanks, Douglas, xiii, xvi, 133, 151, 153, 168, 255, 268, 273
Faith, Percy, 229
Farnsworth, Art, 202
Farouk, King of Egypt, 5
Farrell, Charles, 137, 246
Faulkner, William, 290
Fay, Frank, 73
Faye, Alice, 209, 252-253, 272, 302
Faye, Julia, 245
Fechin, Madam, 51
Fechin, Nicolai, 51
Feldman, Marty, 204
Feliz, Jose Antonio, 237-239
Feliz, Jose Vicente, 237
Feliz, Juan Jose, 237
Feodorovna, Czarina Alexandra, 106
Feodorovna, Czar Nicholas, 105-106
Ferber, Edna, 4

Ferguson, Maynard, 340
Ferguson, Paul, 40
Fields, W. C., 1, 159, 293
Finch, Peter, 259, 266
Fine, Larry, 297
Fitzgerald, F. Scott, 171
Flaherty, Robert, 214
Fleming, Rhonda, 170
Fleming, Victor, 175
Flippen, J. C., 341
Floyd, Joseph, 17
Flynn, Errol, 11, 133-134
Folger, Abigail "Gibby," 34-35
Fonda, Henry, 287, 337
Fontaine, Tony, 210-211
Ford, Glenn, 254, 258, 279, 284
Ford, John, 64, 136, 158, 286-288, 321, 332, 336, 338
Ford, John Anson, 158-159
Ford, Mary, 286
Ford, Wallace, 1
Fortner, Victor, 85-86
Foster, Mabel, 242
Fowler, Gene, 10-11
Fraction, Alma, 86
Fraction, Felicia, 86
Fraembs, Daniel, 219
Frawley, William, 307
Freed, Arthur, 229
Freehling, Allen, 16
Fremont, Jesse Benton, 104
Fremont, John, 104
Friml, Rudolf, 164
Frykowski, Wojtek, 34-35
Furness, Viscountess Thelma, 282-283
Gable, Clark, 37-39, 141, 165-168, 172, 174, 179, 298, 303
Gable, John Clark, 168
Gabor, Eva, 342
Gabor, Zsa Zsa, 140, 342
Gale, June, 334
Gallagher, Tommy, 15
Gallery, Don, 260
Garbo, Greta, 119, 141, 144, 167, 298
Garcetti, Gil, 98
Garcia, Jerry, 70-71
Gardner, Ava, 60-62, 168
Gardner, Reginald, 210
Garland, Judy, 141, 266, 292, 318
Garner, James, 15

Garner, John Nance, 10
Garretson, William, 34
Gaston, Teddy Getty, 18
Gaunt, Loie, 316
Gaye, Marvin, 71
Gaynor, Janet, 137, 246
Gazls-Sax, Joel, 83
Gazzara, Ben, 340
Gazzeri, Ernesto, 192
Geffen, David, 13
Gebre, Astor, 20
Geisler, Jerry, 134
Geller, Bruce, 312
George, Anthony, 338
George, Christopher, 341
George, Gladys, 7
George, Linda Day, 341
Gershwin, George, 154, 303, 334
Getty, J. Paul, 17-19
Getty, J. Paul, Jr., 17
Getty, Sarah, 18
Giannini, A. P., 10
Gibb, Andy, 211
Gibson, Charles Dana, 285
Gibson, Hoot, 286
Gilles, Genevieve, 337
Gillespie, Haven, 208
Gingold, Hermione, 160
Ginsberg, Allen, 57
Gish, Lillian, 212
Gitlin, Todd, 56
Giunta, Ray, 85-88
Glyn, Elinor, 175
Goddard, Paulette, 62
Godfrey, Arthur, 123
Goldman, Ronald Lyle, 42
Goldwyn, Samuel, 153, 244, 266, 298-299, 302
Gorbachev, Mikhail, 330
Gordon, Mack, 331
Gordy, Berry, 16
Gorgeous George, 326-327
Goya, Francisco, 49
Grable, Betty, 143, 170, 188, 209, 252, 281, 302, 306
Graham, Billy, 121, 155
Graham, Martha, 212
Grandison, Dr. Lionel, 30
Granger, Farley, 286
Grant, Cary, 1, 112, 140-141, 169, 284, 298
Grant, Kathryn, 274
Granville, Bonita, 280
Granz, Norman, 109, 332
Grauman, Sid, 170
Grayson, Katherine, 291
Greco, Juliette, 337
Greenstreet, Sydney, 191, 257
Gregg, Augustus "Gus" H., 323
Gregory, Paul, 246
Gregson, Richard, 33
Grey, Lita, 267
Griffith, Christine, 239-240
Griffith, D. W., 255-256, 292
Griffith, Griffith J., 237-241
Griswold, Harvey, 49
Gritnes, Tiny, 109
Grofé, Ferde, 303
Guest, Edgar, 174
Gwenn, Edmund, 112
Hackett, Buddy, 15
Hackett, Joan, 1, 269
Hagman, Larry, 63
Haines, William, 1
Haley, Bill, 71
Haley, Jack, 272
Haliburton, Richard, 5
Halop, Billy, 311
Hamilton, George, 15
Hammer, Armand, xiv, 330-331
Hand, Dora, 60
Hanson, Betty, 134
Hardy, Oliver, 67, 202-203, 325-326
Hargitay, Mariska, 249
Hargitay, Mickey, 248
Harlow, Jean, 3, 36-40, 136, 167-168, 170-171, 298, 303
Harriman, E. H., 233
Harris, Phil, 228
Harris, Richard, 15
Harrison, Rex, 62, 68, 113, 138
Harvey, Laurence, 7
Hatley, T. Marvin, 208
Haver, June, 295
Hawkins, Coleman, 108
Hawkins, Maria, 178
Hawks, Howard, 64
Haydn, Franz Joseph, 45-46
Haymes, Dick, 279
Hayward, Louis, 78

Hayward, Susan, 269
Hayworth, Rita, 254, 278-279, 318
Hazelbarth, Edith, 344
Healy, Ted, 297
Hearst, Millicent Wilson, 9
Hearst, William Randolph, 8-10, 137, 155, 239, 250, 282
Hecht, Harold, 341
Heidt, Horace, Jr., 215
Heidt, Horace M., 215
Hellman, Lillian, 280
Hemingway, Ernest, 134, 243, 337, 339
Hendrix, Jimi, 70
Hendrix, Wanda, 210
Henie, Sonja, 73
Henreid, Paul, 343
Henry, O., 5
Hepburn, Audrey, 65, 318
Hepburn, Katharine, 136-137, 140-141, 169, 243
Herbert, Victor, 258, 303
Herman, Woody, 256
Hersholt, Jean, 163
Hickock, Wild Bill, 94
Hill, George Roy, 333
Hill, James, 279
Hill, John L., II, 103
Hill, John L., III, 103
Hill, John Lamar, Sr., 103-104
Hill, Virginia, 27
Hilton, Conrad N., Jr., 293
Hines, Earl, 109, 272
Hines, Gregory, 142
Hirt, Al, 215
Hitchcock, Alfred, 58, 118
Hitler, Adolph, 118, 290
Hladka, Anna, 17-18
Hodiak, John, 118
Hofmann, Josef, 161
Holliday, Doc, 60
Holliday, Judy, 141
Holly, Buddy, 70, 307
Hoover, Herbert, 10
Hope, Bob, 6, 113, 199, 274
Hopper, Hedda, 282
Horne, Victoria, 188
Horton, Edward Everett, 1
Houdini, Harry, 199
Howard, Curly, 297-298
Howard, Leslie, 153, 172

Howard, Moe, 297-298
Howard, Roy, 10
Howard, Shemp, 297-298
Howard, Trevor, 6
Howe, James Wong, 341
Howes, Archie, 195
Hudson, Gary, 347, 368
Hudson, Marylin, 157, 367
Hughes, Howard, 37, 118, 170
Huntington, Henry E., 233
Hurt, Marlin, 191
Huston, Anjelica, 243
Huston, John, 112, 116, 168, 242-243, 257
Huston, Rhea, 242
Huston, Walter, 112, 243, 294
Hyde, Johnny, 28
Ingram, Rex, 203, 261
Irvine, Myford "Mike," 322
Iturbi, Jose, 289-290
Iwerks, Ub, 131
Jack, Wolfman, 84, 122
Jackson, Jesse, 16
Jacoby, Leo, 312
Jagger, Bianca, 17
Jagger, Mick, 70
James, Harry, 302, 332
Janssen, David, 14-15, 226-227
Jeffries, James J., 305-306
Jessel, George A., 227, 229, 267, 337
Joelson, Moshe, 226
Johnson, Ben, 64, 287, 321
Johnson, Jack, 305
Johnson, Nunnally, 332-333
Jolson, Al, 224-226, 227
Jones, Buck, 286
Jones, Isham, 161
Jones, James, 329
Jones, Jennifer, 7, 169
Jones, Spike, 290
Joplin, Janis, 71, 305
Jordan, Jim, 276
Jordan, Marian I., 276
Judson, Edward, 279
Kahn, Aga, 279
Kahn, Gus, 189
Kahn, Princess Yasmin, 279
Kanin, Garson, 137
Karle, Frankie, 322
Karloff, Boris, 14, 275

Kalmar, Bert, 191
Kasabian, Linda, 35
Kassel, Art, 206
Kath, Terry Allen, 5, 152
Katzenberg, Jeffery, 12
Kaufman, George S., 294
Kaye, Danny, 140
Kazan, Elia, 76
Keaton, Bobby, 267
Keaton, Buster, 199–200, 203, 267, 278, 298
Keeler, Ruby, 226
Keenan, Frank, 158
Keith, Brian, 338
Kellerman, Annette, 281
Kelly, Gene, 15, 170, 279, 318
Kelly, Grace, 241, 274
Kendall, Kay, 138
Kennedy, Arthur, 7, 60
Kennedy, Edgar, 283, 292
Kennedy, John F., 15, 30
Kennedy, Robert F., 30–31
Kent, Atwater, 145
Kenton, Stan, 340
Kerouac, Jack, 57, 297
Kerr, Deborah, 35
Kilbride, Percy, 59
Killian, Victor, 338
Kinelly, Jim, 48
King, B. B., 299
King, Martin Luther, Jr., 15
Kipling, Rudyard, 2, 191
Kitson, Penelope, 18
Klemperer, Otto, 334
Klugman, Jack, 15
Kniestedt, Maria Chacon, 87
Knight, Goodwin, 269
Knight, Ted, 153
Kogut, William, 94
Komack, Jimmy, 24
Korda, Alexander, 153
Koussevitzky, Serge, 291
Kovacs, Ernie, 212–213
Kovacs, Mia, 213
Kramer, Stanley, 136
Krenwinkle, Patricia, 35
Kristofferson, Kris, 71
Kuhlman, Kathryn, 145–146
Kuhn, Hildegard, 18
La Rue, Jack, 290

Ladd, Alan, 174–175, 312
Ladd, Alan, Jr., 175
Ladd, David, 175
Laemmle, Carl, 171, 200, 299
Laine, Frankie, 208
Lake, Arthur, 251
LaMarr, Barbara, 138, 259–260, 289
Lamarr, Hedy, xiii, 1, 327
Lamour, Dorothy, 245, 274
Lancaster, Burt, 341
Lanchester, Elsa, 204–205
Landau, Arthur, 38
Landis, Carole, 63
Lang, Richard, 15
Langdon, Harry, 292
Langham, Ria, 165
Lankershim, Isaac, 231
Lanza, Betty, 291
Lanza, Mario, 271, 291
LaRosa, Julius, 296
Lasky, Jesse L., 244, 265–266
Lasky, Meyer, 26, 269
Lasser, Louise, 338
Laughton, Charles, 153, 204–205
Laurel, Ida K., 202
Laurel, Stan, 67, 202–203, 325–326
Laurie, Annie, 192
Lawford, Patricia Kennedy, 341
Lawford, Peter, 30–31, 141, 329, 337, 341
Lawrence, D. H., 49–51
Lawrence, Martin, 13
Lazar, Irving "Swifty," 340
Leary, Timothy, 56–58, 214
Lebowitz, Fran, 7
Lehrman, Henry, 249
Leigh, Janet, 172
Leigh, Jennifer Jason, 230
Leigh, Vivien, 141, 167, 169
Lemerett, Marian, 162
Lemmon, Jack, 183
Lemmon, Lenore, 25
Lennon, John, 57, 70
Leslie, John, 281
Levant, Oscar, 333–334
Lewis, Jerry, 141, 329
Liberace, 206–208
Liddy, G. Gordon, 57
Lillie, Beatrice, 210
Lincoln, Abraham, 47–48, 104
Linkletter, Art, 58, 214

Linkletter, Diane, 214
Lloyd, Harold, 67, 268
Lockhart, Gene, 283
Lockhart, June, 283
Lockhart, Kathleen, 283
Lockwood, Margaret, 63
Loew, Marcus, 298
Lombard, Carole, 165–168, 169, 209, 292
Lombardo, Guy, 321–322
Long, Richard, 154
Long, Suzan Ball, 154
Longfellow, Henry Wadsworth, 197
Loos, Anita, 266
Lorre, Peter, 14, 257–258, 275
Love, Courtney, 71
Lovejoy, Frank, 288
Loy, Myrna, 39, 136, 167, 298
Lucas, Alexandra, 73
Luce, Clare Boothe, 284
Luciano, Lucky, 26–27, 269, 271, 291
Lugosi, Bela, 14, 271, 274–275
Luhan, Mabel Dodge, 50–51
Lund, Robina, 18
Lupino, Ida, 78
Lyman, Abe, 146
Lyman, Mike, 146
Lynn, Jeffrey, 217
Lyon, Ben, 268
MacArthur, General Douglas, 10
Macaulay, Thomas Babington, 7
MacDonald, Jeanette, 136, 164, 179–180, 258
MacDonald, Marie, 191
Mace, Fred, 292
Machado, Andres, 345
MacLaine, Shirley, 16–17, 142
MacLean, Faith, 22
MacMurray, Fred, 167, 294–295, 307
MacPherson, Jeannie, 245
MacRae, Gordon, 215
Madison, Guy, 64
Maginnes, Mary, 18
Main, Marjorie, 59
Malavasi, Ray, 321
Malotte, Albert Hay, 205
Maltin, Leonard, 203, 253
Mancini, Henry, 79
Mankiewicz, Joseph, 202
Mann, Ted, 170
Mannhardt, Karen, 18

Mannix, Eddie, 25
Mannix, Toni, 24
Mansfield, Jayne, 246–249
Mansfield, Paul, 248
Manson, Charles, 35
Marks, Sadye, 228
Marlow, Jess, 98
Marsala, Joe, 332
Marshall, Lindsey, 83
Marti, Jose, 306
Martin, Dean, 16, 141, 170, 328–330
Martin, Freddy, 321–322
Martin, Harry, 282
Martin, Keith, 98
Martin, Mary, 63–64, 246
Martin, Quinn, 15
Marx, Chico, 124–125, 189
Marx, Groucho, 52, 123–125
Marx, Gummo, 123–125, 189
Marx, Harpo, 124–125, 189
Marx, Zeppo, 124–125, 189
Mason, Perry, 203
Massey, Ilona, 259
Massey, Raymond, 112
Massi, Benny, 15
Masterson, Bat, 60
Masterson, Jim, 60
Mastin, Will, 17
Mathis, June, 261, 264
Matthews, Timothy, 19
Mature, Victor, 245
Maugham, Somerset, 252
Maxwell, Marilyn, 113
Mayer, Louis B., 10, 25, 38, 155, 168, 180, 298–299
McCall, Jack, 94
McCartney, Paul, 84
McClure, Doug, 338
McCormick, Robert, 10
McCrea, Joel, 58–59
McDaniel, Hattie, 105
McGraw, Ali, 7
McLaglen, Victor, 149–150, 287, 321
McLowery, Tom, 60
McNair, Barbara, 178
McNamara, James, 234
McNamara, John, 234
McPherson, Aimee Semple, xiv, 146, 183–186
McPherson, Harry, 184

McQueen, Steve, 34
Medina, Patricia, 68–69
Melcher, Marty, 206
Menjou, Adolph, 242, 280
Meredith, Burgess, 62
Merrill, Gary, 62, 202
Metchnikoff, Elie, 5
Methot, Mayo, 147
Meyer, Ron, 12
Milestone, Lewis, 340
Milland, Ray, 286
Miller, Ann, 278
Miller, Arthur, 28, 168
Millette, Dorothy, 38–39
Millikan, Robert Andrews, 165
Mills, Harry F., 211
Minnelli, Liza, 142
Minter, Mary Miles, 21–23, 140
Mintz, Mike, 85
Mitchell, Cameron, 65
Mitchum, Robert, 337
Mix, Tom, 286
Mizner, Wilson, 3
Monroe, Marilyn, xiv, 27–31, 78–79,
    167–168, 177, 183, 268, 302, 329, 333
Montand, Yves, 28
Montgomery, Blain Julian, 3
Montgomery, Blain Sutton, 3
Montgomery, Elizabeth, 80
Montgomery, George, 77
Montgomery, Robert, 80, 287
Monti, Carlotta, 159
Moore, Archie, 25
Moore, Grace, 266
Moore, Lester, 2
Moore, Owen, 151
Moorehead, Agnes, 80
Morris, Chester, 293
Morris, Mitty, 327
Morrison, Jim, xiv, 69–70, 83
Morrow, Vic, 230
Mudd, Harvey S., 145
Mulligan, Jerry, 340
Mulligan, Richard, 269
Muni, Paul, 235–236
Murphy, Audie, 210
Murphy, Francis, 107–108
Murray, Eunice, 30
Murray, Ken, 205
Mussolini, Benito, 84, 260

Nash, Charles W., 159–160
Nazimova, Alla, 189, 261
Negri, Pola, 118, 264–265
Nelson, Dick, 94
Nelson, Frank, 228
Nelson, Harmon, 202
Nelson, Harriet, 216
Nelson, Ozzie, 216–217, 340
Nelson, Rick, 216
Nesbit, Evelyn Florence, 285–286
Newman, Alfred, 162
Newman, Paul, 34, 74
Ngor, Haing S., 23, 324
Nichols, Red, 205
Nicholson, Jack, 204
Niedorf, Murry, 77
Nimitz, Admiral Chester William, 59
Niven, David, 35, 152, 285
Nixon, President Richard Milhouse, 57,
    122, 155, 157, 314–316, 323
Nolan, Lloyd, 341
Normand, Mabel, 21–22, 117–118,
    292–293
Norris, Eleanor, 200
North, Alex, 76
North, Sheree, 302
Novak, Kim, 254
Novarro, Ramon, 40, 118–119
Nudie, 210
Oakie, Jack, 187–188
Oberon, Merle, 6, 152–153
O'Brien, George, 287
O'Brien, Patrick, 280
O'Connor, Kathy, 316
Odets, Clifford, 139–140
O'Hara, Maureen, 287–288, 321
Oland, Warner, 109
Oldfield, Barney, 281
Oliver, "King," 271–272
Olivier, Laurence, 6, 259
Olsen, Jean, 278
O'Malley, Katherine H., 288
O'Malley, Walter F., 288
O'Neal, Ryan, 7
Ono, Yoko, 57
Orbison, Roy, 340
O'Reilly, Janie, 124
Ormiston, Ken, 185
O'Rourke, Heather, 331
Ory, Edward "Kid," 271–272

Otash, Fred, 31
Otis, Eliza, 233
Otis, General Harrison Gray, 233-235
Owen, Tony, 338
Paar, Jack, 334
Palmer, Lilli, 63, 137-138
Pangborn, Franklin, 191
Panzram, Carl, 5
Parent, Steve, 34-35
Parker, Charlie, 108
Parker, Dorothy, 1, 4
Parker, Tom, 55
Parks, Larry, 226
Parsons, Louella O., 8, 10, 282
Pasternak, Joe, 4
Payne, John, 73
Peale, Norman Vincent, 121
Peavey, Henry, 21
Peck, Gregory, 15, 169, 285
Peckinpah, Sam, 59
Penner, Joe, 162
Peppard, George, 15, 65
Perkins, Anthony, 74
Perviance, Edna, 21
Peters, Elizabeth, 165
Peters, Susan, 187
Peterson, Oscar, 108
Pezon, Jean, 205
Pfeiffer, Michelle, 13
Philips, Mary, 147
Phillips, Betty, 153
Phillips, Lou Diamond, 308
Piatigorsky, Gregor, 341
Pickford, Mary, 21, 127, 140, 150-152, 255-256, 273, 288
Pio, Pico, 344
Pitts, Zasu, 260, 288-289
Pleshette, Suzanne, 15
Polanski, Paul Richard, 34, 271
Polanski, Roman, 34-35
Porter, Cole, 302
Powell, Dick, 138, 173
Powell, Eleanor, 258-259, 318
Powell, Jane, 318
Powell, William, 37, 39-40, 142, 167, 299
Power, Deborah Anne, 253
Power, Tyrone, Jr., 252-254, 269
Prentice, Evelyn, 284
Presley, Elvis, 54-56, 305, 316
Price, Matlock, 264

Price, Vincent, 74-75, 258
Principal, Victoria, 211
Prinze, Freddie, 23-24, 209-210
Purdom, Edmund, 291
Quine, Richard, 187
Quinn, Anthony, 11, 285
Radner, Gilda, 65
Raft, George, 26, 149, 209-210, 268
Rambova, Natacha, 263
Randolph, Amanda, 213
Randolph, Lillian, 213
Ransohoff, Martin, 34
Rappe, Virginia, 200, 249
Rasputin, Grigori Efimovich, 105-106
Rasputin, Maria G., 105-107
Rathbone, Basil, 111, 133
Ravagli, Angelo, 50
Raye, Martha, 65, 67
Raymond, Gene, 179
Razaf, Andy, 107
Reagan, President Ronald, 112, 139, 269, 280
Reed, Donna, 78, 338
Reeves, George, 24-26
Reid, Mrs. Ogden, 10
Remarque, Eric Maria, 62
Remick, Lee, 76
Reynolds, Burt, 236
Reynolds, Debbie, 66
Rich, Buddy, 332
Richard, "The Lion-Hearted," King, 46-47
Richardson, J. P., 70, 308
Richardson, Tony, 76
Rickey, Branch, 288
Riddle, Nelson, 236
Righter, Carroll, 269
Ringe, Frederick Hastings, 104
Rinker, Al, 272
Ritt, Martin, 73-74
Rivera, Chita, 142
Roach, Hal, 67, 202-203, 246, 283, 289, 293, 305, 326
Robbins, Harold, 175
Roberts, Rachel, 112-113
Roberts, Simba Wiley, 98
Robinson, Edward G., 6, 267-268
Robinson, Elmer E., 10
Rodin, Auguste, 164
Rogers, Buddy, 151, 256

Rogers, Earl, 157, 240–241
Rogers, George, 27, 170
Rogers, Ginger, 170, 201, 317–318
Rogers, Roy, 4, 81–82, 319
Rogers, Shorty, 340
Rogers, Virginia, 202
Rogers, Will, 67, 105
Roland, Gilbert, 267
Romero, Cesar, 253, 306
Rommel, General Irwin, 337
Rooney, Mickey, 62, 191. 298
Rose, Billy, 67, 278
Rosenbaum, Joseph, 45
Roth, Joe, 12
Rowlands, Gena, 340
Ruby, Harry, 4
Rudolph, Minnie Ripperton, 342
Ruggles, Charlie, 147
Russell, Gail, 65, 327
Russell, Rosalind, 210, 271, 283–284
Ryan, Cornelius, 337
Ryan, Robert, 337
Sakall, S.Z "Chubby," 146
Sands, Edward, 22
Saradon, Susan, 57–58
Satterle, Peggy, 133
Savalas, Telly, 217
Scala, Gia, 284–285
Schanberg, Sydney, 23
Schenck, Joseph, 266–267, 336
Schneider, Leonard, 123
Schulberg, Bud, 139
Schuller, Dr. Robert, 121–122
Schultz, Dutch, 230
Sconce, David, 89–92
Sconce, Jerry, 90, 92
Sconce, Laurianne Lamb, 90, 92
Sebring, Jay, 34–35
Sellers, Peter, 274, 333
Selznick, David O., 169
Semple, Robert, 184
Sennett, Mack, 117, 167, 273, 283, 290, 292–293
Shaw, Artie, 62, 78, 332
Shaw, George Bernard, xiii, 1, 5
Shawn, Dick, 227
Shearer, Douglas, 172
Shearer, Norma, 141, 144, 167, 171–172, 252, 284
Shelby, Charlotte, 21–22, 140

Sheridan, Ann, 110–112
Sherman, Benjamin, 204
Sherman, Moses A., 186
Sherry, Barbara Davis, 202
Sherry, William, 202
Shirley, Anne, 73
Shoenberg, Arnold, 334
Shore, Dinah, 77, 140
Shore, Shirley, 77
Sidney, Sylvia, 136
Siegel, Benjamin "Bugsy," xiv, 26–27, 209, 268–269
Siegel, Hannah, 181
Silverheels, Jay, 112
Silvers, Phil, 311–312
Simpson, Don, 11–13
Simpson, Nicole Brown, 42
Simpson, O. J., 42
Simpson, Wallis Warfield, 282
Sinatra, Frank, 4, 6, 16, 28, 60, 141, 274, 329, 341
Sinatra, Nancy, 15
Singleton, Penny, 251
Sjoberg, Kurt R., 87
Smerling, Judge Terry, 91
Smith, Alexis, 76–77
Smith, Gladys Marie, 151
Smith, Maurice, 77
Smith, Will, 13
Snider, Paul, 339
Soloviev, Boris, 105–106
Sondheim, Stephen, 74, 77
Soo, Jack, 213
Southbrough, Lord and Lady, 17
Speriglio, Milo, 24
Spillane, Mickey, 236
Spreckels, Kay, 168
Sproul, Robert G., 10
St. Denis, Ruth, 212
St. Johns, Adela Rogers, 10, 23, 37, 128–129, 155–157, 168, 239–240, 253, 260, 263
St. Johns, Elaine, 157
St. Johns, Richard, 157
Stack, James L., 210
Stack, Robert, 15
Stanwyck, Barbara, 72–73, 139, 245
Steele, Dawn, 12
Steiglitz, Alfred, 50
Stein, Gertrude, 69

Steinberg, David, 16
Steiner, Max, 161
Stengel, Charles "Casey" Dillon, 142–143
Stevens, Connie, 153
Stevens, Craig, 77
Stevens, Rise, 259
Stewart, Jimmy, 170, 338
Stiltz, Bud, 233
Stompanato, Johnny, 78, 230
Stone, Lewis, 1
Stratten, Dorothy, 339
Straube, Luisa, 309
Streisand, Barbra, 298
Stuart, Slam, 109
Sturges, Preston, 1
Styka, Jan, 165, 191
Sully, Manna Beth, 255
Sulzberger, Arthur Hayes, 10
Summerville, Slim, 200, 292
Sunday, Billy, 121
Swain, Mack, 292
Swanson, Gloria, 170, 245, 292
Swegles, Lewis C., 48
Switzer, G. Fred, 233
Switzer, Carl "Alfalfa," 231, 233
Talmadge, Constance, 266–267
Talmadge, Natalie, 200, 266
Talmadge, Norma, 170, 227, 266
Talman, William, 203
Tata, Joey, 15
Tate, Sharon, 34–35, 37, 271, 276, 288
Tatum, Art, 108–109
Taylor, Elizabeth, 7, 64, 170, 293
Taylor, John, 316
Taylor, Robert, 72–73, 138–139, 141, 174
Taylor, William Desmond, 21–23, 118,
     140, 257, 293
Teagarden, Jack, 272
Teissier, Mary, 18
Temple, Shirley, 306
Terry-Thomas, 62
Thalberg, Irving G., 118, 124–125, 136,
     171–172, 298
Thaw, Harry, 285
Theroux, Peter, xiii
Thiess, Ursula, 139
Thomas, Danny, 66, 67, 69, 213
Thomas, Dylan, 5
Thomas, Marlo, 69

Thomas, William B., 305
Thompson, Ben, 59
Thornton, Willie Mae "Big Mama," 305
Thundercloud, Chief, 162
Tibbett, Lawrence, 188–189
Tiomkin, Dimitri, 191
Tisch, Steve, 12
Todd, Mike, 138
Topping, Bob, 78
Torpin, Henry, 335
Tracy, Spencer, 37, 39, 134–137, 141,
     171, 179, 280, 298, 303
Traubel, Helen, 342
Travolta, Helen C., 215
Travolta, John, 215
Truelove, Trudy, 57
Tucker, Forrest, 210
Tung, C.Y., 17
Turner, Joe, 109
Turner, Lana, 78, 230
Turpin, Ben, 292
Underwood, Agness, 137
Valens, Ritchie, 2, 70, 307–308
Valentino, Rudolph, 81, 118, 259,
     261–265
Vallee, Rudy, 216, 264
Vanderbilt, Gloria Morgan, 271, 282–283
Vanderbilt, Reginald, 282
Van Nuys, I.N., 231
Varsi, Diane, 69
Vaughn, Lloyd, 41
Vereen, Ben, 142
Vidor, Charles, 300
Vidor, King, 144, 255
Von Alvensleben, Marianne, 18
Von Kleinsmid, Rufus B., 165
Von Ronkel, Carol, 25
Von Stroheim, Erich, 289
Wagner, Robert, 31, 33, 324, 338
Wald, Jerry, 139
Walken, Christopher, 33
Wallace, Beryl, 144
Waller, Fats, 107–109
Walsh, Raoul, 11
Ward, Clara, 182
Ward, Gertrude M., 182
Warner, Benjamin, 299
Warner, Harry, 299–300
Warner, Jack, 299–300

Warner, Sam, 299
Warren, Earl, 10
Warren, Harry S., 331
Waters, Ethel, 4, 154–155
Waters, Tom, 90
Watson, "Bluebird," 94
Watson, Tex, 35
Waugh, Evelyn, 81
Wayne, Bruce, 204
Wayne, David, 79
Wayne, John, 6, 64, 80, 170, 174, 177,
    254, 287, 319–321, 327, 337, 338
Wayne, Marilyn, 34
Webb, Clifton, 266
Webb, Jack, 215
Weinstock, Matt, 93
Weiss, Jackie Dashiel, 42–43, 215
Weiss, Max, 59
Weiss, Robert, 42–43, 215
Welk, Lawrence, 295
Welles, Orson, 7, 69, 272, 279
West, Brooks, 341
White, Betty, 77
White, George, 258, 292
White, Stanford, 285–286
Whiteman, Paul, 169, 303
Whiting, Margaret, 191, 322
Whiting, Richard, 191
Whitman, Paul, 273
Whitney, Gertrude, 282
Wiatt, Jim, 12
Wilcox, Horace H., 257
Wilcoxon, Henry, 245
Wilde, Cornel, 245
Wilde, Oscar, 69
Wilder, Billy, 30, 79, 252
Wilder, Gene, 65
Williams, Paul, 104, 225
Williams, Roger, 122
Williams, Willie, 98
Willis, Cora, 195
Wilson, Don, 228
Wilson, Marie, 205
Wilson, Meredith, 160
Wilson, Woodrow, 127
Wimperis, Arthur, 93
Withers, Grant, 162
Wolders, Rob, 153
Wolfe, Jimmy, 237
Wolfe, Thomas, 254

Wong, Anna May, 109
Wood, Ed D., 14, 275
Wood, Natalie, 31–34, 53, 337–338
Woollcott, Alexander, 4
Wrather, Jack, 280
Wyler, William, 191, 210
Wymore, Patrice, 134
Wynn, Ed, 4, 158
Wynn, Francis Xavier Aloysius James
    Jeremiah Keenan, 158
Yogananda, Paramahansa, 160
York, Dick, 80
Yorty, Mayor Sam, 128
Young, Elizabeth Louise, 189–190
Young, Loretta, 136, 162, 167, 252
Young, Robert, 77, 189–190
Younger, Edward, 97
Yule, Joe, 191
Yussupov, Prince, 106
Zanuck, Darryl F., 335–337
Zanuck, Richard, 337
Zanuck, Virginia, 335–337
Zappa, Frank, 341
Ziegfeld, Florenz, 5, 144
Ziffren, Paul, 15
Zook, Greg, 94–95
Zook, Richard, 94
Zukor, Adolph, 266

# About the Authors

Margaret Burk

Margaret Tante Burk was born in Savannah, Georgia, and educated at Northwestern University in Chicago. As a young woman she migrated to California where she plans to remain forever.

Margaret has many "firsts" to her credit. She was the first woman president of the Wilshire Chamber of Commerce; the first woman vice-president of a Los Angeles financial institution; and the first woman voted into membership of Lion's International.

She has held leadership roles in many Southern California civic and community organizations, including the Los Angeles Community Advisory Committee, the Professional Women of the Philharmonic, and the Hancock Park Historical Society.

Margaret was an executive with the Ambassador Hotel in Los Angeles for 21 years. Then she and partner Marylin Hudson formed Burk/Hudson Public Relations and later founded and manage Round Table West, America's largest book and author club.

A writer and columnist for many years, her book credits include *Are the Stars Out Tonight?, The Story of the Famous Ambassador and Cocoanut Grove, Hollywood's Hotel,* and *Hollywood Presbyterian Hospital, the "Heart" of Hollywood.* She has always had a fascination for cemeteries—who's there and what they are up to.

Gary Hudson

Gary Hudson grew up working on family ranches in Utah, Wyoming and Nevada. He is a graduate of the University of Idaho and served as an artillery officer with the U.S. Army in Bavaria.

Gary began his career as a writer with *Road and Track* magazine and has served as creative director of three Los Angeles advertising agencies. In the 1970s he began his career as a writer, producer and director. His credits include TV productions for Comworld, Fox, Motown, ABC, NBC and CBS television, as well as films for Columbia, Cannon, Atlantic and Tri-Star. He has published two novels, *Limehouse* and *A Killing on Catalina.*